What Every Therapist Needs to Know

What Every Therapist Needs to Know

Michael Karson

ROWMAN & LITTLEFIELD
Lanham • Boulder • New York • London

Published by Rowman & Littlefield
An imprint of The Rowman & Littlefield Publishing Group, Inc.
4501 Forbes Boulevard, Suite 200, Lanham, Maryland 20706
www.rowman.com

Unit A, Whitacre Mews, 26-34 Stannary Street, London SE11 4AB

British Library Cataloguing in Publication Information Available

Library of Congress Cataloging-in-Publication Data

Names: Karson, Michael, author.
Title: What every therapist needs to know / Michael Karson.
Description: Lanham : Rowman & Littlefield, [2018] | Includes bibliographical references and index.
Identifiers: LCCN 2018007394 (print) | LCCN 2018009087 (ebook) | ISBN 9781538106570 (ebook) | ISBN 9781538106556 (cloth : alk. paper) | ISBN 9781538106563 (paper : alk. paper)
Subjects: | MESH: Psychotherapy—methods | Psychological Theory | Professional Role | Professional-Patient Relations
Classification: LCC RC480 (ebook) | LCC RC480 (print) | NLM WM 420 | DDC 616.89/14—dc23
LC record available at https://lccn.loc.gov/2018007394

∞ ™ The paper used in this publication meets the minimum requirements of American National Standard for Information Sciences Permanence of Paper for Printed Library Materials, ANSI/NISO Z39.48-1992.

Printed in the United States of America

For Janna, weaver of tales.

Two are better than one.—Ecclesiastes 4:9.

It is not the critic who counts; not the man
who points out how the strong man stumbles,
or where the doer of deeds could have done them better.
The credit belongs to the man who is actually in the arena.
—Theodore Roosevelt

(Just to be clear, I refer by quoting this to therapists
as opposed to researchers, and especially therapists
who get involved in problematic patterns as opposed to therapists
who merely monitor patients and criticize their parents.)

Contents

Preface

Busy therapists want to get better at what they do. Should they spend their precious time and mental energy reading a book on eating disorders, attending a conference on trauma, or watching Ozu's *Tokyo Story*? Realizing they can't read (or watch) everything that flies across their screens, they feel a pull to decide either that reading is unimportant or that whatever amount they have already read is enough.

One inspiration for *What Every Therapist Needs to Know* came from a consultation I initiated with a former supervisor after a patient told me that her cutting was getting worse. "Look how worried she has you," my supervisor said in her dry manner. "What a triumph for her." Understanding the cutting not just as something the patient was doing to herself but also as a communication to *me* now seems like something I should have known before I even met the patient. Since then, I've noticed how often you can boil therapy topics down to what you really need to know. A therapist who runs into a relevant case—a self-injurious patient, in this example—can read up on the topic to supplement his or her baseline knowledge. That way of reading psychology—with a specific problem or patient in mind—is bound to be more productive, but therapists need to know how to use their emotional reactions as indicators of a behavior's meaning. The patient and I were able to return to a therapeutic collaboration once we identified what I had done to make her think she was in a power struggle with me.

As I've gotten older, I've consulted with therapists across a broad range of experience levels. I see repeating patterns and developmental arcs, but the main thing I see that determines expertise—attained and maintained—is the desire to keep getting better. Supervisees and consultees ask me for things to read, but my list (psychology articles and books, novels, short stories, histories, and philosophies) has grown so long that it is too much to expect anyone to get through it. This book is my condensation of everything I know into essentials for the busy practitioner. For trainees, I hope it provides a vista of the human comedy and our efforts at useful intervention within it. I also hope it provides a sense of the odyssey that lies ahead, a source of ideas not so much to adopt as to chew over. For more advanced therapists, I hope it jars the complacency of competence into the adventure of discovery. We have chosen a field that cannot be mastered in a single lifetime, and there are many benefits that derive from that fact once we learn to laugh at our own pretensions.

The scope of the book is grand, more like an atlas or almanac than an ethnography or treatise. It can be read sequentially to provide a perspective on the scope of therapeutic practice, but it can also be read as a compendium of short takes to stimulate discussion and thinking. These are the topics that I have repeatedly covered in supervision, consultation, and psychotherapy training. The result, I hope, can be used as a handbook for therapists looking to brush up or challenge their own thinking on any of the topics, or as a survey for beginners and those who have managed to preserve a "beginner's mind" (in Zen, *shoshin*).

One of the big ideas in psychology is that psychology elucidates not only the problems that it studies or treats but also the process of studying and treating them. We apply our clinical theories not only to the patient's life but also to the therapy encounter. This thinking led to my starting the book with the psychology of becoming a better therapist. In chapter 1 I introduce the metaphor of the spiral staircase and address some of the psychological variables that keep people from climbing it, including ambivalence about competition, perfectionism, complacency, and cognitive biases. I also discuss productive ways of thinking about the kind of therapy this book is about and the implications for those ideas on how to get better at it.

People come for therapy because of life problems, and some familiarity with the sorts of things that lead people to seek therapy is important. In chapter 2 I review ideas about the most common themes in presenting complaints, including power, sex, money, death, food, and diversity. These are discussion-opening ideas about the human condition that cannot replace wide reading in literature and history but can at least be brought into sessions in a condensed form as a reference point for understanding patients' life problems.

Psychotherapy addresses psychological problems; other therapies and interventions address other kinds of problems. In chapter 3 I review the basics of psychology as it applies to therapy. The chapter covers common diagnoses, diagnosis itself, and the theoretical orientations that make sense of symptomatic behavior and disruptive emotions. I also deal with the major forces that, in contemporary practice, are reframing psychological problems as biological (i.e., brain science) and reframing psychotherapy as generic rather than individualized (i.e., so-called evidence-based practice). The current movement is in the direction of implicit claims that the treatment manual matters more than the therapist. Chapter 4 reminds the reader of the importance of the therapist, whose personality is explored there.

In chapter 5 we look at psychotherapy as a form of conflict resolution, where *conflict* refers to the presence of incompatible goals (wanting, say, to be both unassuming and victorious, or bold and invisible), and *resolution* refers to unpacking goals to gratify their components as much as is feasible. This is the old idea that symptoms obtain something at too great a cost, and symptom resolution often involves a less costly form of achieving the symptom's goals. This chapter also explores conflicts that arise within the therapy dyad.

Outcome research consistently links psychotherapy effectiveness to the working alliance, the subject of chapter 6. Here we nail down what the alliance really means and how to enhance it by developing individualized case formulations. The chapter also covers goal setting, connecting the therapy process to its goals, and enhancing relational bonds in the dyad. Psychotherapy is improved, as are all systems, by clarity around the roles; good therapists distinguish psychotherapy from a purely professional relationship, which typically will not support the level of intimacy that therapy needs, and from a social relationship, which typically occasions tact and saving face, both of which impede taking off the social mask and revealing the patient's inner life. The set of implicit rules that support a therapeutic relationship—the frame—is the subject of chapter 7.

In chapter 8 I cover technique: what therapists actually say in sessions. This includes slowing things down (in order to speed up progress) and understanding the advantages of focusing on process over content; I also suggest what to say when you don't know what to say. I discuss the form of useful interpretations and their purpose. I also present the things I actually say in a typical first session.

In chapter 9 I explore the issue of how to tell whether what you did with a patient worked, what I call *evidence-responsive practice*, where the relevant evidence comes from the patient and not from some study conducted by researchers who don't see patients themselves. Too often we look to patients and supervisors for praise when we ought to be looking at the immediate effect of what we just did on the patient or on the relationship for information about whether it was a good thing to do. Relevant effects can include variations in the alliance around relating therapeutically and metaphorical communication by patients about their responses to us.

Interpreting stories as metaphorical feedback is pretty rarefied practice. Art builds on craft, music on scales, karate on painting the fence and waxing the car, and therapy on understanding people, managing the frame, and tending to the working alliance. Once you know how to run a therapy, you can worry about attending to metaphorical speech occasioned by the last thing you did. Therefore, I think the foundation of the early chapters is needed to appreciate the power of understanding the patient's speech as a window into the meaning of the therapeutic interaction (as a function of its occasioning environment, as the behaviorists would say).

What Every Therapist Needs to Know contains my opinions, the kind of science that relies on digestion of what we as a profession think we know about a topic, but they are not *just* my opinions. They are a distillation of four decades of reading, practicing, and supervising, the ways I have been most effective in communicating to other therapists; big, expansively explained ideas make good foundations, but nutshell summaries are more useful in sessions.

I'm a therapy connoisseur, a purist, but I'm on your side because I recognize that therapy is hard and that in many ways *trying* to do it well is a crucial step toward *doing* it well (because patients respond to our efforts, not just to our skills). So I'm not a perfectionist. One thing I like about therapy is that because it's a relationship, you can't be a genius at it any more than you can be a genius dad or genius girlfriend. And, like a well-mannered usage maven, I don't go around correcting other people's punctuation or therapy technique unless I'm asked—which I have been uncommonly often, not just in thousands of supervised sessions and not just in my own therapies, but in more than 10,000 child welfare case conferences. In these, by far the most common responses from therapists working with children or parents to my query, "What are you working on?" has been either embarrassed silence or something too generic to be useful, like "trauma" or, annoyingly, "the trauma of having her children removed"—rather than, say, the tendency to do what she did to get her children removed.

You don't have to be a connoisseur to become an expert therapist, but it helps, just as it helps in every other field of human endeavor. Caring that the egg on your bibimbap, the Korean rice dish, has just the right consistency both to serve as a sauce and to taste cooked motivates you to learn to cook it right. The trick is to be a connoisseur without being arrogant, and that just means revealing your appreciation of fine distinctions only when asked. (By definition, patients, supervisees, students, and consultees are asking.)

Acknowledgments

The Corner Coffee Bakery off Colfax in Denver provided the occasioning environment for much of the verbal behavior contained in this book. The coffee accounts for many of its good sentences, the distracting bakery for many of its bad ones.

Janna Goodwin, Ioannis Ioannou, Emily Fogle, Lisa Abbrecht, and Matt Abbrecht influenced the manuscript with affectionate criticism. Jonathan Shedler and Janna influenced it with long conversations over a long period of time, as did my colleagues Judy Fox, Lavita Nadkarni, Shelly Smith-Acuña, Peter Buirski, Kim Gorgens, and John McNeill, and my supervisees, too numerous to name here, so many of whom are dear to me. My own supervisors set the stage for me to learn how to do therapy from my patients.

Chapter One

Knowing Something about Learning Therapy

Whoever hates to be corrected is stupid.—Proverbs 12:1

THE SPIRAL STAIRCASE

A seminar student reported in June that her patient said he had something embarrassing to tell her. I suggested remaining silent. She pointed out that in the same situation the previous September, I had suggested she reflect out loud on the patient's dilemma. Now I was telling her the opposite. I replied that reflection was correct back in September and silence was correct now. What had changed over the course of nine months was the student's understanding of the working alliance and the consequent development in the therapy relationship of a sense of partnership, that the two of them were doing something *together*. Back in September, when the pair still thought she was doing therapy *on* him rather than *with* him, she had to say something to address the conflict. She could now rely on this alliance with this patient; silence with him now communicated that she was listening, not that she was uninvolved. He already knew that his job at the moment was to discuss his embarrassment. Learning something in one area of therapy knowledge (the working alliance) had affected another area (technique).

I once attended a conference led by family therapist Sal Minuchin. Minuchin has a model of how family members should behave—which roles they should be in—and then he cajoles, tricks, induces, and guides them into playing their roles. I raised my hand and said that I understood his technique had never varied much, but I wondered if his model of what roles people should play had changed over the years. Minuchin said that feminism had

had a profound impact on his image of a functioning family. This was another example of learning something new in one area (gender) with profound effects on another area (goal setting). I report this example because if Minuchin could learn something new when he was already renowned and successful, so can you and I.

Here is a depiction of the therapist's journey that also, with a few modifications, applies to the patient's. Imagine a giant circular staircase, something like the Washington Monument if the walls were made of glass, or like the cleaning scaffold around it if it were a spiral you could walk up. As you go up the spiral—or helix, actually—you can see new things farther away, and you get a new perspective on the things you could already see. The giant helix stands in the center of a field, surrounded by other geographical features in various directions, corresponding to the chapters in this book. When you get around far enough to see, say, to the northeast, it changes your understanding of what you saw to the east; for example, you may see a factory spilling pollution in a creek and realize why the people you saw earlier weren't fishing in that creek. As you go on, you get higher on the staircase and gain new perspectives. What you thought was a sawmill from two stories up now seems to be a water treatment facility in the southeast; this changes your understanding of the factory's polluting behavior, since its pollution is cleaned up by the water treatment plant, and people avoid drinking the water in the creek only between the two buildings. The higher you go up the helix, the more you understand.

Meanwhile, each trip around the spiral staircase faces a direction you've seen before, a view of a problem you might consider from time to time that looks different depending on how high you have gone and how well you understand the other landscapes relevant to the problem. Such problems include whether to treat symptoms as physical or psychological, how to deal with misfortune, whether to extend a session when the patient is crying, and how to have a meaningful life knowing you're going to die. This book cannot possibly address these issues at the exact level each reader is ready to consider them. Instead, my agenda is to simplify these issues, partly to consolidate what you already know and partly to make what is to come less daunting.

The overarching problem in therapist development and in therapy itself is motivating the person to keep going around the helix and up the stairs. Unlike a real spiral staircase, the learning curve that therapists must ascend to increase mastery of their craft is invisible. It is relatively easy, compared to other professions, for therapists to fool themselves into thinking they have summited. In fact, ours is a profession in which some leading authorities claim that experience doesn't matter and a manual is all you need. Therapists are often like kids who can't imagine anything could be better than what their parents serve them—because they have never tasted anyone else's cooking. Or they're like the parents whose kids gobble up what they provide— delighted with ketchup, butter, and ice cream—unable to imagine that they could be serving better food. Nonetheless, empirical research suggests that the elements of expertise in therapy are the same as in other fields (Miller, Hubble, & Duncan 2008; Wampold & Brown, 2005). It's not innate talent or years of experience or the quality of training (although these help): It's the desire to improve. This desire has three components: appraising oneself realistically, engaging in deliberate practice (especially focusing on mistakes), and getting and valuing feedback on one's performance. The desire for praise is the enemy.

Trainees constantly receive the message that there is no staircase. Many of these messages come from Big Pharma, health insurers, and clinical researchers, each for their own reasons invested in claiming that psychotherapy is the rare human enterprise in which experience doesn't matter (Shedler, 2015). Even within the culture of therapists, some supervisors tell students that everything they do is helpful, and that if their patients keep coming for sessions then something must be working—whereas in reality there are many reasons patients keep coming, most notably because therapists often provide comfort rather than change. Therapists of course attribute progress in therapy to the therapy, but they often attribute any lack of progress to the patient or the patient's mother; if lack of progress is not the therapist's responsibility, then there is no staircase to climb. Therapists sometimes claim that the patient must do the work of therapy, which always makes me wonder what the therapist is taking money for. The answer is typically that they charge to provide a place for the patient to do the work. The implication is that once you learn to rent an office, there are no further steps to ascend.

If therapists' licenses and terminal degrees are imprimaturs of expertise, an odd culture around disagreement arises. Training programs rarely arrange for supervisors to discuss cases in public, so trainees rarely see productive disputation among practitioners. In some places, many clinicians greet the simple statement "I disagree with you" as if a bomb has gone off. In others, clinicians can claim expertise only by refuting, rather than discussing, others' ideas. The pretense that everyone is equally expert implicitly communicates that learning something new is status lowering rather than a gift we can offer each other, and this makes therapists avoid dialogue about what they're doing.

Wherever you are on the spiral staircase, the staircase itself looks nearly the same (except at the very bottom). It's always daunting to look up and consider how much more you have to learn. You can always insist that there are no further stairs, that you are at the top. Because a major part of the method of climbing is to identify and examine mistakes, at some levels of proficiency mistakes are all you see, while at other levels it is easy to ignore mistakes, partly because there are fewer of them (Miller et al., 2008) and partly because unlike people whose work is public, therapists can arrange to ignore them. It seems ridiculous to some people when interns in their fourth year of training claim to have summited, but many of their patients believe them. Truth be told, it's no more ridiculous than when forty-fourth-year students like me do it.

You can camp out on a landing and decide there's no need to keep trudging up the stairs. The problem then is that climbing has become a trudge and not an adventure. It's much more satisfying to look down the staircase to enjoy how far you've come than to look up and see how far you have to go. If teachers have rewarded you your whole life for knowing things rather than for wondering about them, you will find it embarrassing to admit how much you have to learn. If you take pleasure in what you already know, the vastness of what you don't know will always frustrate and repel you. If you take pleasure in finding things out, in physicist Richard Feynman's felicitous phrasing, you will live an encouraging life of adventure because you will never run out of stairs to ascend. Similarly, when therapists begin doing therapy, they often want to tell their patients what they know. It's only later, after they have seen that the patient can access most of what is known on the internet, that they realize their wondering curiosity is their greatest asset.

THE COSTS OF NOT KNOWING

The more you claim to know, the easier it is to lose face by not knowing something (Goffman, 1959). The less you claim to know, the fewer referrals you'll garner. Most therapists hit on the solution of acting as if they know a lot but not making any specific, discreditable claims. This is facilitated early in a therapist's career by clinging to a theoretical orientation or treatment approach that allays the dreadful feeling of being lost: "As long as I name emotions"—or explore thoughts or talk about the immediate present or discuss childhood or what have you—"I am doing good work." All therapists cherish the map they've used to get this far, partly because it is responsible for their successes and partly because cognitive dissonance blames failures on something besides the map they are using. This goes double for patients. It's hard enough to question a map's validity if an admired supervisor or brilliant theoretician handed it to you; it's even harder if it's a Rand McNally map and you happen to be a Rand or a McNally. Climbing the spiral staircase requires an acknowledgment of terra incognita, unmapped territories, a dismal enterprise for those whose maps claim to be comprehensive.

WHY AGGRESSION IS REQUIRED

Aggression gets a bad name because of its association with cruelty and violence, but every human trait has its dark side. If *anger* is the emotional state in which damage to others and property becomes reinforcing, then *aggression* is the name we give to behavior that might hurt others' feelings or property. This includes ambition, the desire for hierarchy, the distaste for hierarchy, self-expression, assertiveness, standing up for something, and—our focus for the moment—achievement. Requiring late-career therapists to adopt a purely collegial posture with younger colleagues, without elements of mentorship or teaching, often avoids aggression, a hierarchical awareness of a staircase and the older colleague's relative position on it. Of course, in this comment, *older* should mean "meaningfully experienced"; many older professionals are not in fact higher up the staircase because their own distaste for its daunting size made them stop looking up. One good way to tell if a therapist is still climbing is to find out how much he or she currently reads in the areas of psychology, philosophy, history, and especially literature. My one job interview question is, "What are you doing this year to ensure that you will be a better clinician next year?"

The field of psychotherapy attracts an unusually large number of people who are uncomfortable with aggression, those who choose the field because they identify with the soothing caregiver or with the victim who craves soothing. Many of them have been victims of vicious aggression; they may construe all aggression as vicious and want to protect patients from it. Gone are the days when Freud could describe the therapist as a conquistador; nowadays, therapists want to be midwives or, even worse, caretakers, spreading good thoughts among the suffering, disinclined to inquire whether they are effective as long as they are nice. The claim that one is going to change another person is aggressive—and often avoided. Treatment manuals alleviate therapists of the onus of implementing a change agenda by placing it on the manual, much as a parent trying to establish a bedtime routine might blame a book on baby care for the child's initial discomfort.

Clinical training—at least in psychology, counseling, and social work—is in a backlash from the days of the all-knowing analyst pontificating about the patient's childhood and inner workings. These therapists would pretend, even to themselves, to have summited the spiral staircase; the patients, by comparison, were a mess, wrong about everything. These therapists were so keenly comfortable with the hierarchy that they used it to disguise their own humanity. Now, therapy is so egalitarian that many therapists think that it's forbidden even to specify what the patient does to create or maintain his or her problems. The therapist treats the patient as a perfect, misunderstood specimen who knows at least as well as the therapist how to conduct a productive relationship. This apparent honoring of patients undermines their motivation to ascend their own staircases. My view is that therapists can learn much about motivating patients up their staircases by examining what puts therapists in the mood to read books like this one, or to read literature rather than tweets and Facebook posts. Different people will have their own ways of depicting these moments, but hope and adventure will be a part of them all, and escaping from reality will be a common hindrance.

In much of contemporary psychotherapy, *excellence* is a dirty word. In many programs focused on so-called evidence-based treatment—which has become a synonym for manualized or at least simplified treatments developed for clinical conditions rather than for the people who have them—excellence is relevant only to writing the manual. The whole idea of a treatment manual or a programmed approach is that therapeutic expertise is not needed to implement it. Some colleagues treat the desire to become excellent as if you were trying to surpass both them and your patients. This is, of course, exactly what it means, but clinicians hear it in a pathologizing context, as if you had just said that you want to be the best member of a family. When Tom Brady discusses his pursuit of excellence, nobody chides him for making the other quarterbacks feel bad. Shouldn't a therapist be excellent at understanding symptoms, wise about people, and extraordinary at relationship maintenance?

In my admittedly idealized memory of graduate school, our professors were expert clinicians who showed us their work. They weren't trying to teach us clinical skills so much as trying to inspire us to put in the 10,000 hours with feedback that we would need to learn clinical skills. In my memory, each of us committed to becoming a master clinician, aware that this could take decades. What we did not do was to lock our arms in protest against supervisors for making us feel bad that we were not already experts. One year, in my current therapy seminar, the first student to show videotape looked nervous, and another student reassured her that the video was "going to be great." "Whoa!" I said, "it's not going to be 'great'; she's a third-year. It's going to be 'fine.'" The enemy of excellence is the message that one is already excellent. This is as true in the journey to becoming an excellent person as it is in the journey to becoming an excellent therapist.

Therapists also require aggression, because therapists, not unlike doctors and dentists, must frequently make patients feel pain and discomfort. Therapists who balk at this thought seem right for the job. Those who jump at the chance and those who run from it are either too aggressive or not aggressive enough. The pain takes two primary forms. One is that effective therapists bring patients closer to upsetting experiences, painful affects, and discomfiting aspects of themselves. The other is that good therapists are constantly disrupting their patients' master narratives about who they are and how their world works. They may do this passively, through cultivating a process of self-discovery, or actively, by pointing out discrepancies and impossible roles in their patients' stories. Many patients come for therapy after a long period of pampering and protecting the part of them that has to change. These might be the combat veterans who nurse their victimhood by refusing to discuss it, the angry young people who feed the tigers that others would cage, or the divas who sense that others want them to be ordinary. The whole thrust of therapy is to upend these narratives, to show patients not only that they are failing but that they are playing for the wrong team. That takes a certain amount of nerve.

An analogy to political echo chambers seems relevant here. Nations stay divided, and divisions get deeper, when internet algorithms and the quest for comfort keep people from talking to each other and exposing themselves to different points of view. Comfort seeking impedes growth. It takes a therapist comfortable with aggression, deconstruction, and upset to keep the therapy from becoming an echo chamber. That goes double for aggression, since it is often aggression itself that is most warded off or unintegrated in the patient's psychological functioning, as sex used to be in Freud's day.

EXPERTISE

Surely, one good strategy to motivate us to ascend the spiral staircase is to find role models who themselves keep going up it. How to spot them is a tricky matter, though, because they often appear outwardly to be much like the clinicians who have stopped climbing and are merely getting older and not better. Thus, I've noticed a tendency of master clinicians to stop talking about their work. They see complexity where others look for simple answers. They are wary of teaching others who have not asked for lessons. Others claim that there is no spiral staircase, requiring experts to pretend that all therapists are equal, which discourages them, as does the expectation that they talk in case conferences as if beginners' ideas are always good ones. As a result, master clinicians may look like their old, doddering, inattentive counterparts. Still, if you ask them straight up, eagerly and humbly, for input into a clinical situation, they will say something useful and unexpected.

Because real experts constantly look up the spiral staircase and not down it, they underestimate their own expertise (Kruger & Dunning, 1999). Their most obvious characteristic is their focus on their own mistakes, on what they themselves could do better. This lack of self-satisfaction is doubly important in therapists because the therapist's willingness to look at his or her own contribution to whatever may be going wrong translates into a productive working relationship with the patient. A lack of self-satisfaction will also make a better bowler or software engineer, but the bowling pins and the computer don't cooperate as a function of how you make them feel about working with you. Now, having said that age doesn't matter as much as interest in collaborative feedback, I have to mention that therapists might need 10 years and 10,000 hours (Ericsson, 2006) to reach proficiency.

PROBLEMS WITH LOCATING YOURSELF ON THE SPIRAL STAIRCASE

One feels almost a compulsion to take stock of one's position on the spiral staircase, so social and competitive is our species, and assessing an accurate baseline is a crucial step toward expertise (Ericsson, 2006). Interfering with an accurate self-assessment are a few cognitive bias problems. One is the bias we feel toward what we have already done and said (Kahneman, 2011). Therapists justify their practice, however skillful it has or has not been, by forcing it to fit a master narrative of their own helpfulness and efficacy. If they need to be seen as experts, or if they need to believe there is no such thing as expertise in psychotherapy—that it is all a matter of taste—or if they need to believe that they are always starry-eyed novices (presumably to avoid any hint of hubris), they recall or ignore their successes or failures to bolster the master narrative.

Another hindrance to self-assessment is that people of lesser competence lack the expertise necessary to accurately appraise their abilities (Kruger & Dunning, 1999). Meanwhile, people of greater competence find certain tasks easy and assume that these are equally easy for others. These effects are even more pronounced in psychotherapy because the missing component for the incompetent is not only competence itself but also the metacognitive capacity to self-assess at all. A therapist's lack of self-reflection not only makes it impossible to recognize his or her own incompetence, it hinders competent performance of therapy directly as well, since patients need therapists who can appraise themselves. Again, for the expert, the effect of the trait is compounded. Benign assumptions about others and identification with others are what make experts think that others can do what they do. These tendencies are part and parcel of therapeutic expertise: The same traits that make good therapists make it hard for them to recognize that they are better than average.

Finally, there is the problem sometimes called *earned dogmatism* (Ottati, Price, Wilson, & Sumaktoyo, 2015). After undergoing a series of easy tests, people assume that they are more expert than they actually are in the subject area of the tests. In our current training system of inflated grading and tender feedback, the entire educational system—but especially first-year supervision—begins to look like a series of easy tests that make it very difficult for trainees to accurately appraise their ability. The tendency to ask *patients* how the therapy is going—which is uncomfortably close to asking children to rate parenting techniques and discovering that they prefer staying up late and skipping vegetables—leads to excessive praise for questionable practice. Research that celebrates slight, statistically measurable change rather than actual patient improvement (Shedler, 2015) turns therapies into easy tests that make clinicians overestimate their expertise. Only a glutton for corrective feedback can find it in a system that tells you what you want to hear.

It's not clear that there is any reason to locate oneself on the spiral staircase when it comes to an enterprise like therapy, whose staircase is taller than any human could live long enough to mount. Perhaps the more important point, as I've mentioned, is that the staircase itself looks the same wherever you are on it. It's probably more productive to think about the next step, the last misstep, and the exciting and disruptive new information available from the next vantage point than it is to think about how far you've come or how far you have to go. Still, it can be helpful for therapists to ask themselves how good they should be at therapy in their second, tenth, or forty-fourth year. The answer usually calms their perfectionistic expectations. I try to get trainees to watch themselves on video with affection rather than embarrassment, to feel sympathetic toward the therapists they used to be, even if that was only yesterday's version. I want them to feel affectionately sympathetic about their old therapist-selves during sessions, even after a few seconds, so patients can learn to think of themselves similarly.

THE KIND OF THERAPY THIS BOOK IS ABOUT

Before heading up the spiral staircase, we need to make sure we are on the right one, so for the remainder of this chapter we will explore what kind of therapy I am talking about and what kinds of people and situations it is for. A simple, useful model for understanding the relationship between people and environments links activating events (*A*) to beliefs the person has about the situation (*B*) to consequences (*C*) of interest, the last including overt actions and emotional responses (Ellis & Harper, 1975). You could substitute *between* for *beliefs* to make the model less cognitive, where *between* would stand for personality, learning history, old maps, organizing principles, or patterns—whatever the person brings to link situations and behaviors that accounts for the fact that we don't all react the same way to the same environment. People generally come for therapy because of problematic *C*'s: unpleasant emotions or whatever behavior they keep trying or avoiding without success.

In what I call *A-therapy*, therapists focus on patients' involvement with activating events. They teach an alcoholic to avoid bars, for example, or a battered woman to leave her relationship. They help the person to avoid fights or to schedule activities to skip the despair of weekend evenings. In what I call *C-therapy*, therapists address the problematic consequence directly. Most notably, this includes medications to eradicate problematic anxiety and depression. It might also include relaxation techniques, counting to ten before expressing anger, or finding more suitable outlets for unwanted impulses. The problem with all C-therapies is that anxiety, depression, and anger might be the alarm signaling that there is something wrong, and soothing the problematic emotion might be like disabling a burglar alarm that wakes you up at night rather than dealing with the burglar. In fact, many patients seek therapy because their self-administered C-therapies—which may include drugs, avoidances, and engrossing bad habits—have gone awry. C-therapy—relieving stress or discomfort—is what people mean when they say football or dancing is their "therapy."

The type of therapy this book is about is *B-therapy*, or what we might call *psychotherapy*, where the objective is to change the way people react to situations. This can lead to problem solving, conflict resolution, or proactive changes in the environment (pursuing pleasure rather than avoiding discomfort). There's a difference between psychotherapy and case management, between working as a physical therapist and a personal aide. Presumably, the latter retrieves patients' newspapers from their porches to meet their needs and the former helps patients get their own papers. The idea is to change people by interacting with them in the therapist's office. Thus, my focus in this book also excludes those situations in which the therapy needs to occur in the problematic environment, such as exposure therapies to scary places. I also exclude therapies where the therapist needs to import the problematic situation into the therapist's office for direct intervention, which is a way of characterizing family therapy and couples therapy. Minuchin (1974), discussing families, said that effective therapy requires the presence of the person who *wants* to change, the person who *has* to change, and the person who *can* change. Individual therapy makes sense if the patient is all three of these people.

Complex treatment cases can include the kind of therapy this book is about. For example, a trauma victim might have a case manager who coordinates couples psychoeducation, yoga lessons, group therapy, neurofeedback, and massage therapy, plus individual therapy of the sort that I am writing about. A child molester can be monitored by a probation officer and required to attend offense-specific groups, ongoing assessment, some kind of redemptive sentencing program, plus a confidential individual therapy—although as far as I know, this has rarely been allowed. The same goes, changed as needed, for medical patients, asylum seekers, and battered women.

NINE WAYS TO THINK ABOUT PSYCHOTHERAPY

People are more likely to climb a staircase when they have a concept of the journey ahead and where it's going, a topic we will explore elsewhere with respect to patients. Here, we can make the therapist's staircase more inviting through the review of encouraging (and overlapping) rationales for why talking to patients can help them with their life problems. Notice that *getting advice* is not on this list. Virtually everyone has gotten plenty of advice—if not from friends or authority figures, then from a web search—before calling a therapist. Freud invented psychoanalysis because good advice doesn't work with people who become patients.

These conceptual schemes rely on patients screwing up the therapy in the same way they screw up everything else. Much of what we'll cover about the frame and technique in subsequent chapters facilitates the patient's replication of problematic life patterns in therapy. Virtually all therapists want to work on the life problem in vivo—old-fashioned behaviorists want to treat fear of flying *on* an airplane, couples therapists wait for typical fights to emerge, family therapists ask kids to reenact their symptoms, and so on. My view, in agreement with the psychoanalysts and with Bateson (1972a), is that an ambiguous, authoritative, mutual, tightly framed therapy is bound to evoke the relational patterns that trouble the person.

The following ways of thinking about therapy provide something beyond problem solving in the sense often associated with so-called empirically supported treatments. They resemble the kind of doctoring relationship that promotes health and doesn't just deal with disease as it arises. All of the traits promoted in this list lead to "aging well" (Vaillant, 2002), the fruits of all-too-rare longitudinal studies of entire lifetimes. In other words, therapy is about promoting psychological health, not just about alleviating symptoms. The meaning of *health* varies from therapist to therapist, but articulating its features is a good start to cultivating it.

1. Intimacy Exposure

Many people come for help because they function poorly in intimate encounters such as romance, childrearing, or close friendships. A simplified approach notes that people have hurt them in intimate relationships, and so now they panic when getting close to people, just as someone injured in an elevator might avoid elevators or behave erratically in them. Gentle but insistent exposure to an elevator is the answer to that hypothetical; gentle but insistent exposure to intimacy is the answer for many actual patients. Elevator exposure won't work if the elevator in question is too specific or if the elevator therapist is too soothing, since the patient will then learn only that one particular elevator is safe or that elevators are safe only when reassurance is available. The implication is that the intimacy exposure in therapy must not be too specific or reassuring, either.

2. "I Know What to Do, but I'm Not That Type of Person."

One reason advice often fails is that people already know what to do, and the problem is that they can't see themselves doing it. A common reason for ignoring advice is that the patient loses face if he could have solved his problem all along so easily, by being big-hearted toward his wife, a good loser at work, or a rational counter of calories. Patients need "a graceful way out" (Haley, 1976, p. 212). This might mean a narrative: Of course you are a sore loser because of the way your parents raised you or because of existential fears of being alone, but now you have invested in our difficult and emotionally evocative relationship so that, finally, unlike before, when you were still in the throes of your whatever, you can face making allowances or losing a contest or counting calories with equanimity.

Less sardonically, there is often a mismatch between what one ought to do and how one sees oneself. A conqueror who devastates his or her opponents cannot be a good loser. One who is an exception to the physical laws of the universe cannot count calories. Therapy is a place where one can find out who one is, whether by examining one's beliefs about oneself or by producing oneself through spontaneous speech. A *unique* view of oneself might compensate for one's essential ordinariness.

Self-discovery enhances self-control. Without affectionate self-knowledge, efforts at self-control paint the self in a negative light, as if one is intrinsically greedy, rapacious, or cruel and the task is to keep the beast in check. Patients resent these characterizations, implied by many self-control efforts, and rebel against them. Self-awareness paints the self to be controlled in a more positive light, and creates a stronger alliance between the controlling self and the self to be controlled. Self-awareness also allows people to tailor their efforts at self-control to fit them better, and nearly everyone responds better to contextualized, personalized guidance than to generic, impersonal rules.

3. Misreading Situations

Many people would make more allowances for their spouse's idiosyncrasies if only they could keep in mind that the spouse is not trying to ruin their lives, dominate them, or trap them. These people may have flexible or well-rounded views of themselves, but they misread certain situations. Who can say whether your spouse is really behaving arrogantly as opposed to expressing irritation about being treated like a tyrant, or whether your colleagues are really acting like sniping backstabbers rather than reacting to your hunkering suspiciousness? In therapy, the dyad can jointly explore erroneous assumptions. Patients learn their idiosyncratic ways of misreading certain situations, and they learn to question whether their first read is accurate. This works only if therapists can allow errors to emerge, and only if therapists can accept their own occasional tyrannies, arrogations, and so on, so as not to require the patient to misread the therapy.

4. Conflict Resolution

A common precursor to seeking therapy is a conflict that the person doesn't know how to address. This might be an adverse life experience that contradicts one's expectations, internal incompatible wishes, or emotions that do not fit one's claims about who one is. Psychotherapy teaches patients three conflict resolution skills: (1) It is better to approach and address psychological conflict than to avoid it. (2) Meta-communication—talking things over—including the creation of a calm space to air all aspects of a conflict, is often all that's needed for resolution. (3) Optimal conflict resolution in ongoing relationships is principled (Fisher & Ury, 1981) rather than positional—it references values like fairness and satisfaction rather than maximal gain. Zooming in too close to one's immediate emotional experience fuels conflict, and zooming out too far, where emotions become a headline and not a story, makes conflicts hard to resolve. Therapy teaches patients a useful distance from themselves, close enough to feel and far enough to consider, because the therapist engages the patient from that distance.

5. Reparenting

Many life problems follow from the way we treat ourselves. If we ignore our impulses, they emerge in contorted ways, or they wither. If we disapprove of them, they emerge without our guidance. If we champion them, they emerge at the expense of other agendas. So don't take *reparenting* literally: It's not fixing what the patient's parents did; it's changing how patients currently parent themselves. The therapeutic stance of welcoming curiosity achieves much of this. What people need in their heads is a therapeutic parental voice that one can only half-jokingly boil down to asking themselves two questions: "Honey, what sounds good?" and "Honey, is that a good idea?"

6. Changing Narratives

A good scientific theory accounts for the most salient facts and generates guides to successful action (Skinner, 1957). A good life narrative does much the same thing, accounting for facts and serving as a kind of guidebook. Inevitably, theories and life lessons become outdated as new situations are encountered and idiosyncratic rules are exposed. Some internal guidebooks are nearly empty (in conditions known as *identity diffusion*), some apply a few rules of conduct to nearly every situation indiscriminately (in conditions known as *personality disorders*), and most include flexible rules adaptable to many situations but still susceptible to misuse in confusing, emotional, or ambiguous circumstances.

Most therapies include discussions of patients' life stories or at least discussions of certain situations. Even if therapists do not directly address the maps or rules that patients use, implicit editing occurs when therapists address mismatches between narratives and current situations. The strongest form of changing narratives occurs when the therapy encounter becomes a major turning point in the narrative. Most stories take the form "Once upon a time," followed by "then, one day" (Hicks, 2010). The life story might turn on major events: "Then, one day, I fell in love" or "left home" or "traveled to Tibet" or "got cancer." Successful therapy often involves, in its generic form, the therapy as a turning point: "Then, one day, I met my therapist and found that many things I believed about myself and about relating to others were untrue."

Because of *cognitive dissonance*—the discomfort caused by conflicting beliefs, often resolved by trashing one of them—painful narratives are ironically harder to change than happy ones. It's easier for a family that has not sacrificed a service member to question whether entry into the war was a good idea. The more unfit the parents, the more dissonance they cause, and the more splitting they produce. (*Splitting* is the maintenance of a positive or negative image by splitting off from it all disconfirming information.) If your mother gives you a map that leads to a dead end, you fix her mistake. If it leads off a cliff, you hate to think your mother almost killed you, so you suspect that the map was accurate, and someone else put the cliff there to mess with you.

7. Collaboration

Many life problems stem from collaboration deficiencies. Patients may not know how to collaborate on dates or how to pick likely mates. They may not know how to make a relationship a team or how to maintain romances or friendships. They may not know that true love is built, not found. They may not know how to collaborate with coworkers or bosses and may have trouble finding or maintaining rewarding employment. In these cases, the therapeutic working alliance is not only the key to successful treatment, it is the window into the problem. Patients screw up the therapeutic collaboration just as they screw up other collaborations; establishing and repairing the therapeutic alliance changes patients in ways that will enable them to establish and repair other relationships.

8. Self-Exposure

Everyone has an identity, a self-image that suits his or her definition of a good person and the expectations of others. And every identity casts a shadow (Jung, 1969 [1938]). People waste a lot of energy on keeping the shadow hidden, especially from themselves, and they sacrifice a lot of satisfaction by shunning the shadow, which often contains virtuous aggression, sexual gratification, and unmet needs. To Horney (1950), the very definition of *neurosis* is the energy spent on polishing one's identity claims instead of embracing the real self. Therapy can be a place to meet the real self, optimally evoked by a private and nonjudgmental therapist and optimally accepted by getting to know it. Self-love can grow out of self-understanding, which requires self-exposure. A consequent decrease in self-avoidance channels energy into getting one's needs met rather than pretending those needs don't exist.

9. Play

Many life problems reflect an incapacity to play, which is the opposite not of work, but of depression (Sutton-Smith, 1997). Play requires versatility around the framing of interactions, meaning that bared teeth don't *have* to mean a real threat and swearing doesn't *have* to mean a sin (Bateson, 1972b [1954]). Play also requires an ability to accept an arbitrary frame for the time being, Coleridge's suspension of disbelief. Play is often defeated by the insistence on frames such as obedience or morality or correctness; consider a two-year-old girl banging chess pieces while a parent, invested in chess as a different kind of interaction, tells her she is not playing, but is disrupting. Thus, to play is to impose a frame that the person recognizes as a frame and not just as the way things are (Goffman, 1974). Therapists teach patients to play by talking about things without taking action outside the frame, much as a theatrical play evokes emotional response that would be weakened if audience members felt obligated to warn Caesar of Brutus's plans. Therapists promote play by setting the therapy apart from life, by drawing out and honoring fantasies, by following the rules of the interaction, and by taking the occasion seriously while it lasts—much as adults teach children to play.

PATIENT SELECTION

These ways of looking at how therapy works imply some of the requirements for patients. For example, a patient who is not just alarmed but freaked out by intimacy can't benefit from closeness to the therapist. In fact, Linehan (1993) invented dialectical behavior therapy (DBT) to manage this reaction. Patients who are freaked out by recalling traumatic events can be treated with modifications (discussed under "Trauma"). Like trauma victims, many people will need other services ancillary to psychotherapy; these range from medical interventions to interventions that address other nonpsychological problems that interfere with basic needs or that make attendance to therapy impractical. Patients must be able to attend; among those who can't are people in cultures that don't condone regular meetings with a stranger for intimate conversations.

Patients with biological illnesses, such as cancer, multiple sclerosis, schizophrenia, or bipolar disorder, cannot cure the illness in psychotherapy. However, psychotherapy can help many of them cope with the illness. Patients such as hard-core psychopaths, who cannot accept even the most basic frame of therapy as a discussion about the patient's psychological difficulties, cannot benefit from it.

Many clinicians are not trained to recommend a variety of therapies or approaches; they either do what the patient requests or they say they have a way of working that they deploy in all cases. Therapists don't have to choose between dominating patients and deferring to them. The immediate point is that patients appropriate for personality work or changes in response styles are also those not better suited for something else. This includes those seeking relief only for specific problems, although many present this way and turn out to need more. For example, a woman living a well-adjusted life could lose her job since she is afraid of getting on her commuter bus. Sometimes she'll need exposure work or brief cognitive treatment to get on the bus; other times she'll need to explore whether getting on the bus to keep a job she hates is really a good idea. Often, she'll need to work on why it's so hard for her to consider holistically what's best for her.

Also excluded from dyadic therapy are people so embedded in a network of relationships that the therapist must address the whole system. This applies to a huge percentage of children and a lot of married people. Therapists can identify many such exclusions by the specificity of mutually defined goals. In the case of the woman discussed above, if the goal is to keep the job, then they can do exposure work on the bus she's afraid to ride to work. If the goal is to change a tendency to force herself to comply with suffocating demands, then they can do psychotherapy. If the goal is to improve a specific relationship, the therapist should work with the couple; if the goal is to change a tendency that affects many relationships, the therapist should work with the individual (and perhaps have a colleague work with the couple).

THERAPIST SELECTION

Ideas about therapy imply requirements of the therapist, too. Psychological mindedness—the capacity to view people, especially oneself, as a set of selves rather than as a unitary or monolithic entity—is crucial for welcoming marginalized aspects of the self into therapy. There must be a capacity for intimacy, a broad conception of the human condition and what it means to be a person, gluttony for feedback, a tendency to approach conflict, welcoming curiosity, an appreciation for and understanding of metaphor, self-knowledge, and an ability to collaborate and play even in trying circumstances. Essential is the ability to take strong emotions in stride. I lament the extent to which our selection procedures in training programs ignore these traits.

In a renowned TED Talk, Edmondson (2014) distinguishes a "psychologically safe workplace"—a "learning zone" that promotes inclusive dialogue and the voicing of nonconforming ideas—from zones of anxiety, comfort, and apathy. Good therapists create learning zones, but many therapists produce anxiety zones (when their cooing fails to soothe) or comfort zones (when their cooing succeeds at soothing). Many therapists produce apathy zones when the two parties fail to connect with each other, patients obstinately sticking with it and therapists claiming that change is up to the patient. Edmondson says that three traits characterize leaders who can develop a productive workplace. Leaders must construe the workplace as a learning environment instead of an execution environment. This distinguishes psychotherapists from manualized therapists, where the former must understand a unique problem and the latter merely implement a solution. Leaders must also be fallible and curious, coinciding pretty well with the image of therapists who never summit the spiral staircase and always wonder what's around the bend, what is overlooked or excluded, and what their privilege may be blinding them to.

OWNING THE STAIRCASE

A good way to start up the therapy staircase is to learn to say what pretty much any therapist would say to pretty much any patient. "How do you feel about that?" fits into this category, even though I don't recommend ever saying that particular sentence at any time in a therapist's career. Therapists can start up the staircase by slowing down the discussion of problems, homing in on specific moments and images, and summarizing the stories they're told. They might revert to saying, "Let's see where your thoughts go from here" when they have nothing else to say and it's their turn to talk. Silence is also golden, and therapists have the right to remain silent.

Later, therapists learn to say what any therapist would say to this *particular* patient. A good way to employ clinical theory is to say what the theorist might say to that particular patient, whether that theorist be Beck, Ellis, Horney, Selvini, Madanes, Kohut, or whoever. Therapists could include their clinical supervisors here if they were lucky enough to have supervisors who told them what they would actually say at given moments. Next, therapists learn to say what *they* would say to that particular patient. This starts when they are so familiar with the role of therapist that they find themselves able to improvise without violating the role, much as actors who know their parts inside out can handle mistakes or accidents while staying in character. The therapist alone climbs this portion of his or her personal spiral staircase. This can remove some of the competitive aspects of climbing, since there is no longer anyone below or above the climber. It can also remove some of the incentives for climbing, and legion are the therapists whose reliance on “the relationship” is code for complacency.

Chapter Two

Knowing Something about Humans

The major difference between rats and people is that rats learn from experience.—B. F. Skinner

One of the ironies revealed by the nationwide drift of psychotherapy practice from relationships to manuals is the attitude that good therapists need not have any particular expertise in the human condition. Later on, we'll explore the technique of summarizing a patient's story, memory, or interaction in a single sentence, but for now let's examine the grandest example of a summary: Scanning all of history, what is the human story about? Is it a story about meaning and emptiness? Of good versus evil? Of living with a knowledge of death? Of oppression—man's inhumanity to man? Living peacefully with other aggressors? Attachment and suffering? Sin and redemption?

These and other lenses inform the core questions of philosophy, the answers or approaches to which cannot help but affect therapists' work, because it is impossible to set aside our worldview. What therapists can do instead of trying to hide their philosophies is to learn different worldviews and to subject their own to the reactions of others. The idea is to select one that fits the occasion rather than merely relying on the ones that therapists are most comfortable with. Breadth of perspective can come from listening to other people and from travel, but ultimately these methods are slow and constricted compared to reading.

The whole point of literature (versus melodrama, or what Stephen King calls *salami*) is to make visible the inner workings of human affairs. Your own thoughts and feelings will always be specially available to you in a way that no one else's are, and you might get glimpses of the intimate functioning of several other people in your life. Certainly, one of the main rewards of a career in therapy is the chance to learn about other people, which is why I call therapy *applied literature* and not a branch of medicine. Literature gives you a chance to expand your intimate circle dramatically. Also, the people perceiving, collating, and reporting data on the inner life of individuals are typically, as with therapy patients, the people themselves—and of course most people are only so-so at it. In good literature, the reporting party is an expert observer and describer of human affairs. You learn not only about other people, but also how to think about them. Eliot's *Middlemarch* doesn't just show you the inner worlds of recognizable characters; it teaches you how to think about a variety of people with affection and acceptance.

The following whirlwind tour of some of the great human topics that relate to practicing psychotherapy would be ridiculous if presented as a comprehensive guide, and of limited utility if presented as a sampler. Instead, it's meant to illustrate, in the space available, the *kind* of thinking that forms a foundation for psychology and therapy. Let's think about important topics in a manner that is deeply considered, vetted by friendly debate, and revisable. It's too much to require wisdom of ourselves, but we can insist on wisdom seeking.

Knowledge about humans informs therapy not only in the manner and bearing of therapists, but also in the areas they choose to explore. Experts in sleep hygiene can focus on the patients' bedtime routines without turning the relationship into an advice column, using expertise to inform the inquiry. Knowing something about mating can lead to a focus on how patients experience themselves on dated and not just on their potential partners' appeal. Knowing something about people opens many avenues in therapy. Therapists often say, "Take me to the moment when . . ." and "What does that moment remind you of? Paint us a picture of yourself at that moment." Knowledgeable therapists choose productive moments to focus on.

DEVELOPMENT

Be suspicious of *development*; it often disguises a sense of superiority. When people promulgate theories of racial identity development or moral development, they rarely specify stages they have not yet mastered. What they often mean is that if you disagree with them, it's because you are immature. I certainly hope the metaphor of the spiral staircase explicitly places me somewhere on it and not at its nonexistent summit. Still, development nicely describes what happens from conception to young adulthood, when the brain matures, and it is a useful metaphor for what happens thereafter, even if culture and not biology largely defines adult development.

One aspect of development useful to consider is the trajectory of assuming ownership of one's body. Ownership of oneself, like ownership of land, comprises a bundle of rights. These range from doing one's hair to choosing which food, drink, and drugs to ingest, to sexual contact and, for women, reproductive rights. People start off owning none of themselves and end up, in the United States, owning mostly all of themselves, but no one completely owns the body, even those of a privileged race or gender. Just as zoning laws or neighborly expectations abrogate the right to paint your house a ridiculous color or to emit an odor of garbage, so statutes, racism, sexism, and cultural courtesies limit dominion over one's body. Much sexism is expressed as a reduced degree of self-ownership afforded to women and girls, much racism as a reduced sense of personal safety (Coates, 2015).

Parents are generally one step behind children on the subject of dominion over the self. When parents finally learn the rules and expectations of raising three-year-olds, the kids turn four. Now the children want control over more rights: the right to choose what to wear, for example, or the right to cut their hair. Many eating disorders rest on confusion about who owns the body.

POWER THEORY

In every human system, whether as grand as a nation or as tiny as a single individual, whether as lasting as the Catholic Church or as evanescent as strangers in an elevator, implicit and explicit rules emerge that at first are designed to benefit the system but inevitably drift to benefit the hegemony of rule makers. According to the political theory underlying the US government, this is inevitable, a function of how things look to the powerful in any system, which begins as blindness to the plight of the powerless and ends with contempt for them. When an individual or a small group makes, enforces, and interprets rules, it is the definition of tyranny (Madison, 1945 [1788]), because the usual hallmarks of tyranny inevitably follow from power.

Therapists, like parents, make, enforce, and interpret rules. Unlike politicians' relationship with the populace, their concern for their patients and children offers some checks on tyranny, but therapists can usefully construe many life problems as the result of an exploitation of power. Parents, then schools, then social groups, then employers mistreat, neglect, or spoil children, students, and adults, respectively. Many therapists react to their power to harm patients by relinquishing this power, but surely a better response is to use it wisely. Therapists should monopolize rule making and rule enforcing, but they can share the work of interpretation with patients. The well-known goal is to be authoritative rather than authoritarian or permissive (Baumrind, 1968).

Aside from instances of sexual exploitation, physical abuse, or lawsuits, power dynamics play out in therapy around the authority to define the situation, to say what's going on: The therapist starts a session late and chides the patient for being too sensitive, too rigid, or too dependent. I often ask students to raise their hands if they are or have been in therapy. I ask them to keep their hands up if their therapist ever did anything that annoyed them; most do. I ask them to keep their hands up if they told their therapist they were annoyed; few do. I think most patients hint at criticizing the therapist, but, like employees who sense that the boss isn't really interested in corrective feedback, they soon give up. It fascinates me that the First Amendment includes not only the freedoms of speech, religion, and assembly, but also the right to complain ("to petition the government for a redress of grievances"). Clinicians often diagnose patients who complain as oppositional, rebellious, or borderline, without considering the righteousness of the complaint.

Privilege is any luxury of power, but its essence is blindness, the luxury of not having to think about race, sex, or inclusion. White privilege will occasionally garner better customer service, but mainly it frees white people from wondering why the service is so poor. Therapeutic privilege is the luxury of not having to wonder whether the last thing you said was useful. It relies on the patient's discretion. At its worst, this discretion becomes unconscious, like a child's idealization of a parent's corporal punishment ("it showed she loved me") or neglect ("we learned to fend for ourselves") or pampering ("I felt like a princess"). The main way to overcome privilege without relinquishing power is for therapists to seek feedback about the immediate effects of their behavior on patients and not to assume it's all good. The essence of therapeutic privilege is the oft-heard claim that the patient must be getting something out of therapy; otherwise he or she would stop attending. In fact, there are many bad reasons for patients to persist. Indeed, many patients begin therapy with a charade of wanting to change while really blaming other people for their disadvantageous conduct. Therapists often collude with them by blaming their parents, but the cure for conditions wrought by parents who misused their power is to be honest and corrective when one misuses one's own power.

Just as a society marginalizes certain members as a solution to the political problem that people cannot accept each other, and just as that marginalization itself becomes a political problem, individuals marginalize aspects of themselves and then have to work on psychological integration. If you have six children and one of them is angry and jealous, will it work on a family outing to pretend that they are all peaceful and hope for the best? Of course not. In fact, it will make the angry child even angrier and more sullen when once again the anger comes as a disruptive surprise. In a real family, you can leave the angry child with a sitter (which will also increase the anger). In your own psychology, you cannot arrange to leave the angry part of the system behind. Therapists must constantly monitor their all-too-human tendency to exclude discomfiting aspects of the patient's functioning and then to ignore having done so.

STIGMA AND SAVING FACE

Humans are social creatures who (probably) evolved to survive in pairs (Fletcher, Simpson, Campbell, & Overall, 2015), with those pairs embedded in packs of 30 to 90 individuals (Diamond, 2013). Maintenance of the pack requires careful management of the power differentials discussed above. It also depends on other people's reactions being enormously important to us. It doesn't matter whether there are genes that make us social or whether it's a function of our prolonged infancies (and, therefore, prolonged dependencies, as everything we need for the first several years is provided in a social context, i.e., by other people). Either way, we locate ourselves in social networks.

We typically value the social reinforcers of attention, affection, and approval if we have been lucky enough to associate these with the biological reinforcers of food, agreeable touch, and shelter. We also value the social reinforcer of obedience if we have been lucky enough to know people whose compliance with our wishes led to rewards. We (almost) *all* value saving face (Goffman, 1959), because social reinforcers depend on our acceptance by others.

The face you save combines the face your system gives you and the face you covet. We can translate these into trying to pull off the role you find yourself in and trying to pull off the role you wish you were in. You lose face when an audience discredits your performance by not responding in the reciprocal role. A *stigma* (Goffman, 1963) is any identity element—anything you are or have done—that discredits your performance of a given role on a specific occasion. For example, you lose face as an engaging faculty member when students look bored, unless you redefine the role of faculty by reading PowerPoint slides instead of talking to students, in which case their boredom credits your performance of an information-conveying faculty member. You lose face when you try to perform *good person* and your audience's knowledge of an indiscretion of yours keeps them from smiling at you, showing you courtesy, and so on.

It's hard for therapists to learn how to play the role of therapist. Patients don't help much, at least in the short run. Patients are ambivalent about the reciprocal, vulnerable role, so they often respond positively when therapists mishandle the role of therapist by indulging, entertaining, or distracting them, or when they define it in such a way that it doesn't induce patients to take off their masks and tell their stories. Thus, therapists must learn how to distinguish when their audience credits or discredits their performance, and how to distinguish which role is credited or discredited.

Typically, I start teaching the therapy role by exploring the student and professor roles or the trainee and supervisor roles. I find that some trainees misunderstand (or promote an unhelpful version of) the student role and what discredits it. They seem to believe that you save face as a student by getting answers right and lose face by getting answers wrong. This leads to an avoidant, or deadly, classroom (Goodwin, 2001). A parallel problem is how you lose face in most of life by revealing that you have a personal psychology, that you acted on motives that were ugly or that you weren't aware of. In the culture of psychology, it ought to cause a loss of face to make ridiculous claims of self-mastery and self-awareness, but of course that's not true. Many acknowledgments of having a personal psychology—of being subject to the laws of behavior—are lip service. The allure of being always *right* once drew clinicians to the field, giving rise to the image of the Viennese analyst with beard and pipe. Nowadays, the allure of being always *good* draws some of them: the belief that every saccharine thing they do is helpful, like a parent who serves only Kool-Aid and points to the children's enthusiasm for it as evidence of good parenting. When Planck said that science progresses one funeral at a time, he meant that scientists should change their minds when confronted with new evidence, but they don't; it's new scientists who weigh all the available evidence. Scientists are all too human when it comes to balancing the science culture's demand for humility against the larger culture's admiration of being right. Clinicians, too, forgo the clinical culture's insistence that they themselves are subject to psychology, and they strive instead for the larger culture's admiration of people who claim to be above all that.

A more useful face for a student than being right is being willing to change, to learn from mistakes. I want to present my work not as if I'm modeling at a fashion show but as if I am asking a close friend if my outfit suits the occasion we are about to attend: "Should I change?" A better face for faculty shows pleasure in watching people wrestle with difficult ideas. It's hard to implement these role definitions if students or other professors think one's humanity discredits the performance of faculty member, or if students snicker and act superior when one of their classmates says something stupid. Real, lasting stupidity derives from a hatred of being wrong.

Therapists should define and maintain the patient role as one in which their performance *cannot* be discredited by anything they say (Goffman, 1967). This allows them to expose identity elements stigmatized elsewhere without a loss of face. The therapist's role is designed to encourage this.

STATUS

A crucial feature of every role is the status with which we play it (Johnstone, 1981; Karson, 2008). You can be a high-status president like Barack Obama or Ronald Reagan or a low-status one like Jimmy Carter or George W. Bush. High-status does not mean superior or unapproachable—it means striding with confidence like Obama; low-status means carrying your own luggage like Carter. Either way, you have the same power and functions, but one *looks* more important and adult than the other. A waitress can play high or low while reciting the exact same specials and clearing away the exact same dishes. There are many subtleties to status play, but the broad outlines will suffice to understand the concept.

In *vis-à-vis* status play, you portray yourself compared to the other person as more powerful or important, less so, or equally so. How you play status may vary from moment to moment or topic to topic, but in general most people default to a particular level depending on how their current and formative social networks have responded. It's not too hard to see how our culture generally rewards men for playing high and women for playing low. This makes it harder for women to perform authority roles such as therapist or classroom teacher beyond elementary school, and harder for men to pull off subordinate roles (unless wearing a uniform).

General status play claims or repudiates importance by comparisons to the behavior of children, since in all societies (but not all families) children are less powerful than adults. High-status players distinguish themselves from children; low-status players imitate them. Things that children cannot refrain from doing include stillness, so it is generally a low-status maneuver to fidget, move your head, or touch your face. Children reveal their desires, try to please the powerful, and cannot disguise the fact that they have bodies. Any nonintentional calling of attention to the body, including sounds and odors, is status lowering. Commenting unexpectedly, regardless of tone, on people's appearance, skin color, or age puts them in their bodies and lowers their status.

Therapy patients respond best when the therapist communicates that he or she can take patients' problems and revelations in stride, and that he or she has the power to help patients. In individual therapy, the therapist should almost always play status higher than the patient's portrayal of status. The movie *The King's Speech* provides a brilliant rendition of a therapist performing higher status than even a king. In family therapy, *joining* often requires equal or lower-status play in the famous *one-down* posture (Fisch, Weakland, Watzlawick, & Segal, 1982). In family therapy, the therapist seeks entry into the family culture and must adapt to it; in individual therapy, the therapist entices entry into the therapist's culture and the patient must adapt.

Therapy as a profession often attracts low-status players—born helpers and former patients. Much initial training for these people involves reframing high-status play not as one-upping the patient but as empathically understanding the patient's need for a strong therapist. When you get an "owie" as a kid, you don't want your mom to weep or run for help; when you are suffering in therapy, you want a therapist who takes it in stride. Further, high-status ambiguity—exploring the patient's reaction rather than clarifying what you meant—in the therapist's performance is key to eliciting peculiarities in the patient's approach to people, and it is also key to ensuring that intimacy exposure will generalize to other situations with other people. You want the patient to learn that he or she is not repulsive, rather than that *you* are especially tolerant. Stillness and reserve foster ambiguity.

DIVERSITY AND MULTICULTURALISM

Culture is a set of implicit and explicit contingencies of social reinforcement. A contingency is an if/then effect. "If you touch the fire it will burn you" is a natural or geographic or nonsocial contingency. "If you pick your teeth at the table, others will look at you with disgust" is a cultural contingency. An important fact about culture and diversity is that social contingencies vary from place to place more than you expect them to. People do all sorts of deviant things not because of pathological motives but because of the universal motives of seeking social approval and avoiding social stigma.

Therapists can't develop a useful treatment plan until they know—or at least make a working guess at—what is motivating a problem behavior. Angry parents may mistreat children in order to hurt them; other parents may mistreat children in order to gain social approval from other parents, as in rubbing hot coins on a child's arm to cure an illness. Of course, some parents use coining to disguise their anger at the child with a harmful practice that looks like cultural conformity. Therapists will not always be right in their assessments, but they will be right more often if they consider the alternatives.

It's also important to recognize that you yourself have a culture, a largely arbitrary and invented definition of what it means to be a good person, of how people should behave in various situations. Indeed, my definition of cultural competence is *not* knowing some facts about Haiti before treating a Haitian American or attending a workshop on Costa Ricans before treating a Costa Rican (Karson, 2006a). To me, the essence of cultural competence is knowing your *own* assumptions and cultural injunctions, and especially knowing that they are arbitrary, nothing more (or less) than people's preferences. A good way to learn this is to share your cultural rules with people you respect who don't share them. If you're Christian, read Nietzsche; if you're not, read Matthew. That advice assumes you can read dialogically and not just to memorize facts for quizzes; if you can't, you might need to acquire this skill before practicing psychotherapy, which requires dialogic engagement with other people's ideas and stories.

Cultures vary in the ways they define a good person, so they also vary in what stigmatizes the performance of being a good person. Understanding these stigmas—for example, lust and dominance in women or vulnerability in men—will keep therapists alert to which parts of the patient the therapy still excludes even when it looks like it is going well. Nearly everyone comes for therapy because of stigma. When society discredits one's role as a normal citizen (as in racism and sexism), it can wear down people's sense of belonging, intrude on their ability to get engrossed in what they are doing, and make then angry. When it's their family or social circle, it can eat away at their sense of wholeness. Either way, people need spaces that don't stigmatize them. Therapy is such a place especially for those stigmatized by families and close associates. When Freud said that a goal of therapy was to replace neurotic suffering with common unhappiness, he meant that therapy for the politically oppressed (or the grieving or the physically ill) should relieve any corollary self-blame or rage, while unhappiness and proportional anger about discrimination or misfortune should not be pathologized. Political activism and other coping strategies are appropriate for political oppression, not psychotherapy.

Parker (2016) began her poem "For the White Person Who Wants to Know How to Be My Friend" with two simple rules: "The first thing you do is to forget that I'm Black. Second, you must never forget that I'm Black." This duality is not all that hard to achieve. I've never met a black American patient who seemed not to notice my being white, so I'd bring it up in the first session, after agreeing on a case formulation and treatment plan. "I'm white," I'd say. With other people of other races, other ethnicities, the other sex, and so on, I'm not always sure whether to say anything. If I do, I acknowledge about myself only what is obvious, not my sexual orientation, religion, and so on. If I make a mistake and raise an issue that was not on the person's mind, I do so in good faith, ready to explore the meaning of my highlighting something from my own agenda or misattunement. If I fail to raise the issue, at least I try not to say things that make sense to say only to white people, straight people, and so on. If I accidentally say such a thing, I am prepared to acknowledge that misattunement as well.

A disappointing development in multicultural studies insists that therapists can't treat someone from a different group unless they "obtain the training, experience, consultation, or supervision necessary to ensure the competence of their services" (American Psychological Association, 2002, 2.01b). Such consultation includes learning the stereotypes about various groups, based on the wrong idea that all people in wheelchairs, or all Mexican Americans, are alike. The rule lists so many groups, from gender to national origin, that the implication is that you can treat only yourself. This is even more alarming when you think of the implications for therapists of color, who may not be qualified to treat white people (Karson, 2008). An analogous disappointing attitude demonizes fiction writers who create characters unlike themselves (Shriver, 2016).

RELIGION

Organized religion typically functions as an institution of social control (Skinner, 1953) distinct from government in that statutes are openly and obviously the creation of humans while religious rules of conduct purport to be created by deities or by nature (Harari, 2015). Religion, like any system of control, provides communal benefits (Haidt, 2012) and some costs, including the psychological cost of stigmatizing certain aspects of the human condition. Science, in contrast to religion, is about behaving effectively, not about how we *should* behave (Skinner, 1957). If a therapist and a patient can agree on goals and a fee, then books like this one can help therapists practice more effectively. Science can weigh in on the likelihood of therapy working and how to do it better, but whether to do therapy at all is not a question for science.

Religions often promote a definition of a good person that no human can achieve (contra the spiral staircase metaphor, which discredits perfection rather than goodness or even excellence). This built-in failure is good for the institution—no one ever graduates—but bad for individuals, whose performance of a good person is constantly discredited, if only to themselves or their priests. Only humans, with our grand imagination, could define a good human as one who excludes some of our most obvious traits, such as sex and aggression, claiming we are really angels and not animals. "It would hardly occur to a cocker spaniel that he is really an Irish setter" (Horney, 1950, p. 23). Our therapeutic efforts to encourage patients to invest in themselves and not in an impossibly idealized version of themselves may run afoul of religious training. Such conflicts can be as grand as "It is selfish for a woman to pursue a career" or as small as "God wants me to get good grades." In honoring the humanity of a patient, a religious crisis may ensue.

Religion also frequently arises in therapy because religions often forbid or require goals and processes that conflict with therapeutic goals and processes. Therapists can manage religious requirements as they do societal or familial ones, with the usual strategy of overseeing inquiry into when, not whether, to apply old rules and to rely on old maps. A shorter path may be available with religious rules, since there is usually some religious authority with a more humanistic view than the patient's current one. Commonly for Christians, that authority is Jesus. Otherwise, there is often some other minister, priest, rabbi, elder, shaman, or imam who thinks homosexuality, masturbation, fantasy, virtuous aggression, or play is just fine. Still, we must acknowledge that the main clinical theories, and humanism itself, can produce a religious conflict. This occurs either because they antireligiously debase glorified values to the status of mere human preferences ("I'm not sure that honoring your father is working for you"), or because clinicians adhere to humanism or a clinical theory as if it were a religion, using its values to frame the human condition in a way that they don't see as arbitrary but as the way things really are. This is *theory fusion* (Karson, 2008), when a theoretical approach seems not like a useful narrative but the way things really are, as if an organizing principle, a core belief, or even an operant is not a construct but a *thing*. A good solution is to learn many theories, just as multilingualism can prevent fusing a thing and its name. If you can play your song in only one key, it's a hymn.

AGGRESSION

People are scary. Even a shark will leave you unharmed if it's not hungry, but a human might not. One of the most difficult things about civilization is the requirement that we must suppress the impulse to attack people simply because we don't know them (Freud, 1930/1961). It turns out we are capable of assuming benign intentions in strangers (especially if they look like us in some important way), but it requires management of our aggressive nature. A major management strategy has been to demonize aggression, to promote sheep and sacrificers as idols, canonizing victims as martyrs. Gratifying the public's preference for strong men, heroes, and generals also works, since it keeps people in the posture of sheep. One widespread effect of this demonization is the way the word *aggression* has come to mean violence or angry incursion rather than its virtuous counterparts: the quest for mastery and protection, including ambition, achievement, sturdiness, and assertiveness.

To counter this effect, let's use the term *virtuous aggression* to describe self-defense, defense of others, holding one's ground, resisting oppression, and so on. Therapy often requires virtuous aggression from the therapist—exploring versus dispersing conflict, collecting the fee, and ending sessions on time. These things all injure patients, as they should. Of course, they don't "injure" patients if that phrase calls to mind abusing or exploiting them, and therapists who insist on being utterly benign tend to think of all injury as abuse. Therapists' virtuous aggression injures patients in the sense that most patients would rather avoid unpleasant topics, payments, and untimely departures. To maintain an agenda despite injuring others requires making peace with injuring others.

Supervisors waste a lot of time and energy trying to convince trainees that infliction of injury is not injury at all. I don't imagine surgical residents need a lot of coaxing and rationalization to get them to cut people, because the kind of people who become surgeons don't twist themselves into knots at the idea. Many therapy trainees act as if ending sessions on time or broaching sensitive topics is a vicious thing to do, like parents who crumble at the first sign of frustration. I'd rather train them to accept their own aggression and to appreciate its utility than to train them to think it's all a kind of sweetness after all. Similarly, I don't want to practice a therapy that attempts to achieve goals with only positive reinforcements. I want patients and trainees to learn to take bad weather in stride and to navigate rough water; I don't want to just get them safely to port. No competent athletic coach would arrange only for positive outcomes, because that would leave athletes unprepared for setbacks. I certainly don't want to insult students or patients, but telling the former when they have made a mistake and charging the latter a fee, and for both groups ending class and sessions on time, are not things I want to shy away from, either.

SEX

Sex has a few meanings relevant to psychotherapy. I'll discuss whether a person is a boy or a girl, a man or a woman, below, under the topic of *gender*. Here, I want to focus on erotic feelings and on the whole romantic (and often reproductive) enterprise.

A surprisingly large number of people seek therapy because of romantic woes. There are many reasons for this phenomenon, from cultural signals that single people are defective or that marriage is the end of "every happy plot" to longings, however inspired, for a teammate to go through life with. Also, of course, people in good romantic relationships already have someone to talk to, do intimacy exposure with, and so on. In therapy, it's often useful to consider whether the problem is primarily one of relationship maintenance, mate selection, or romance maintenance.

Some people don't know how to have friends, much less a spouse. In skills training, they can learn to take turns talking, to observe boundaries, and so on. In psychotherapy, the work removes barriers to friendship. These might include a self-experience as unlikeable or expectations or relational patterns that preclude connection and collaboration, such as insistence on playing a role, like conquistador or butterfly, that interferes with emotional connection.

When the problem is mate selection—choosing the wrong people—the case formulation emerges from consideration of the moments in the early stage of relationships when the patient overlooked red flags. These often include a failure to consider one's own experience in courtship and focusing instead only on the other person's appeal. Unwarranted assumptions and fears about what other people are up to are also often in play. Either of these can lead to an open-ended or relational therapy. Patients can use therapy to learn to observe themselves better, and they can use the ambiguity in the therapy relationship to unearth and explore their erroneous assumptions and fears.

Couples therapy often best addresses problems in relationship maintenance. This is true even when one of the partners acknowledges responsibility for the couple's troubles because of psychological tendencies. There is no reason that a couple can't examine and embrace a member's psychology, and doing it together can be restorative for the relationship, not just for the individual. However, there is often no couple to treat in these situations, because problems in relationship maintenance have left the patient alone. Also, couples therapy is best when the goals are couple oriented, when the person wants to change that particular relationship. Sometimes, the patterns of relating that lead to problems in relationship maintenance are widespread. For example, a woman gets bored with any partner she can get to settle down, seeking adventure rather than intimacy in her primary romance. The same woman patches together a work life that eschews any sort of daily grind and, while she is not an alcoholic, socializes only with enough alcohol to get tipsy. Here, the pervasive pattern of adventure is interfering with several life goals; if she could discover that not all routines are deadly, it could help her at work and socially, not just in her love life. Psychotherapy, reliably framed, is ideal for such a discovery, if the therapist can resist the temptation to break the rules with her.

Therapists ought to know something about the range of sexual fantasies and practices, if only not to look shocked if patients muster the courage to tell them what they actually think about and do. This is part of the larger implication of psychological mindedness: not taking people at face value and adopting a welcoming curiosity about what they're hiding.

One reading of history has it that until the invention of agriculture around 12,000 years ago, there wasn't enough food to sustain certain roles in human societies. These include master-slave relationships and their derivative patriarchal ones (Diamond, 2013). Without a way to store value, whether in granaries or banks, slavery must have been scarce. Would-be masters had little incentive to dominate or rob within their own tribe once they had their fill for the day. Prior to agriculture, for about 60,000 years humans were physically and cognitively modern, living in bands of 30 to 90 people (Harari, 2015). It's unclear in that context what the evolutionary purpose of sexual pleasure was. It's certainly not necessary for reproduction. Many species reproduce without sexual pleasure, and people left many infants behind when childrearing was inconvenient because of lean years or because other infants needed nurturing (Diamond, 2013), evidence they were having sex for pleasure and not for procreation. Sexual pleasure in chimps seems to raise questions about paternity, because females mate with so many males, which ensures decent treatment of infants by adult males, since most of them in a given band may be the father (Dawkins, 1976).

In our own species, sexual pleasure may foster pair-bonding (Fletcher et al., 2015); the foraging life is easier when someone has your back, and children are more likely to make it to adulthood in the care of a couple: "Two are better than one, because they have a good reward for their toil. For if they fall, one will lift up the other; but woe to one who is alone and falls and does not have another to help" (Eccl 4:9–10). Genes that confer extreme pleasure under one's own control or the control of a loved one could also tilt the pain-pleasure balance enough to keep people thinking that the struggle to stay alive is worth it. People with erotic genes would then be more likely to stay alive long enough to raise or help raise children, who would then inherit intense eroticism from those parents. (Notice how this idea normalizes gay couples, whose eroticism is also in the service of pairing and pleasure.) Admittedly, though, it's difficult to peer back through the lens of our own cultures to see what sex might have been like when people were foragers, but studies of more contemporary foragers lend support to these views (Diamond, 2013).

Sex is such a powerful reinforcer that, as Skinner (1953) teaches us, when people punish or constrain sex, those punishments become conditioned reinforcers. Many sexual fantasies illustrate this, from masochistic desires to lose one's beloved, to rape fantasies and bondage games. Difficulty sorting out what's originally sexual from what's conditioned is the basis for much advertising, which associates sexy people with a product. Sorting these out in therapy can help patients engage in the pursuit of other rewards. For example, many people find naughtiness attractive, presumably because society construes their own sexuality as naughty, and they wind up hurt and frustrated when they pursue naughty people. Accompanying reinforcers are often better obtained in fantasy form, or in naughty sex with a reliable partner. Therapy can help frame these desires for rogues as play by discussing the desires in a way that takes them seriously but not requiring actual rogues to gratify them.

The method of therapy is to establish a relationship (described in chapters 6–8) that encourages patients to share what's on their minds. When thoughts turn to sex, therapists ought first to inspect their own possible sexualization of the relationship. The reason good therapists are so firm—I would say reliable—about certain elements of the relationship is that patients often interpret departures as social or sexual overtures. Any hint of social relating evokes repertoires of tact, politeness, and saving face that interfere with honest reporting of the patient's inner thoughts. Any hint of sexual possibility will either oppress patients or induce them to check their appearance, also inhibiting the doffing of the social mask. When patients sexualize the relationship, they are often following the therapist's lead.

Of course, therapists will meet some patients who strike them as particularly attractive. Depending on therapists' own histories of sexual relating, they may become hypnotized, tantalized, attracted, or merely pleased. In brief treatment or couples therapy, they will have to manage these feelings just as they would if they were attracted to the spouse of a friend or to someone at work who is unavailable. In relational therapy, these feelings will interfere with the intimacy and lack of agenda therapists are trying to establish. The best strategy is to evoke the part of the patient's selfhood that is in pain: the frightened or sad or lonely child, the angry or jilted child, the neglected parts of the self. Therapy is about welcoming these aspects of the personality into the community of the self, so getting to it will help with erotic feelings. If the therapist finds lonely or neglected children attractive, this might be the wrong field for that person.

Often patients wrestle with similar feelings of attraction. The same strategies will usually work for them, namely, cleaning up the therapy frame and focusing on the work. However, sex in therapy is just one example of the many ways that patients and therapists compare themselves to each other. Envy may be the biggest ignored topic in therapy, besides (perhaps) money. Our sensitivity to status and our biological design for sex and aggression makes us reactive to signals of superiority from other people. Many patients are perfectly aware that their therapists would not give them the time of day if not for the fee. Many (but fewer) therapists are perfectly aware that their patients would not be interested in intimacy with them if not for the pain that motivates them. In other words, each might be out of the other's league on the dating market. Adding to this dynamic is the patient's tendency to glamorize the therapist's life, to imagine financial and romantic success. Patients complain about work and love to someone who seems to have no troubles in those areas, since therapists ideally are seen while fully engaged in their work and while comfortably offering intimacy.

Sexualizing the therapy is often a status move. Status is lowered by being put in your body, and reminding a therapist that he or she has a sex life can make him or her less threatening. Many people are uncomfortable with seeing women in positions of power, so they put women in power in their bodies by sexualizing or evaluating their appearance. Management of overt sexualization of the therapy is tricky, because talking about what's going on is also sexy. It's like making a documentary about pornography; these typically *become* pornography (Karson, 2008). Still, "I wonder what you imagine this is like for me" can be a useful thing to say.

Finally, after cleaning up their own acts and getting down to work, therapists can focus on the *function* of the sexualization of the therapy by observing the immediate context of its occurrence. Depending on the amount of collaboration in the therapy, this can range from a simple observation ("You were thinking about your sister and then switched to sex") to an interpretation ("an example of your filling your mind with distracting thoughts when you feel unloved"). It's tempting to avoid all this by pairing patients with therapists so as not to evoke sexual feelings, but this avoids the potential redemption from a relationship that manages rather than avoids eroticism.

I often ask trainees what they would say if a four-year-old niece or nephew expressed a wish to marry them. They usually find the best answer: "What would that be like?" The idea is that if patients are only *speaking* ("staying in the chair"), they are not violating any of our rules, regardless of what they say. (Threats of violence and reports of child or elder abuse are exceptions.) Many things come up in therapy, including sex, that the therapist wants to make go away but which need exploring, or at least a hearing.

GENDER

Sex is whether you are a boy or a girl, a man or a woman. Some people are neither or both, but almost everyone is one or the other. *Gender* is how you perform the role associated with your sex (Butler, 1990; Goffman, 1959). *Masculine* and *feminine* often describe gender, but these terms have become so tied to a specific sex that their introduction does little to free people to separate gender from sex. *Yin* and *yang* have their advantages. Best, though, is to avoid terminology altogether and to think of gender as the repertoire of behavior that has been differentially reinforced because of sex. Gender refers to the behaviors that families and communities require or forbid boys or girls to do *because* they are boys or girls.

Sex (male or female) is profoundly important in our society, and even more important in other societies. If society organized roles as tightly around earlobes as it does around sex, then the first thing parents would want to know about a new baby would be attached or unattached, not boy or girl (Karson, 2008). Because of this, people are profoundly concerned not only with whether they are successfully performing the role they are in situationally and the role of good person generally, they are also profoundly concerned with whether they are successfully performing the role of man or woman. The importance of the performance heightens the consequences of failure, and people are extremely sensitive to the presence of identity elements that discredits them as "real" men or "real" women.

Gender pathology refers to life problems associated with social contingencies that vary with sex. Sensitive boys and tough girls have trouble fitting in with some communities. Women who worry they are too authoritative in meetings and men who worry excessively about not getting a promotion are caught in pathologies of gender. Thus, gender is an important therapy topic, and patients can derive much relief from distinguishing personal pathology from gender pathology. Relational therapy can elucidate what kind of man or woman the patient really is, in contrast to what the patient is supposed to be. Rewards will accrue from treating oneself as a knight or a princess in a metaphorical, playful frame rather than in a bound-to-fail, literal frame.

Gender is also an important consideration in technique—what the therapist does while doing the therapy. Good therapists perform the role androgynously, with the tender acceptance necessary to bathe the exploration of the self in welcoming curiosity and with the reliable strength to communicate that they can hold together and take in stride the patient's disparate selves. Some therapists are too much one way or another, varying between Freud's previously mentioned claim to be a conquistador and the "you poor dear" relinquishment of authority and power.

The field of psychotherapy tends to cultivate yin (i.e., stereotypically feminine) gender performances, so—male or female—therapists might find themselves stymied in their efforts to portray strength to their patients. Female students sometimes bully each other (with eye rolling and critical text messaging) for speaking out in class. One occasionally detects a bizarre kind of pride around which trainee is most easily triggered and offended by other people's stories; one would think that a therapist would find prestige in hearing difficult material without getting too upset rather than in falling apart over it. Some students perceive direct feedback as an assault—and I don't mean feedback criticizing the trainee's personal psychology or intelligence; I mean statements like "I wonder if there's another way to look at that." Increasingly, student applications contain declarations of mental illness or psychological problems as good reasons to seek a career as a therapist. Born caregivers in the cohort organize around not hurting the feelings of these students rather than around learning a difficult skill.

HOMOSEXUALITY

Gay people are just like straight people, and vice versa. In addition to whatever life problems bring them to therapy, they may suffer from gender pathologies (see above) since their selection of a same-sex mate may discredit the performance of their sex role in circles that are important to them. They may have suffered the same stigmatization that straight people do when revealing sexual preferences, which is why straight people so rarely talk about what they do in bed. Straight couples can hide their interest in sex by looking as if they are merely conforming to social mating patterns; gay couples communicate that sex must be important enough to them to go to the trouble of mating with a same-sex partner. When gay people suffer enhanced stigmatization because of their sexual orientation, society may prohibit them from playing normal roles like teacher, soldier, or good person. Therapists must not pile on by disallowing their gay patients from having normal problems; not everything they do involves their sexuality.

A recent nationally discussed question that doesn't interest me is whether the government ought to force therapists who hate gay people to treat them.

To me, the important question is whether therapists who hate gay people or gay sex ought to practice at all.

VIOLENCE

Violence, like anxiety and depression, comes in different personalities. Psychopathic violence is goal oriented and enjoys inflicting pain. A psychopath is like a wolf among sheep and worries only about the rancher's shotgun. Narcissistic violence restores power to the individual, either by inducing fear or by having one's way. It is essentially a tantrum. Much battering is of this sort, with the perpetrator, feeling powerless and infantile, relieved of that feeling by intimidating the person who intimidates him or her. Many batterers are disguising their vulnerability to humiliation from, say, a partner's potential disapproval or infidelity by asserting control over the partner. The fact of the battery humiliates the batterer, so the partner's visible injuries and fears further humiliate and enrage the batterer. Paranoid violence rectifies a perceived injustice. People who shoot up theaters, schools, and workplaces are very much like action movie heroes. In an action movie, injustices are piled up on the hero until viewers find themselves rooting for a violent resolution. The only difference is that most people do not perceive the paranoid's injustices as injustices.

It's generally a mistake to try to predict violence (Heilbrun, Marczyk, & DeMatteo, 2002). Instead, authorities should implement prudent, sensible responses to any concern with the understanding that the person must comply or face some consequence. For example, a therapist doesn't have to guess whether a patient is going to attack her when he accosts her in the parking lot. Instead, she should explain that she can't work like this because it worries her, and they need an agreement that it won't happen again or the therapy will be over. Therapists can institute a therapy frame only with those people who can wait (or can learn to wait) until the next session to speak their minds (or who call them only in emergencies). Similarly, therapists preoccupied with the question of whether a patient is going to attack someone else can't provide a therapeutic environment, so the therapist and the patient need to come to an agreement about how they can put the therapist's mind at rest. (As in trauma work, therapists may need to have a colleague involved to conduct the part of the treatment that is not relational psychotherapy.) Therapists could address many confidentiality binds with a treatment contract that authorizes the release of information whenever violence is a concern (Morris, 2016), whether or not the concern rises to the level requiring statutory disclosure, with a clause that therapy depends on keeping the confidentiality exception in place.

SUICIDE

Suicide, like much else in psychotherapy, is better considered a multicharacter drama than a solo performance. Suicide is a form of murder in which perpetrator and victim happen to occupy the same skin. As with other violence, the reasons for it vary with personality and can suggest a direction for intervention. We can infer the type of suicide from the patient's history and imagination.

Some people kill themselves as a form of euthanasia, to put themselves out of physical or emotional misery. They need an objective assessment of the costs and benefits of doing so, including the costs and benefits for others close to them. Many friends and relatives are not as burdened by the patient's illness or depression as they appear to be. The dyad should also consider the odds of remission. Many miserable people underestimate the chances of things getting better, and objective data can help.

Some people kill themselves out of shame, much as a Spartan mother would supposedly kill a son who returned from battle a coward. It's the patient's own pride that is usually a problem. When police arrested a well-known psychologist for sex crimes, there were not many life roles left that he could play without having the attempted performance discredited by his record. Still, when he killed himself, it was also a declaration that he was better than that; the ultimate effort to disown an identity element is to kill it. These people need reconciliation between the parts of the self, something that relational therapy is just right for. I don't have much sympathy when people blame horrible crimes on anyone but the perpetrator, but if people blame one particular part of the perpetrator, that seems different. If the ashamed psychologist hadn't been so prideful in the first place, he might have accommodated the rights of the women he was secretly taping.

Some people execute themselves for bad conduct not because they are ashamed but in a search for justice. They may feel, for instance, that they don't deserve to enjoy life because of something they've done. These people need to understand that while punishment is in order, they are leaving the sentence to a biased judge. I have a few times staged a trial in therapy and collaborated with patients on a just sentence, emphasizing features of what might be restorative to the victim and rehabilitative for the patient.

Ultimately, every story is different, and clinicians must specify the exact reasons for the murderous impulse for each patient. Framing it as one part of the patient doing something to another part of the patient helps clarify what is going on and what the therapist can do about it (Karson, 2001; Schwartz, 2001).

DEATH

The smart way to live is as if you will survive for about as long as local mortality tables say you will. It would be foolish to undertake a project like getting skilled at psychotherapy if you expected to die by age 25, and it is foolish to smoke tobacco if you can otherwise expect to live to 80. Again, a multicharacter approach is useful, so economists talk about the relationship between the present self (the smoker, say) and a future self (who doesn't want emphysema). Therapists can welcome both selves into the therapy and arrange for mutual understanding between them. They can suggest to patients that their behavior would make more sense if patients believed they were going to live forever (if overly abstemious) or only for a few more years (if overly impulsive). In my view, work-life balance need not always be achieved in the present; it can also be sought over the course of the life-span, bearing down with little sleep while establishing a profession and raising children, relaxing before and after the high-stress phase of life.

Death and serious illness provide common examples of the Freudian injunction to replace neurotic suffering with common unhappiness. Grief is healthy, whether conceived as loss or behavioral extinction. There is often little for therapists to do but wait for it to pass, just as a friend may have to suspend the typical agenda of the friendship during moments or even periods of grief. Similarly, patients often share good news in therapy that has little or nothing to do with the work. Accountants, dentists, and gardeners will want to get back to their work after a decent interval when their clients or patients share good news, and therapists should too, although other professionals will say, "That's great!" while therapists ought to know that silver linings often come with clouds. It is often useful to ask for a picture of grief, a description of what is going on in the patient's mind while he or she is crying about a lost loved one. You might get simple grief, as in, "I was thinking of how much she made me laugh," but you might get something more psychologically complex, as in, "I was thinking of how I never told her how much she meant to me." The latter may relate to the focus of the therapy, or may even open a new focus, and becomes grist for the therapy mill.

Nothing good will happen ever again once we die, but nothing bad will ever happen either. It's not that we should actually look forward to its arrival (although a period of decrepitude may encourage that), but that the entire therapy enterprise is one of making the most of situations one is in rather than merely wishing one were elsewhere. Part of every situation is the inevitability of dying. Men often have a harder time of it in our culture, since death may represent defeat, and debility is unmanly.

LOVE

Love is both an emotion and a relational model. When abusive parents say they love their children, there's no way of knowing what they feel, but we can certainly question whether the relational model obtains. The essence of the model is that the other person's happiness and well-being operate as reinforcement for oneself, and injuries to the person are aversive. You know how you are happy for people who get good news but you're also kind of resentful of them? When you are only or almost only happy, that's called *love*. *Romantic love* is the same thing plus sex. In other words, just as anger is the name of the emotion in which injury is reinforcing, love is the name of the emotion in which injury is especially aversive. If you love your car, you hate to see it dinged. Ideally, with a partner, the feeling is mutual, and signs of one's own well-being reinforce the other person.

In love, the other person becomes an important source of reinforcement. Sharing secrets about oneself, the ultimate honesty, enhances this, and it generates the feeling of being truly loved but risks rejection. Therapy is a cure through love, as Freud once said, in the sense that sharing and accepting secrets deepens the relationship. A major source of conflict in life derives from the natural tendency to control the source of reinforcement. The paradox that many happy couples and parents learn and even celebrate is that the very quality that makes other people's reciprocation of love so meaningful—their humanity—makes them impossible to control.

Therapists, parents, and romantic partners must learn a circumspect definition of injury if they are to avoid overindulging the objects of their affection. Patients and children may be upset if they don't get their way, and only a broader conception of the benefits of not always getting one's way will reconcile limit setting with the emotion of love. This is true also of overly complimentary clinical supervisors. We teach children to manage growth-inducing emotional injuries as parallel to the muscular strains of athletic training by viewing the injuries that way ourselves.

The relational model of love engenders care and protection. It need not involve the emotion of love, but it is easier to maintain if the emotion is present, since the emotion means that the caregiver will be rewarded by signs from the beloved of being cared for and protected. The caregiver may impose the same model without the emotion, just as a martial arts master can fight without anger. The reward might be the approval of peers for good caregiving, or signs of improved functioning from the person in question rather than signs of happiness.

When love goes wrong, it's often because the emotion was misnamed and love was never in the picture. It's not too hard to see that many abusive parents hate their children, but their associates have taught them to insist they love their children. If the psychologist infers hatred, nearly everyone rebukes him or her, because it is a violation of cultural norms to question whether a parent loves a child. Some judges and attorneys react as if the psychologist were saying that *their* mothers didn't love *them*. The question of what kind of love it is can clarify domestic violence. In many cases, the batterer loves the victim the way one loves one's new car and the victim loves the batterer the way some monotheists love their God. The treatment is to distinguish the victim from a car and the batterer from a god, although the latter is hard to do when he or she really does have the power of life and death over the victim.

I balk when therapists tell me that their patients have to learn to love themselves before they can accept love from others. How are they supposed to know how to love themselves? Instead, they need to experience the therapist's love to learn how to love themselves. The word *love* is too evocative to use in therapy, but the relational model and the emotion can occur. Many patients come for therapy not because they squirm when loved but because they don't know how to love others. Therapy is an opportunity to love and be loved with certain built-in protections against exploitation.

A clear, consistent frame facilitates engrossment and intensifies emotion (Goffman, 1974). Rigid rules make board games and sporting events emotionally evocative, and participants in the former and even spectators in the latter can get extremely angry. There are a lot of reasons it's easier to fall in love with a character in a movie than with a real person, and one important reason is that the experience is tightly framed. Yes, you only see the character at his or her best—the witty conversation and not the chores—but also important is the knowledge that the intensity of the emotion need not last long and the framing absolves the character from providing anything in return. Many couples stumble because they feel awkward about framing their relationship. You don't have to tell the love of your life (or your children) that you feel this way about two hours a day and otherwise would be fine amusing yourself on your own, but a mature couple that wants its love to last does not make impossible demands on each other to refute this truism that the emotion of love is consistent but not constant. Therapists and patients can love each other more intensely and reasonably at the same time by tightly framing the relationship.

MONEY

Money is the ultimate socially constructed phenomenon and generalized reinforcer. It has value only because other people think it does, and it can be exchanged for so many different things that its value is almost equivalent to whatever you might want. Any dissatisfaction, any deprivation, any wish potentiates money as a reinforcer. Because we acclimate to whatever we have, additional money is almost always reinforcing. As with anything that looks like an addiction, it is unhealthy to put too many eggs in one reinforcement basket. An array of rewards ensures that no single reward will dominate, and it also ensures that people will have something to spend money on to rival the desire for accrual. Many people spend as if there is no tomorrow; others save as if they have forever to convert money into goods and services (see "Death," above).

Therapists can't be that helpful with patients' complexes about money if they can't talk about the fee. Winnicott (1972) once said that wherever there is love, there is hate, because love implies the potential to be hurt, and people naturally feel hatred for that which can hurt them. In therapy, the time boundary and the fee should fully express the therapist's hatred of the patient. Therapists should charge enough to make them glad to be working with the patient, and enough to offset any resentment they might feel for giving up their time and for relinquishing any forms of self-indulgence that interfere with therapy, such as gossiping and talking about themselves. Of course, when therapists start their practices, the money has more value to them because it allays their fears about paying their rent, so they can be satisfied with having to charge less. Later, as their time becomes more valuable to others and to themselves, they will want more money to take on another patient in their practice.

WORK

"Work organizes life" (Clinton, 1993). Gainful employment is a solution to poverty not only because it provides money, but also because it combats the aimlessness of poverty by providing a structure to the week, a sense of purpose, a network of relationships, and a positive identity element. These same features can assist with anxiety, depression, negative self-definitions, and mental illness. When something has gone wrong at work because of the patient's psychology, the same problematic pattern can interfere with working in therapy. If the dyad can change the pattern to enable more productive working in therapy, that will apply to the patient's work life as well. If the dyad merely fixes the noticeable problem in therapy—by making accommodations, offering reassurances, or avoiding therapy in favor of a more comfortable way of relating—rather than change the pattern, the solution will not apply to the patient's work life.

Frequently, the problem is that the patient is working just fine, but not getting engrossment, purpose, or satisfaction from work. As with mating, we can usefully view this as a problem in either selecting the right job or maintaining its potential satisfactions. Some jobs are just not suited to the patient, but the patient did not sufficiently consult his or her inner self about what kind of work would be satisfying. For example, an artist who took a job as a graphic designer that did not allow her to express her artistic agenda but that also depleted her energy for art by the end of the day might find happiness in a corporate job with predictable hours and affectionate relationships, leaving her with plenty of time and energy to sculpt. Other jobs could be a source of vitality and satisfaction, but the patient's psychology gets in the way. This is the problem that many therapists call *burnout*, but which often has to do with losing interest in climbing the spiral staircase.

FOOD AND EATING DISORDERS

We are hard-wired to eat the whole thing, to take advantage of our fat cell storage system in case we can't find food tomorrow. In foraging troops of 30 to 90 people, there was little risk of obesity. Even if foragers discovered a giant cache of honey, they would divide it into manageable portions. As food has become cheaper in the United States and work has become less physical, obesity has become a major health problem. Sugar kills far more people in the United States every year than guns do.

Weight is a function of calories in and calories out. (Day to day, salty foods and some medications and hormones may produce water retention, but in the longer run, there is no way around the first law of thermodynamics.) Calories out includes basal metabolism and exercise, and exercise has the added benefit of building muscle mass, which burns more calories than flab even at rest. People have bottomless appetites for weight-loss systems that involve eating something and little interest in systems that involve not eating as much. The existential desire to tap dance our way out of the laws of nature is nowhere more evident than here.

Many American children are never hungry, so they lack opportunities to learn to manage their deprivations. They eat because food tastes good. Those who are indifferent to food hardly eat at all, and those who aren't eat too much. I found that by depriving my kids of food after school (or limiting them to a very small snack), they would be cheerful and talkative at dinner and compliment me on my cooking. Eventually, they learned to stop eating when they weren't hungry, but I don't see how you can learn this if you don't know what hunger is.

Many children are too hungry and eat everything, like foragers. Food, like any reinforcement for any kind of person, can become too much the focus of reward to the exclusion of rewards that are harder to obtain. Money, food, sex, love, and even laughter can lose their appetitive qualities and serve as negative reinforcement, a way to concentrate on something to avoid something else. In other words, people concentrate on them because they are available and not because they are the itch that needs scratching. Good therapists heed this distinction, and bring up whatever it is that a fascinating topic is avoiding. Also, if a patient is skinny or obese, therapists should think not just about whether they themselves could stand to lose a few pounds, as humans are wont to do, but also about whether the patient might have a strange relationship with food.

One of the most socially transgressive comments a therapist can make regards the patient's weight. At the start of therapy, the therapist might introduce the patient to the general transgressions of therapy, or the therapist might delay the implementation of therapy until clearing up professional issues (such as dangerously low or high weight), analogous to postponing therapy for a depressed patient until suicide has been dealt with. Later, once therapy is underway, significant weight changes are harder to address. In our culture, it's a lot easier to say, "You're losing weight" than it is to say, "You're gaining weight." The more obvious the issue in either direction, the more the therapist is obliged to say something. Therapists can often handle this by going meta: "I'm not sure how it would feel for me to comment on your weight." Assuming the working alliance is in reasonably good repair, it's often best just to plow ahead with a straightforward comment while preparing to process the moment retroactively.

As noted above, under "Development," we can understand many eating disorders as expressing confusion about who owns the patient's body. I've noticed two main variations when the parents claim more ownership than the child can stand. (Often the claim is made around the issue of sex but the reaction is expressed around food.) In the first, the child proves ownership by taking control of ingestion. This is like a homeowner, told by the zoning board that he or she can't build a deck, who responds by painting the house a horrid color, shutting off the water supply, and letting the lawn go feral: *I'll show you whose house it is*. Since eating seems to please the parents, the child often finds that the only way to express ownership is to refuse to eat or digest, just as you can truly know you own something only if you can do something with it that others don't want you to do. The other main variant is the child's refusal to take any responsibility for eating, like a homeowner who wouldn't dream of telling a neighbor which kind of tree to plant on the neighbor's lawn, as a way of signaling nonownership, the problem being the treatment of one's own body as if it is the neighbor's or the parents'. Here, the child capitulates to the parental insistence of ownership, and the parents' efforts to promote healthy eating unfortunately seem to claim even more of an ownership interest in the child's body. The parents' concern about the child's immaturity to make good decisions keeps them from transferring ownership rights. When the child leaves home, he or she eats whatever is available and doesn't know how to monitor his or her intake.

SLEEP

Sleep deprivation causes psychological problems like anxiety and depression, which, in turn, interfere with sleep. It's not often aligned with the therapist's role to give advice, but even the most nondirective therapist is authorized to wonder why a patient hasn't explored sleep hygiene on the internet. If a patient sought therapy for depression or anxiety and the therapist discovered that there was domestic violence or substance abuse (which, like sleep, exacerbate anxiety and depression), the therapist would be wise to include the major problem in the goal statement and case formulation. Though far less dramatic, sleep disturbances often deserve this kind of focus, since they compound other problems. Cognitive behavioral therapy for insomnia includes sensible and practical ideas such as not napping and getting out of bed when fretting. Patients can pick up most of it online; its cognitive-behavioral component corrects unproductive beliefs about sleep itself.

The case formulation can inform unproductive beliefs about sleep to keep the therapist in a consistent therapeutic role, whether addressing the main problem or addressing sleep difficulties. For example, a depressed patient may think that a good night's sleep is undeserved for the same reasons that a good love life or gratifying work are undeserved. A narcissist may lie awake rehearsing the insults suffered through the day, fuming about the world's refusal to recognize his or her importance; falling asleep would signal an acceptance of the insults that the patient fights. An anxious patient lies awake worrying about what might go wrong tomorrow, missing out on the pleasures of sleep as he or she misses out on other pleasures by worrying. In each case, the therapist need not isolate the patterns that interfere with sleep. Instead, the undeserving, retaliatory, or uncertain patient produces the same constellation of self and other in the life problem, in bed, and in the therapy office. The therapist can use the therapy relationship as a window not only into the life problem but also into the sleep disturbance.

Chapter Three

Knowing Something about Psychology

No one asks how to motivate a baby. A baby naturally explores everything it can get at, unless restraining forces have already been at work. And this tendency doesn't die out, it's wiped out.—B. F. Skinner

People come for therapy because of behavioral problems, where *behavioral* means things they do, including feeling emotions, worrying, avoiding conflict, and so on. Knowing something about why people behave as they do can lead to productive ideas about intervention. Lately, approaches other than understanding the problem and devising a solution have captured the field, so I'll deal with these before we proceed.

EVIDENCE-BASED PRACTICE

Psychotherapy is more like residential architecture than like curing a disease because psychological problems like anxiety and depression (versus biological problems like schizophrenia and bipolar disorder) are more like having a kitchen that doesn't meet your needs than they are like scurvy or cholera. Terms like *evidence-based practice* and *empirically supported treatment* sound good—who could be against evidence or empiricism?—but what they actually mean applied to therapy is manualized treatment, or, at the least, *not relational* (Shedler, 2010). A good architect will not look into a book with only four or five prefab kitchens and suggest the one closest to your needs. A good architect will instead listen to your description of your lifestyle—and, more importantly, observe it—and make design suggestions accordingly. He or she will not classify you according to vaguely relevant variables and prescribe a design solution based on the category you are in. Of course, there is a fee for this, but you get a kitchen that will meet your needs for decades.

It's fine when therapists shrug and admit they are doing the best they can for what the patient can afford; what's annoying are claims that the prefab model is the superior product.

Evidence-based practice is supposed to mean an integration of science, practitioner skill, and patient values (American Psychological Association, 2012). When your doctor and you decide whether to have a mammogram (if you're a woman) or a prostate cancer screening test (if you're a man), the underlying science and the doctor's skill (at reading the results and at performing potential surgeries) produce the evidence needed to make a decision. The evidence includes the chances of finding a major problem and the chances of averting that problem with medical intervention. The evidence also includes the worry and hassle of undergoing the screen and following up on positive results that turn out to be either incorrect (there's nothing really wrong) or so bad that there's nothing to do. Only you, the patient, can weigh this evidence. You can see how this only remotely applies to the decision about whether to undergo psychotherapy. For one thing, the success of therapy depends a lot more on the particular therapist than most medical procedures depend on the particular doctor. For another, each depression is more different from the next than each prostate or breast cancer is. Finally, undergoing the procedure in therapy is a benefit, while in medicine it's a cost.

Some would say that manualized treatments counter this problem, since they seek to remove the importance of the particular therapist from the equation. The gold standard here is the randomized clinical trial, invented by James Lind in 1753. Lind carefully controlled the diets of sailors and found that none of those receiving citrus got scurvy (wherefore Brits are often called Limeys for their association with that fruit). Are anxiety and depression really like scurvy? Or is each one unique? Is a sailor consuming citrus like an anxious person on medication?

Here's where I think we often mistake the alarm for the burglar, as I've already noted. Occasionally, a burglar alarm is defective and the smart thing to do is to disconnect it. Of course, even then it's not a long-term solution if burglars worry you. Usually the alarm is working fine and disconnecting it is a bad idea. Depression and anxiety are alarms that indicate that there is something wrong with the person's life. That thing, and not the indicator, should be addressed. Sometimes, of course, there's little harm in muffling the alarm, especially when, as in trauma, it goes off full-blast at the least gust of wind, but generally, the patient will lose interest in fixing what's really wrong once the alarm is turned off.

The evidence base for relational therapy is actually stronger than for manualized treatments (Shedler, 2010; Wachtel, 2010). The best predictor for the success of a manualized treatment is the willingness of the therapist to set aside the manual (Ablon & Jones, 1998, 2002). Cognitive behavioral therapies have never been successful in randomized trials (Shedler, 2015), press reports notwithstanding. Antidepressants and antianxiety drugs are also ineffective, the former from the start and the latter after a few weeks (Whitaker & Cosgrove, 2015). Virtually every psychotherapy treatment that researchers have subjected to scientific scrutiny has passed muster, so we're really talking about empirically supported treatments and those that are not yet empirically supported (W. Pinsof, personal communication, 2015).

A recipe or a manual is not enough to make a good meal. You also need someone who can cook. No recipe can teach you the point at which to stop mixing the batter, how to fry an egg over easy, or how much salt to add when correcting the seasoning.

BRAIN SCIENCE

Science, for better and worse, is a human activity and is therefore subject to all the cognitive distortions and biases that flesh is heir to. Indeed, one way to characterize the psychoanalytic transition from classical to relational analysis is that under the former the analyst's humanity was a constant disappointment, a departure from an ideal, while under the latter it is central to the approach. Similarly, scientists, being people, constantly seek an ideal of certainty when the best they can ever do is to probe the environment and interpret the response.

Focus on the brain serves the desire to find a fundamental way of looking at things, to say what is *really* going on. It's not that *you* like chocolate; chocolate has a certain effect on your *brain.* "Liking chocolate" seems less concrete to brain scientists (and depressives) than activating a brain feature, less like something that adrift psychologists can sink their teeth into. The problem with brain science is not that it's a different way of punctuating experience, but that it claims to be the *fundamental* way of punctuating experience. This leads to all sorts of nonsense, such as looking at functional MRIs instead of genetic and experiential histories with similar events to find out what is really going on when your boss summons you or a lover whispers your name. The great drawback of brain science is that it is irrelevant to psychotherapy, because there is nothing we can do to the brain when we are stuck in the environment. And if we ever did invent a drug that had a direct effect on the brain (besides general stimulation, tranquilization, and leveling), would we really want it? Wouldn't we prefer to discover how to love each other over how to dose each other?

An angry Rottweiler accosts me as I check my mailbox, barely restrained by a leash tied to a stake in the ground. Genetic programming plus a history with barking dogs makes me fearful. When brain scientists say that what is really going on is an electrochemical reaction in certain areas of my brain, they seem to imply that the solution to my trouble will be to take a downer before checking my mailbox. When I say that what is really going on is an intrusion by my neighbor, I imply that she should get a stronger leash, train her dog not to growl, or get rid of it. Locating depression and anxiety in patients' brains makes a similar implication that they should bathe their brains in drugs rather than change their environments and their response tendencies. Of course, if you wanted to give a tranquilizer to the Rottweiler, I wouldn't mind.

Still, sometimes the brain isn't working correctly. I think of this only when the situation makes no sense to me psychologically, but it's certainly acceptable, before settling on a psychological case formulation, to inquire about head injuries and neurological symptoms. Psychotherapy depends on a psychological explanation of the life problem.

MENTAL ILLNESS

Some diagnoses are best thought of as illnesses because their causes are most productively considered biological. These include schizophrenia, autism, almost all bipolar disorders, many cases of hyperactivity, and a small percentage of depression and anxiety cases. I don't call what you do with people who have these illnesses psychotherapy, at least not with respect to the illness itself. The illness itself is like cancer or lupus or any other illness, in that the patient needs to learn strategies for managing the disease. When the disease is psychiatric, practitioners trained in psychology are often in a better position than purely medical staff to conduct this training. So there are two distinct roles, often filled by the same person: the treatment of the illness and the training of the patient to manage the illness.

Medical patients often need yet a third professional: a psychotherapist to assist the patient and the family in coping with the illness by helping them manage their *neurotic* reactions to it. These may include catastrophizing, blaming, and despondency. Sadness and fear are healthy, though unpleasant, reactions to illness; depression and anxiety are problematic reactions. It is not easy for therapists to get people to tell them their crazy ideas, wild fantasies, and strange explanations for upsetting events. This kind of disclosure often requires a separate therapist, one who can provide actual privacy and won't share the information, even with other providers.

When therapists treat problematic behavior patterns as diseases, a few benefits and many drawbacks ensue. One benefit is that in the disease model, no one blames the patient for the depression, anxiety, or addiction. This is less of a benefit among people who don't divide the world into behavior that is blameworthy and behavior that is not and who instead seek to explain behavior and intervene accordingly. To these people, blame is irrelevant; this is what we mean by a neutral or nonjudgmental therapist: not that the therapist approves or sympathizes with the patient's behavior but that blame and approval are not relevant. Another benefit is that the disease label can induce patients into treatment when they are worried not about whether there is something they can do, but about whether they are to blame. It can also (famously, among alcoholics) induce patients to stop fighting about whether they have the condition and to surrender to its presence in their lives.

One drawback to the disease model for behavioral problems is that excusing people from blame also seems to excuse them from doing anything about the problem. More importantly, the main motivators for treatment of problematic behavior patterns are the distress they arouse in the patient and the annoyance they arouse in others. Calling depression and anxiety *diseases* signals to patients that they should tolerate the subjective distress or rely on drugs to make it go away. It signals to others that it would be monstrous to find the condition annoying. This can lead to treating patients as if they had cancer or a broken leg. Ironically, one of the greatest hindrances to cancer treatment or physical therapy is patients' attitude that there is nothing they can do about it. Good oncologists, gerontologists, and physical therapists often sound more like drill sergeants than like nannies.

EMOTION

The evolutionary strategy that characterizes mammals, and especially apes, is to genetically preprogram as few responses as possible and instead to learn by trial and error or by instruction. The enormous cost of this strategy is an extended childhood during which much of this learning takes place. Parents cannot give birth and move on, and children need care and protection for many years if the genes that require an extended childhood are to survive in a next generation. Humans take the longest of any animal to become self-sufficient, and our brains don't fully mature until our mid-twenties. The advantage of this strategy is the capacity to adapt to changing circumstances, an advantage that offsets the costs of extended childhood.

Behaviorists call adaptive learning *operant conditioning*, referring to behavior—operants—that operate on the environment. They call genetically programmed responses—like heartbeats, reflexes, and blinks to moisten the eyeballs—*respondents*. For operant conditioning to work, environmental contingencies must have an effect; the animal must be able to feel pleasure and pain. Indeed, to a behaviorist, the greatest hindrance to the development of artificial intelligence is the question of how to reward a computer. Whether the feeling occurs in the organs and smooth muscles or in the brain that processes their information or in the interpersonal space that highlights and names the feelings is a matter of punctuation: Different answers have different uses.

Where feelings *occur* is a matter of framing, but there is no doubt as to where they are named. Humans don't come with words; words are operants that verbal communities have to teach people. Children learn what *mad*, *happy*, and *afraid* mean by hearing these words in the types of situations that produce anger, joy, and fear. The verbal training that children receive is only as accurate as their verbal community is observant and empathic; the training children receive makes fine distinctions only if these are available in the verbal community's vocabulary. Sometimes the verbal community—usually the family—has other agendas besides teaching the names of emotions; for example, they may not want to think of their girls as angry or their boys as fearful, so they teach girls that they are "tired" when their frustration shows and boys that they are "weighing their options" when they are afraid.

For this reason, it is generally a mistake to attune to patients by naming their emotions. I'm all for therapists demonstrating that they *get* their patients and what they are feeling (Buirski, 2005), but to do so by saying things like "You seem angry" or "How frustrating" assumes that therapists and patients agree on what these words mean. The emotional states that most need the embrace of attunement are likely to be those that the patient mislabels, since their marginalization implies that they were likely not welcomed and understood by the people who taught the patient their names. Beyond that, the names of emotions categorize feelings, and like all categories and labels, they are useful only to the extent to which all members of the category are alike. For some purposes, categorizing emotions is useful. For example, "I've noticed that whenever you are angry, you cry" might be a useful observation, and it requires a lumping together of various emotional reactions into the category of anger. When it comes to attunement, though, it's almost always better to specify the emotion by citing events that would produce a similar emotion. It's much more empathic to say, "You feel the way a child feels who has her candy snatched away by a bully" or "You feel like a guy being stood up on a blind date" than to say, "You're frustrated." Much therapy technique involves getting patients to tell you the pictures in their heads so these more specific attunements can occur.

Emotional behavior is generally annoying to other people, who therefore often punish it. Yes, the finest moments in life involve other people's emotions, but the fact is that many interpersonal conflicts occur because even our loved ones act human when it is inconvenient for us. Indeed, appreciation of the spouse's agenda fosters marital happiness, as when people manage to remind themselves, when the other spouse empties the dishwasher only halfway or doesn't feel like traveling or doesn't laugh at their jokes, that these same human qualities are what make spousal love so valuable. People punish even joy when it is inconvenient, not just in church but when they are trying to read or sleep, or when it makes a mess. Because emotional behavior is so predictably punished, a central function of therapy is to occasion emotional behavior and not punish it (Skinner, 1953). A crucial trait of a good therapist is the ability to tolerate strong emotions.

ANXIETY AND SELF-ESTEEM

Anxiety, in Skinner's famous dictum, is the feeling associated with not knowing what to do, with not having recourse to a behavior that has been reliably reinforced under current contingencies. If not having a solution were the whole story, people would feel dejected about their misfortune or accepting of their fate rather than anxious, so there must also be a sense that there *is* a solution—something to be done—for anxiety to arise. Generally, circumstances give rise to these expectations, as in performance anxiety about public speaking, where the public speaker is hoping that the speech will go better than it's likely to and is aware that the audience is hoping the same thing. Skills training is a good approach for many such problems. For example, anxious beginning therapists need supervision that lowers their expectations and gives them things to do when they are stuck. For the kinds of problems brought to a therapist, though, it's typically perfectionism that gives rise to looming expectations (Horney, 1950). People develop a system—what Goffman (1974) calls "a corpus of cautionary tales [and] newsy stories [that] elegantly confirm a frame-relevant view of the workings of the world" (p. 563)—for managing the inevitability of death, uncertainty, and our own ordinariness, and then they feel anxious when facts contradict the system.

Anxiety is almost always what I earlier referred to as the burglar alarm and not the burglar. Someone who feels anxiety only when flying but rarely has to fly may be better off with a beta-blocker than therapy, especially if the patient sees therapy as a way to become perfect rather than to discover the costs of compromises in other arenas. For example, perhaps the patient is fearful of not having control of every situation, and perhaps this has kept him or her from falling in love or playing with children without keeping score. Either way—beta-blocker or therapy—there is no need to tell the patient that the problem lies in the way some part of his or her brain does something. Generally, anxiety is the signal that something is wrong. When the thing that is wrong is death, uncertainty, or ordinariness, then accommodating these inevitabilities in his or her narratives better serves the patient. It's not too hard to see how religions have assisted in this process of making sense of these existential issues. Psychotherapy can provide similar benefits by reworking the patient's narrative into one that accepts death, uncertainty, and ordinariness instead of trying to outwit or overcome them.

The opposite of anxiety is the feeling you get when you have skills (reliably reinforced behaviors), a feeling that Skinner described as *self-esteem*. Self-esteem is decidedly not the habit of complimenting oneself or getting compliments from others. Compliments occasionally convey affection, but typically they impair self-esteem because they set the stage where mistakes—i.e., further efforts to develop skills—will invalidate the compliment. I discussed this in chapter 1, but it bears repeating: The only way to get better at something, to develop the skills that replace anxiety, is to make mistakes. Supervision and psychotherapy must be places that occasion mistakes.

Very few patients come for therapy saying that their perfectionistic, face-saving claims on reality are not working for them. Instead, they want our help to bolster those claims, usually by helping them eliminate the evidence that the perfectionistic narrative is false, or by changing their story from one of heroism to one of tragedy, a different kind of heroism (Schafer, 1981). Among the ways therapists have of eliminating this evidence are drugs, relaxation exercises, and mindfulness training. (Relaxation and mindfulness are useful in the service of accepting the inevitable aspects of life, not as ways to make anxiety go away.) Therapy involves getting patients to collaborate not on polishing their armor but on taking it off. Rather common are patients who experience an emotional caress not as a reassuring touch but as a sign that the armor has a hole in it!

A therapist who is afraid of snakes is unlikely to conduct useful exposure therapy with a snake-phobic patient. The patient is more likely to engage in the exposure if the therapist demonstrates that both the snake and the patient's fear are not too alarming. Now, what is true of snakes is also true of mistakes. Perfectionistic therapists are not likely to make mistakes more tolerable, and therapists who claim not to make mistakes—to have mastered the situation to the point of coasting—are not likely to inspire growth or change.

DEPRESSION

In chapter 2 we saw the advantages of treating suicide as a form of homicide in which the killer and the victim occupy the same body. Now, let's extend the metaphor to the conceptualization of depression. Every depression is unique, because every depiction of the defective self and every depiction of the oppressive self is unique, but a general consideration of a defective self and an oppressive self can clarify what's going on. The personality-based view of depression lies somewhere between a unique case conceptualization and general diagnostic categories. Thus, at the broadest level, patients can hate themselves for not living up to their own publicity. Within that concept, narcissists get depressed around failure, histrionic people around being ignored, obsessive-compulsives around losing control, and so on. And then within the example of narcissism, there is an important difference between the man haunted by the image of himself dropping the potentially winning pass in a high school football game and the man haunted by the image of himself wetting his pants while waiting to bat in a Little League game. The label of *narcissism* alerts the therapist to the kind of self-image that the patient is beating him- or herself up over, and the unique case formulation specifies the particular image.

Let's consider four broad categories of depression (cf. Jacobson, 1971). In each case, patients despise themselves for one reason or another that varies from person to person and usually (or always) smacks of hidden perfectionism. Patients might hate themselves for not being smart, attractive, free, charitable, or special enough, for example. Jacobson's categories can help us understand the experienced locus of the conflict between the hating self and the hated self. A common example is the patient who hates his or her body. The problem is sometimes the body, and the patient must learn to change it or live with it, depending on the details. More frequently, the problem is not the image in the mirror but the eyes that appraise the image. The eyes that denigrate the body assume a stance of perfectibility: *If only I weren't saddled with this thick or ugly or aging body, I would be Batman or Wonder Woman.* Ultimately, the therapeutic gaze replaces the pornographic, rejecting, or admiring gaze, although some therapists seem to think that the admiring gaze is therapeutic. Good parents don't *admire* their children's bodies, and healthy people look in the mirror to check for spinach in their teeth, not for the satisfaction one feels when looking at an amazing human specimen or Michelangelo's *David.*

In *neurotic depression*, the person experiences the conflict as internal. The patient looks in the mirror and thinks what a fat or pimply or wrinkly slob she is; she says something incorrect in class and thinks how stupid she is. She moves through life as if she is a short-tempered nanny with an ugly or annoying baby. Her depressive lens for interpreting the reactions of other people makes her feel bad when they are neutral, so instead she wants them to agree with her that the baby is an intolerable burden. The therapist must establish a metacommunicative space, reflecting on the quandary of either agreeing that her inner self is intolerable or inadvertently implying that she could be doing a better job. If, instead, the therapist treats her well, she resents it, like a nanny watching the usually inconsolable baby cooing in someone else's arms. If the therapist suggests she treat herself better, it enrages her, because it implies that the depression is her fault and not a natural reaction to the little brat she happens to be stuck with. She wants the therapist to give the baby a sedative. Therapy provides a new way of relating to the baby, from the therapist's way of relating to it and from the therapist's supervision of her relating to herself.

In *pointlessness*, the patient does not experience the conflict between the hating self and the hated self. The world seems bleak and hopeless at best, a cesspool at worst. Old reinforcers have lost their appeal and no new ones take their place. The oppressive self has abandoned the real self, much as the economy has abandoned the slum or the aristocracy has abandoned the poor. The person glimpses the oppressive self only in occasional fantasies of nobility or triumph, especially in fantasies of the nobility of suffering. Just as you cannot understand slum life without considering the economic abandonment by the larger culture, you cannot understand pointless depression without considering the oppressive, glorified self that is carrying on outside of awareness. Pointless depressives react to others as poor people do to advice givers. If a therapist suggests he confront the glorified self, he looks the way poor Washingtonians would if someone told them to go talk to the president. If a therapist suggests exertion, the patient acts like the therapist blames him for his predicament. If a therapist expresses curiosity, he resents it the way poor people resent anthropologists with clipboards. He wants uppers for excitement or opioids for relief, not ideas. Treatment for this and the remaining types of depression are discussed below, under "Personality Disorders."

In the narcissistic escape from depression, a version—or inversion—of pointlessness, the patient still does not experience the conflict, but here it's the despised self that is out of awareness. Life is like a TV game show, abuzz with prizes and the potential for celebration, ignoring the lives the contestants will return to at the end of the game. When the therapist addresses the emptiness of her excitement, she resents it the way contestants do when reminded they have bills to pay with the prize money. She avoids any conversation about the less fortunate aspects of herself, personifying the glorified self to the extent she can get away with it.

In *despair*, the patient externalizes the conflict. He feels rotten and he is aware that others despise him. At the extreme, in *psychotic depression*, he hears voices telling him that he is worthless, but short of that, he is constantly fighting the unfair expectations of others. He attacks their yardsticks and demands special consideration. He is miserable, and he knows it is someone's fault, but he has no idea that it is he who oppresses himself. Therapists are enraging because they talk about conflict resolution when he thinks what's needed is revolution. When therapists tell him to modulate the anger that is wrecking his life, he hears an aristocrat telling the poor to be patient. He feels like a prisoner in the Bastille, and he focuses his attention and vitriol on those he thinks oppress him, especially on those who seem to be happy, eating cake, mocking his despair.

The psychology of the problem—in this case, depression—is also typically the psychology of reacting to solutions. Self-blamers insist on total acceptance of their plight as a tragedy, and they experience any effort to change them as a kind of blame. People who find relief when told that depression is not their fault—that it's a disease or a function of chemistry—experience any effort to help them change as an unfair expectation. Narcissists experience empathy with the real self as an affront to their glory, and people adrift in pointlessness find any breath of hope to be unbearably pointless.

Kierkegaard (1983 [1849]) said that one solution to the existential dilemma of integrating an infinite mind with a finite body is to deny the body, a solution he called *schizophrenia* (when the word meant something else); he called the solution of denying infinitude *depression.* It is characteristic of all forms of depression to be too much a physical creature and not enough of a spiritual, emotional, or psychological one. The patient prefers physical framings of the problem, and chemistry is a more appealing source of treatment for many depressives than psychology. Chemical solutions maintain the depressive frame (even if they worked, which apparently they don't, per Whitaker & Cosgrove, 2015), whereas philosophical solutions challenge it.

TRAUMA

Psychological nomenclature often describes unpleasant conditions. Through conditioning, the terms for the conditions also become aversive. For example, *intellectual disability* now describes what clinicians have called—each term constituting a new effort at neutral, nonpejorative description—*idiocy*, being a *moron*, *imbecility*, and *mental retardation.* On the other hand, the use of anything less than an extreme term can seem to minimize a patient's suffering. There is a class of suffering, however, that we need to distinguish from others, because we need to treat people in the class differently from most patients. We used to call these special circumstances *shock*, and now we call them *trauma.* However, clinicians have applied the latter term to so many setbacks in life that it no longer distinguishes the people who need a different approach. Not every disaster is a trauma.

We should use *trauma* to describe shocking events that disrupt the integration of the narrative self, the body, and the connection with external reality, a disruption often observed in fight-flight-freeze reactions triggered by reminders of the shocking event. A reaction is *triggered* not if the response is merely occasioned by the stimulus but if, in addition, the narrative self is suspended or dissociated during the event. A trauma may be quite mild, and a nontrauma may be emotionally devastating. For example, a teenager was shagging flies on a baseball field when a long drive from a nearby batting practice struck him in the side of the face. The physical damage was minimal—not even a bruise—but for two days thereafter, glints of sunshine off store windows triggered a reaction in which he threw himself on the ground without thinking. After two days, the effect of peripheral light extinguished. Conversely, a man witnessed the death of his child from falling off a balcony. His grief made him question all his ideas about life and his sense of responsibility made him suicidal, but he was able to describe the dreadful event without dissociating and he was tortured by memories but not by flashbacks. Surely, the man elicits our sympathy more than the teenager, but it was the teenager who had a trauma and the man who had a different kind of setback.

As noted, the utility of the term lies in its direction of the treatment. As in several other situations, the patient may need more than one clinician, one for case management and one for psychotherapy. The case manager helps the person reset the broken alarm system often associated with trauma. There are many ideas for achieving this, but they typically break down into helping people reconnect with their own bodies and social networks (Van der Kolk, 2015). For the body, I prefer martial arts, although massage, dance, and exercise can also be useful. I prefer martial arts because of its implicit empowerment and focus on what to do in dangerous situations. One of the challenges with reestablishing social networks is the victim's sense that only other victims can understand, when typically that is a way down rather than out of the rabbit hole of letting the trauma dominate one's narrative. (*Victim* is another term that has become aversive by association.)

In psychotherapy itself, retelling the event has exposure benefits, but the challenge is that the patient often dissociates while saying what happened (Peebles, 2012). The idea is to remember without reliving, as Dr. Keyworth put it on *The West Wing*. The therapist must be more concerned about the patient's varying psychological presence than about getting the details about what happened. Trauma victims are often confused about their own agency, and this is made worse by a world that seems obsessed with either blaming them or declaring them blameless. Victims who feel responsible often fare better than those who feel helpless, presumably because of the sense of agency preserved in the former attitude (Janoff-Bulman, 1982). Therapists, as always but with heightened purpose, need to avoid either blaming or declaring blamelessness. Indeed, terrible things the person thought or did during the episode often makes the trauma worse (Van der Kolk, 2015), and a declaration of blamelessness communicates that the person should not share their guilty secrets.

Trauma is like living in a horror movie. Simple acts like checking the refrigerator for a snack in the middle of the night or saying goodbye to a friend at the end of a lunch date can seem imbued with frightening possibilities. Therapists must be aware of the potential for normal acts and, especially, small mistakes to have emotionally devastating consequences, and they must devote even more attention than usual to ensuring an alliance around talking things over rather than reacting to them.

NONSUICIDAL SELF-INJURY

Nonsuicidal self-injury (NSSI) refers to behavior maintained by the physical pain it causes to the person. Tattoos, piercing, and nail biting, in contrast, typically occur *despite* the pain. The pain may be a conditioned positive reinforcer, as in masochism's link to sexual pleasure, but almost always NSSI refers to pain as a negative reinforcer, a distraction from emotional pain or from numbness. It is a pain that, compared to other life pains, feels chosen rather than suffered, transient rather than permanent, and measured rather than bottomless. NSSI gratifies the hating self at the expense of the hated self, much like child abuse gratifies the parent at the expense of the child. There is a certain triumphant aspect to NSSI's secretiveness, a mockery of convention such as what an abductor might feel at work on a weekday, knowing what awaits him at home.

This sense of triumph is the greatest hurdle for treatment, since the patient doesn't want to stop doing it. Keeping it a secret, even from the therapist, makes the patient feel special, *in* on something in a world that otherwise tends to exclude the patient. When that is true, it is crucial for the therapy to become something secret and special that the patient is in on, which means a tight frame. A therapist's attempt to make the therapy that special place through making exceptions rather than tightly framing it can backfire when the day inevitably comes that the therapist is not willing to live up to the implied promises of availability and permanence. The tight frame allows a neutrality that a special relationship can't provide, and the therapist's earnest efforts to stop NSSI enhance the pleasure of getting away with it. When there is an incest history, the patient often plays the parts of the abusive parent and the victimized child, while the therapist is cast as the unaware parent. Even without an incest history, devastated children often assume that their parents could have done something protective, and mock their current efforts to protect them. NSSI also expresses ownership of the body, as discussed under "Eating Disorders."

In milder form, these dynamics occur in many therapies. Once patients stumble on the consolation of being a tragic hero (Schafer, 1981) or on the compensatory sense that no one has suffered as they have, there is a certain satisfaction associated with defeating the therapist. Therapists must often deal first with the specialness that suffering confers before inducing patients to really ally with them around getting better.

As in suicidal behavior, therapists are often hindered by their distaste for approaching the patient in any way that could be construed as blaming. This paints a portrait of the patient as a helpless victim of NSSI instead of as its perpetrator. Every perpetrator has a sympathetic history, and therapists trying to change them must learn to distinguish blame from the observation that there's something they can do about the problem. Therapists who want to coddle the injured part of the patient while excluding the vicious part find themselves in an alliance with only part of the system. In domestic violence, that might work if the patient does not consider ending the marriage a great cost. In NSSI and suicidality, it's impossible to end the relationship between abuser and abused.

CHILD ABUSE

One thing therapists need to know about child abuse is that (in every jurisdiction that I know about) they have to report it. However, they don't have to investigate it. If the patient mentions spanking a child, the therapist is not obliged to ask if it left a mark (the distinguishing feature of abuse in most states). This is a specific example of the general principle of not dropping the therapy agenda at the first hint of a professional agenda. Another example on this topic is that the state may require informing the patient of the therapist's status as a mandated reporter of child abuse, but in the states I have practiced in, that must occur at the outset of therapy, not before the therapy even begins. Therapists can start therapy by inquiring what they can help with and not with a pile of forms and disclosures. Indeed, it's hard to see how a patient can give informed consent—one of the commonly used forms—until there has been a case formulation and a recommendation for what will happen in treatment. Therapists sometimes worry that the patient will disclose child abuse, elder abuse, or violent intentions before the warning that the therapist will disclose such reports to the proper authorities. This has never happened to me, but I would be comfortable saying, "I don't know where you got the idea that I would keep such a thing a secret." When I get to promising privacy, I spell out the exceptions.

Adverse childhood experiences (Edwards, Holden, Felitti, & Anda, 2003) seem to produce bad outcomes when the child grows up. The research I've read on this topic barely considers that adults whose lives are going poorly might construct a narrative of childhood that emphasizes or even invents maltreatment or misfortune. Longitudinal research (Vaillant, 2002) often suggests that children can overcome adverse events. I'm not condoning child abuse—I've spent a lot of my professional life trying to prevent it, at least as much for its immediate effect on the child as for its potential effect on the eventual adult. I'm saying that in the metaphorical, narrative, literary, relational space of therapy, it's hard to tell what really happened. I'll discuss this under "Journalism versus Literature," but it will bear repeating that the accuracy of eyewitness testimony is highly suspect even when adults are recalling incidents from a week ago. Adult patients' reports of their own abuse as children may depict their current autobiography but they cannot, and need not, be relied upon for literal accuracy.

THEORETIC MULTILINGUALISM

Before discussing the major clinical theories, let's review the importance of learning more than one of them. Expertise is essentially a form of pattern recognition. Exposure to patterns is a way of enhancing the specificity of one's recognition, which is why clinical experience, case conferences, and reading literature and history are so important. However, the language we use to describe patterns also limits our ability to recognize them—this is the famous Sapir-Whorf hypothesis that our language informs our view of the world. The more languages we know, then, the less our pattern recognition is fused to particular phrasing, and the more patterns we can recognize. Different theories are like the country pavilions at Epcot (Karson, 2008), where not only the languages but other cultural practices are different. We call theories different pavilions rather than different countries to emphasize how arbitrary, artificial, and interchangeable they are.

Multilingualism is especially useful in light of ideas about what a case conceptualization is for. Unlike medical diagnosis, which implies a specific, effective treatment regardless of the patient's agreement, a psychological case conceptualization engages the patient's participation and *in addition* implies a treatment. As with a medical diagnosis, the implied treatment may or may not work, and if it doesn't, clinicians must try a new diagnosis or case formulation. Thus, a case conceptualization must be *plausible* rather than accurate (Watzlawick, Weakland, & Fisch, 1974), and therapists should view implied treatments as experiments. If, after giving the problem their best conceptualization, a therapist has to come up with a new one, it will be a lot easier if he or she speaks more than one theoretical language. Another way of thinking of theories is to ask, "What would Skinner say?" or "What would Horney say?" or "What would Selvini say?" The more consultants therapists have on their shoulders, the easier it will be for them to come up with the next plausible hypothesis.

One theory that therapists should always consider is the patient's. People have ideas about why they behave as they do, and ignoring those ideas puts the therapist at a disadvantage when trying to develop a case formulation that the patient will be on board with. The process is like assisting a driver who stops and asks for directions, a map on his lap. You can simply give directions, but you will be more effective if you show him what's wrong with his map. You might point out that he is looking at a map of the wrong city, or that he is on 17th *Avenue* rather than 17th *Street*, or that Lincoln has become a one-way street since that map was made. Honoring the patient's ideas as formerly useful will help him let them go as guides to the present situation. Much of the patient's theory will be unconscious, meaning that he is operating on assumptions that he is not aware of. For example, he may assume that life is a Siberian prison camp, and that the most one can do is seek occasional warmth or sneak a piece of bread. The therapist's own ideas, including the idea that a warm, reciprocal relationship will assist him, assume that life is otherwise. Until the therapist addresses the patient's theory of the situation, the therapist's efforts will seem impossible to him. We'll discuss how to elicit the patient's unconscious assumptions later on, but it amounts to joint exploration of specific moments.

BEHAVIORISM

Behaviorism is a philosophy of the science of psychology. The philosophy really has only one principle—namely, that psychology is a natural science and that scientists can study the field with the same culture of observation, rational thinking, and experiment as other areas of science. Skinner's *radical* behaviorism distinguished itself from Watson's *methodological* behaviorism; what was radical—meaning "thorough" or "to the roots"—about it was the inclusion of human and private behavior (including thinking, feeling, and imagining) and not just the public behavior that psychologists can observe in rats. Skinner explains what the psychologist does, not just what the lab rat does.

The relevant theory (as opposed to the philosophy) is learning theory, which psychologists developed in laboratories. As in other natural sciences, the working assumption is that the variables that govern behavior in one setting govern it in another. The same physics operates on the moon and earth; the same chemistry operates in North America and Australia; the same psychology operates in the therapist's office and in the patient's home.

As noted above, learning theory distinguishes *respondents* (genetically programmed behaviors like reflexes and metabolism) that evolved under contingencies of survival and reproduction from *operants* (learned behaviors that operate on the environment) that evolved under contingencies of reinforcement. Genes that produce useful adaptations help their hosts and themselves survive; other genes go extinct. Behaviors that work well in situations are thereby reinforced or made more probable; other behaviors go extinct.

Some people reject behaviorism because it conflicts with what Harari (2015) calls the prevailing religion of humanism—the worship of the individual and the insistence that the individual has a special standing in the universe that is not just a preferred way of looking at people. Behaviorism conflicts with humanism just as evolution and astronomy conflicted with Catholicism. Evolution insists there is no soul; behaviorism insists there is no mind. What we have learned to call the mind is nothing more than the exercise of the various senses in the absence of external control. You start by smiling when happy and learn how to smile even when there is nothing to smile about. You start by kicking a ball and learn how to kick even when there is no ball. You start by seeing an apple when an apple is there and learn to see an apple even when no apple is there. By seeing things that aren't there and hearing speech not spoken, you generate images and thoughts that you learn to call a mind.

The reason to go to all the trouble of offending people by analogizing (but not equating) them to pigeons is the same reason Copernicus, Galileo, and Darwin offended people. Science, according to Skinner (1957), is a "verbal community especially concerned with verbal behavior which contributes to successful action" (p. 418). We are more effective in dealing with problematic behavior if we focus our attention on the environmental contexts in which it occurs and especially on the reinforcement contingencies in those contexts. This is awfully convenient for psychotherapists, who happen to find themselves in the environment of their patients: By changing what *they themselves* do, therapists can affect patients.

The big idea, as it applies to psychotherapy, is one that many behaviorists seem strangely uninterested in. The therapy office is the occasioning environment, and therapists must understand the things the patient does and says in it in functional relation to that environment if the therapist is to respond to them in a behaviorally informed manner.

COGNITIVE BEHAVIORISM

The big idea in cognitive behavioral therapy (CBT) is that you can change what people do or feel by changing how they think about it. "There is nothing either good or bad but thinking makes it so," says Hamlet when explaining why, to him, Denmark is a prison. It's obvious that this idea is true in many situations. When a clerk tells you the grocery store now stocks your favorite sauce in the Mexican aisle rather than the condiments aisle, you look for it in the Mexican aisle. Indeed, there would be little point in writing or reading this book of advice if there weren't good evidence that changes in thinking lead to changes in behavior. The primary methods of CBT are Beck's collaborative empiricism, in which patients and therapists explore the logic and evidence behind problematic beliefs, and Ellis's disputation, in which therapists teach patients what's wrong with their thinking. Both are attempts to engage the patient in a kind of local science—critical thinking, experimenting, and assumption questioning—to develop more effective action. In practice, patients have typically heard new ways of thinking about behaviors that are problematic enough to bring them to therapy, and therapists must delve into much more complicated schemas and beliefs, such as their patients' attachment to their erroneous schemas and their suspicions about therapists' motives.

As noted in chapter 1, Ellis and Harper's (1975) *ABC* formulation is useful. An activating event or discriminative stimulus (*A*) occurs. A discriminative stimulus is one that defines the situation because the person's history with it has made it relevant. The person has beliefs (*B*) about these kinds of situations. The result is a consequence (*C*) of some interest, which might be a feeling or an overt action. Instead of using *B* to stand for *beliefs*, I use it to stand for *between*, a placeholder for the idea that the person's learning histories, personality patterns, organizing principles, mental maps, cognitive schemas, *or* beliefs mediate the stimulus and affect the result. We saw in chapter 1 that this book is about *B-therapies*, efforts to change response tendencies versus changing activating events or consequential reactions. CBT practice often boils down to two questions: "Are we talking about the right thing?" and "Are we thinking about it productively?"

CBT appeals to health insurers because it justifies short-term therapy and interchangeable staff; it appeals to researchers because they can study it in a shorter time frame, leading to more publications and to grants that are easier to get. Clinicians have always exaggerated its success (Shedler, 2015), like the supposed success of drugs. Still, in the many situations where, for one reason or another, the therapist and patient are not able to implement an open-ended relationship, brief treatment is in order and CBT is well suited to it. We can enhance its effectiveness with a few tweaks.

Events in life unfold as *ABC*s, but in therapy, the program usually runs *CAB*. First, either therapist or patient notices an odd occurrence, something that makes them go *boing*, indicating it is worth talking about. Then, they articulate the relevant context. Then, they articulate the patient's take on the context, whether in the form of an explicit or implied belief, schema, map, or pattern.

A major problem in therapy technique is that patients are reluctant to disclose what really goes through their heads. Here, I want to note that CBT therapists often evaluate or dispute the wrong belief. A common example is the patient's belief: "I am worthless [or unlovable]." Almost no one thinks this. Instead, patients think, "*You* are worthless." It's not just a grammatical difference; the latter statement makes it obvious that there are two characters involved, the self making the statement and the self the statement is made about. Identifying both selves—the object of scorn and the self heaping on the scorn—leads to the sorts of useful multicharacter case conceptualizations discussed above under "Suicide," "Depression," and "Nonsuicidal Self-Injury."

Even better than statements, as *B*s to evaluate or dispute, are pictures. When a patient reveals that she thinks of herself as a "horror show," her therapist can invite a discussion of how she depicts this in her imagination. Then, she and the therapist can evaluate not whether some *phrase* applies to her accurately, but whether an oozing pimple or dirty tampon, for example, really accurately portrays her. This is just as true in relational therapies, where it is the image of the pimple that the therapist must include in the therapeutic, metaphorical hold, not the euphemism for it. Even better than pictures are movies, since they provide context for imagery; by movies, I mean dreams, stories from the week, childhood memories, and fantasies during the session.

The right beliefs to discuss are those that would impel the problematic *C* in everyone, not just the patient. Thus, a man who claims he struck his wife because he believed she was cheating has not told the whole story; we know this because most people would not strike a spouse for unfaithfulness. There would have to be a lot more. The batterer would also have to believe that, for example, his culture required it, or perhaps that he could not influence his wife by talking and that she was not human—the sorts of things that might make him strike a table when he can't get it to stop wobbling. This requirement—that the relevant beliefs would also produce the reaction in others, even the therapist—ensures that the dyad will evaluate or dispute the right beliefs. It also invites a discussion of perfectionism and perfectibility, because most therapists would not themselves do the odd and disadvantageous things that lead their patients to therapy if they were not haunted by or flirting with perfection. Another commonly unexamined but necessary belief involves the patient's belief that he must defend his problematic beliefs. We all use maps to navigate our lives, and much bad behavior includes a belief in their infallibility.

Finally, therapy is more productive when it focuses on *C*s that occur during the session. Whether any *C*, at home or in session, actually occurred remains debatable, but when the focus is on an in-session *C*, at least both parties have firsthand access to the event. What activating event any *C* responded to may also remain up for debate, but again, both parties have access to the occasioning environment when the *C* in question happened in therapy. Usually, it was something the therapist did or said, since the other person is typically the prepotent stimulus when two people meet. That means that exploring in-session *ABC*s enhances intimacy and collaboration, which are major components of therapy. Also, the relevant *B*s when focused on in-session *C*s are more likely to be available than those that have been re-formed by the patient's master narrative over the course of the week. Patients who cannot recall their thoughts or images from the relevant moment can just make them up, because the sorts of things they are likely to invent in a certain context are even more salient than what might actually have occurred to them at the time. This is because the context that occasions the *C* also occasions the invention of *B*s once the patient puts him- or herself back into the moment psychologically. When the focus is on *ABC*s in the session itself, the relevance of invented *B*s is even more on point, since the person does not have to rely on imagination to re-create the situation.

I recognize that my tweaks of CBT make it look like relational psychoanalysis, behavioristic functional analytic psychotherapy, and the systemic tradition of reenacting conflict and drama in the therapy space. These put the therapist in a position to do something about problematic patterns in real time. Of course, I think of all psychotherapy as depending on the patient to reenact problematic patterns where they can be reworked in real time.

PSYCHOANALYSIS

No other branch of science is held as accountable for its passé ideas as psychoanalysis. Physicists do not defend Aristotle or even mainstream ideas from 1900. Nobody blames contemporary behaviorists for Watson's harsh child-rearing recommendations, contemporary systems theorists for their forebears' naive assault on personality, or contemporary CBT therapists for Ellis's bullying. Everything that Freud ever wrote that was wrong is smirked at in college classes all across the country. (Critics now see everything Freud ever wrote that was right as obvious and not psychoanalytic.) Things got so bad at one point that psychoanalysis changed its name to *psychodynamic*, like an ex-con trying to start a new life. Apparently, though, the psychoanalytic approach has the best and most sustainable success rates among therapies (Shedler, 2010). Further, the common factors (Rosenzweig, 1936) that underlie all therapy approaches and account for a large measure of their success (American Psychological Association, 2012) are essentially psychoanalytic techniques. Instead of saying that the best measure of the potential utility of a psychotherapy is the extent to which it is psychoanalytic, however, critics take the effective parts of psychoanalytic technique and call them something else (the common factors).

Psychoanalytic therapy (annoyingly, you're not allowed to call it *psychoanalysis* or yourself a *psychoanalyst* unless a psychoanalytic institute has certified you) has seven features, according to expert consensus (Shedler, 2010), besides the obvious one of meeting with a patient on a regular basis to talk. These include a focus on emotion, exploration of resistance (attempts to avoid unpleasant or difficult topics), identification of psychological patterns and themes, discussion of childhood, focus on the patient's interpersonal relationships, focus on the therapy relationship itself, and focus on the patient's fantasy life. Psychoanalytic theory has always been concerned with internal conflict—that is, on incompatible goals, such as desiring to have one's way while also desiring to be seen as a good person.

Even to consider that people have incompatible goals was revolutionary at the time in medicine—Freud acknowledged that artists and writers have always known this. Indeed, one way to look at Freud's monumental achievement is to say that he demonstrated the relevance of philosophy and literature to clinical practice. Even today, some people, are shocked and humiliated by the idea that they are not of a single mind, that they are not the final authority on themselves—that we are much more our own press secretaries than our own anthropologists. This, plus the arrogance of psychoanalysts who claim to be exceptions to this humbling truth about ourselves, is one of the main reasons for the denigration of the approach. Also, researchers can't study it quickly and health insurers can't manualize it, so it doesn't appeal to them.

Contemporary psychoanalysis can be summed up in a single sentence: We treat ourselves as we were treated, and the only way to really learn to treat ourselves differently is to be treated differently. There's nothing magical or unscientific about this. In fact, it's often said that Freud was the one theorist that Skinner never criticized (although he did rephrase a lot of Freud's ideas to eliminate their mentalisms before he could agree with them). We learn to treat *everything*, including ourselves, by observing how others treat it and by experiencing the effects of treating things one way or another. We may treat ourselves as royalty, as garbage, or as human beings in various situations, and things go better when we treat ourselves as other people expect us to be treated. The second half of the one-sentence summary merely notes that we can get only so far by talking about how others treated us and that real change comes from others treating us differently, which we can facilitate by curbing our annoying behavior, seeking the company of people who would really like us if they got to know us, and hiring a competent therapist. All technique derives from the effort to invite patients to produce their mistreated selves in therapy and to treat those selves as we would have the patient treat them.

SYSTEMS THEORY

The relevance of systems theory to individual therapy is sharply limited, since a systemic approach would often imply seeing more than one person at a time or adopting a coaching rather than a therapy relationship. One way to summarize systems theory is to say that reality does not consist of things in relationships with each other; reality consists of relationships occupied by things. This implies that personality is not that important compared to the structures and functions and connections of the relevant system. This leads to changing the system and not to changing an individual's response tendencies.

It's often hard for clinicians trained in individual psychology to think systemically. A bridge for behaviorists is to consider that contingencies in the immediate environment may not be as relevant to maintaining problematic behavior as the responses of various people who may not be present. Practitioners of other approaches that champion or even worship the importance of the individual may balk at the idea that the individual doesn't matter in the analysis. Classic examples are the depressed parent whose depression creates teamwork in the rest of the family, or the anxious child whose parents can engage each other around blame instead of appearing to be on the brink of separation.

In systemic terms, if a patient is self-conscious or a trainee is anxious, it tells us more about what it's like to be a patient or a trainee than it does about the individual patient or the particular trainee—or it tells us more about what it's like to be *our* patient or *our* trainee. Bosses (and therapists) are arrogant not (only) because arrogant people seek authority but because being the boss puts them in a position where underlings agree with them, laugh at their jokes, and kowtow to them, which would make most people arrogant. People get depressed not (only) because they despise their imperfections but because their role in relevant systems is something like whipping boy or maid or hopeless dreamer or psychotherapy patient of the "you poor dear" type of therapist, which would make most people depressed. When a cohort of clinical trainees consists of strong and creative individuals who act fragile, the problem is in the system.

Where systems theory shines in a discussion of individual therapy is in its illumination of the therapy system itself. This includes the conflicts that arise around defining what kind of situation it is and what kinds of roles are available. When Bateson (1972a) said that the main thing going on in therapy is the teaching of metacommunication, he meant the important skill of resolving conflicts about roles and situations by talking them over. All systems struggle when roles are ambiguous (Minuchin, 1974), so while therapy must appear ambiguous to elicit framing errors by the patient, it must be clear to the therapist that providing ambiguity is part of the job. This is no different from a painting teacher who tells you to paint what you want rather than directing you paint a particular object. Each has advantages, but the advantages disappear if the teacher forgets which kind of instruction she is offering.

We typically communicate with other people about how we are defining our role and the situation not by talking it over and negotiating a settlement, but by subtly imposing our definition of the situation on each other. Every communication has a *report function* and a *command function* (Bateson, 1972a). The former involves informational content about anything other than the nature of the relationship between the parties, while the latter involves information about that relationship. A husband says to his wife, "Your keys are in your purse" (location of keys is the report function), but he can say it as if the wife is a ditz, a child, a doddering old fool, or a friend who wants to find her keys (command function).

One hallmark of systemic thinking is the ability to characterize a group of people without characterizing the individuals involved: for example, "This isn't a family so much as a boot camp." This language doesn't suggest that a parent has a need to be a drill sergeant or that the children want to be recruits. It may turn out that the mother will find a different way or place to be bossy, but it may be that everyone is promulgating an unwanted pattern. A common solution is for one person to stay in the desired role—of parent or child—even when pulled to act like a drill sergeant or recruit. Often, no one in the system is capable of this, so the therapist enters the system and either induces such moves or insists on keeping to the therapist role when pressured to act like the commandant or the press. Systems theory in individual sessions should make therapists wonder what kind of relationship the therapy has become and how to get it back to the one it should be.

DIAGNOSIS

The purpose of diagnosis is to suggest a treatment. We can diagnose by categorizing people, which guarantees that we will not tailor the treatment protocol for the individual, or by understanding the function of the symptoms in context, which guarantees that we will. Categorizing appeals to many clinicians because it's easier than understanding the meaning or function of a problem and because it makes them feel like experts when they apply criteria from the *Diagnostic and Statistical Manual of Mental Disorders* (DSM; American Psychiatric Association, 2013). Of course, researchers did not derive those criteria empirically but by polling experts who had the skill of distinguishing one diagnosis from another. If therapists are intent on categorical diagnosis, shouldn't they try to become one of those experts?

The diagnostic manuals for most branches of medicine, including even the psychiatric section of the International Classification of Diseases (ICD), do not explain what the diagnoses mean. They are just coding lists for reporting incidents of various diseases. They assume that the doctors who apply them learned how to recognize the diseases while in training. Only psychiatrists have criteria, as in the DSM, and even with listed criteria the agreement rates among expert diagnosticians as to whether a particular patient has the disorder are so low that the publisher of the DSM had to redefine what constitutes adequate agreement.

Because of the inclusion of criteria, it's unclear whether the DSM *defines* the various disorders or whether it's a way of *testing* for them. If the former, then the criteria are by definition correct: Anyone who meets the criteria has the disorder and anyone who doesn't, doesn't. However, that cannot be, because the DSM tells you right up front that it's not a book of definitions; it says you can still diagnose a disorder if your clinical judgment tells you to. It seems, then, like a book of tests. Experts developed the criteria to maximally identify those who have the disorder and maximally exclude those who don't. That means there must be an error rate, some number of false positives and false negatives associated with each criteria set; if so, why don't they publish the error rates?

We're not going to review Bayes' theorem here, but suffice it to say that psychiatric disorders are fairly rare in the general population, and Bayes proved that the odds of a diagnosis being correct are worse with rare disorders. That's why we don't do general screenings for HIV; even an amazingly accurate test like that one would produce many thousands of false positive results if doctors screened everyone. That's also why mammograms and prostate screenings come in and out of favor. There simply is no psychological or psychiatric test anywhere near as accurate as the HIV test. Therapists should never defer to the DSM on diagnosis; they should undertake to understand what a particular disorder is and whether it is a useful description of the patient's difficulty.

The big problem in diagnosis is that there are too many categories, so each of them is rare. That makes it unlikely that two clinicians will agree, and it makes it harder to get it right. You might also say that there are too few diagnoses, in the sense that a unique case formulation is desirable for every therapy patient. In cancer treatment currently, oncologists treat every cancer as unique (Mukherjee, 2016), and every patient gets a drug mix selected particularly for him or her. A small number of diagnoses would allow for general direction of the therapy while still implying that it is providing only a bird's-eye view and that the therapist needs more details. A diagnosis of *psychological problems* would be the ultimate example, implying therapy and nothing more. If there are several categories of depression to use for diagnosis, and if each has numerous specifiers (such as severity and duration), then selecting one of them seems to signal the end of diagnostic work. Indeed, therapists don't even need depression as a diagnosis; they can usefully restrict themselves to four major categories (Peebles, 2012). We might call these biology, trauma, neurosis, and personality disorder. Within the category of biology are schizophrenia, bipolar disorder, and a lot of hyperactivity cases. We've reviewed trauma above. Neurosis refers to psychological problems in people who are generally healthy psychologically, which means, in effect, the capacity to accept the therapist as someone to help them change their response tendencies and not as someone to gratify their needs or stand in their way. The most important differential diagnosis in most psychotherapy is between neurosis and personality disorder.

PERSONALITY DISORDERS

What Personality Disorders Are

A personality disorder is a long-standing and inflexible personality pattern. Personality, in turn, is whatever makes a person respond idiosyncratically to a given situation (Cattell, 1946). It refers to the ways people differ from each other in what they do, as opposed to the ways situations differ from each other. A personality pattern is a typical way of responding to a particular kind of situation, but we can as easily consider it a typical way of *construing* situations. Making sense of an environment is, in behavioral terms, just another way of responding to it, but it's a particularly important way of responding to it, because once you understand how someone is making sense of a situation, you'll have a pretty good idea of their response alternatives. We use the term *personality disorder* when a particular way of making sense of situations has become so widespread and inflexible that it interferes with the ability to makes sense of situations as they are. The person with a personality disorder illustrates the adage "If all you have is a hammer, everything looks like a nail." Inflexible expectations constrict the ability to see things as they are. Thus, the problem is often not the problem but the framing of the problem; for example, a man who complained that his wife kept her distance had a problem in that he framed every interchange with her in terms of whether she really loved him.

The amount of interference with accurately seeing things needed to merit the label *personality disorder* is a matter of judgment. The DSM requires that this reliance on expectations has to be extensive enough to cause significant personal distress or dysfunction, but it's unclear why this is a requirement. Even a medical model will diagnose, say, heart disease if the heart does just fine at rest but diagnostic tests determine that exertion would kill the person. Analogously, a person with a personality disorder can be asymptomatic, but we should still use the label if we think the person's behavior would be dysfunctional or distressing should their environment change in some reasonably expectable way.

Extending the analogy, a person with heart disease that makes exertion painful or difficult will live a sedentary life, and it can be hard to tell that this is not merely a preference. People with personality disorders may live lives in which their preferred way of making sense of reality fits most situations: for example, someone with obsessive-compulsive personality disorder who gets a regimented job that requires orderliness (bookkeeping, say, or software engineering) and mates with a slob or a free spirit whose very presence defines the obsessive-compulsive as the clean or reliable one. Unless you do something unregimented with these people—charades or finger painting, say—you might not know whether their lifestyle keeps them functional. Psychologists often mistake a lack of symptoms for health (Karson, 1980; Shedler, Mayman, & Manis, 1993).

The metaphor of maps and territories is useful for understanding how psychological patterns play out. Disadvantageous behavior is often a function of using an outdated map on new terrain—trying to get around Denver with a map from the 1980s, say. These are everyday occurrences. Using a map of Denver to get around Portland, another medium-sized city, is neurotic. Using a map of Denver to get around everywhere is personality disordered. If people insist on using a map of Denver, they can disguise their personality disorders by never leaving Denver.

Some of the more common maps that people use to navigate reality have names derived from clinical observation. Narcissism, for example, has several forms; one of them is a tendency to see an excessive number of situations as signaling either adoration or disparagement. Everyone is narcissistic sometimes. If someone calls you stupid and ugly in a public forum, you are likely to respond narcissistically, getting angry at the source of disparagement and seeking signs from others that you are worthwhile. Same goes for hitting on someone, even a loving partner: The vulnerability can put you on a precipice of exaltation versus debasement. We're all occasionally neurotically narcissistic, taking a long line at the grocery store as an affront to our sense of importance or mistaking correction by a teacher for an insult. The term *personality disorder* implies that the individual treats a large number of situations as narcissistic encounters.

Obsessive-compulsives treat a huge number of situations as toilets, where things are viewed through a lens of order versus filth. Histrionic people see many situations as sexual triangles. Paranoids nearly always think they're in an action movie. Borderlines think a huge number of situations are about abandonment and compulsively test the durability of relationships. They are in a constant panic brought on by identity diffusion (Kernberg, 1984), just as you would be if you woke up in the morning, went to the bathroom to brush your teeth, and saw no reflection in the mirror.

For many people with personality disorders, the map they use does not have a common name or pattern. A man I worked with was hindered in life by his belief that attractive women signaled his sexual inadequacy, and he could only reestablish his sense of adequacy by avoiding all desire or by challenging male authority figures. In a memory from high school, he noticed that he could see the bra of a classmate through the buttons of her blouse, and he reacted by challenging a teacher's computation. This unique depiction of the pattern was more useful in working with him than any label would have been. Indeed, even when a person's typical map fits squarely with one of the well-known personality disorders, it's better to use the person's unique depiction of the pattern rather than the diagnostic label. One narcissist may see himself as a little boy who has just cried at school, an image of the self that he wards off with claims of hypermaturity, while another may see himself as too short to reach the cookies, which he compensates for with daring acts of athleticism.

One important aspect of personality disorders is that they constantly annoy other people, both those who don't have a personality disorder and those who have one that doesn't align with the one in question. They just don't have the flexibility that we want from other people; they constrict the range of roles we can play with them. Also, people with personality disorders rarely if ever engage in genuine self-reflection or authentic metacommunication. Smart people with personality disorders learn to imitate self-reflection, but they don't really ask themselves whether they could have handled a situation better (masochists and depressives ask themselves these things, but with reproach rather than curiosity), whether there's something wrong with them, and whether consideration for others is insufficiently important to them (or, for masochists and depressives, whether consideration for others is too important to them). When discussing a conflict, personality-disordered individuals are rarely genuinely collaborative. When they agree to a time-out to discuss the problem, they are still trying to get their way rather than come to a meeting of minds. Again, we are all like this sometimes—especially when angry or afraid—but people with personality disorders fundamentally lack the skill of observing themselves with anything approaching affectionate objectivity, presumably because they lack the experience of others observing them this way.

Origins

From the psychoanalytic-developmental perspective, personality disorders are not so much created as they are the way we all start life and usually develop beyond. Children, as it were, are born with personality disorders, although you wouldn't call them *disorders* unless the children failed to outgrow them. Even within this approach, there are several ways to think about child development. An appealing one suggests that there are three major tasks of human development. First, infants learn to distinguish what is them from what is not them. This occurs primarily by trying to move things. The hand and the leg move in ways that the door and the trees do not. This task gets confusing when Mom or Dad's movements are also under operant control; the child adjusts her mouth to fit the nipple, but the mother also adjusts the nipple to fit the mouth. Crying brings the parents; laughter makes them smile. We call these errors *loose boundaries*, which originate in the state in which the infant has some control over the movement of parents that is hard to distinguish from her control over her own body. None of us learns perfectly to distinguish what is us from what is not us; it's relatively easy to double-check visual anomalies (so visual hallucinations are rare), but it's sometimes hard to tell whether you really heard or smelled something. Still, we call people who don't fundamentally master this first task of development *psychotic*.

The second task of development is to create an organized system of all the things that are in fact part of the self—our physicality, our thoughts, our emotions, our memories. Steady, nurturing caregivers facilitate this task because each aspect of the self that gets paired with an accepting, emotionally present parent more easily finds a place in the integration of the self. It's easy to blame parents if some aspect of the self is not includable in the child's self-organization, and indeed, many parents cannot bring themselves to see their children as sexual, aggressive, needy, or autonomous. Some children get so angry so early (usually because of abuse or abandonment, but also because of temperament) that no amount of acceptance can lead to integration of the anger with the rest of the self. None of us learns perfectly to accept what is ours, especially in the face of rejection, disappointment, or failure. We used to call people who don't fundamentally master this second task *borderline* (on the border of psychosis), but that term now denotes a specific type of personality disorder, so that now we might call them *severely personality disordered.*

The third task of development is to create an organized system accounting for all the things that are in fact part of other people—their physicality, their thoughts, and so on. The groundwork for accomplishing this task occurs early in life, probably before age five, but it doesn't really come to fruition until adolescence, when people negotiate with each other around their roles as the main characters of their own lives and supporting cast members in the lives of others. An eventual effect of a secure attachment is a concern for the attachment figures that is broader than the immediate issue of what they can do for the child. No one perfectly masters this task; it's too time-consuming to consider the fullness and complexity of every human you meet. We used to call people who fundamentally fail to master this third task *narcissistic*, but that label, too, now denotes a specific personality disorder, so now we might call them *mildly personality disordered* or simply *personality disordered.* We refer to people who basically master all three tasks sometimes as *healthy* and sometimes as *neurotic* (because everyone has complexes or conflicting unconscious wishes or irrational ideas).

Behaviorists might construe personality disorders as a pursuit of peculiar reinforcers or a narrow array of reinforcers. Through conditioning, most children associate the biological reinforcers, when parents supply them in a reliable and nurturing frame, with the typical secondary social reinforcers of attention, affection, approval, and obedience. If caregivers supply the biological reinforcers (food, drink, cuddling, sleep, and sex) in a social frame that is begrudging, hostile, unpredictable, or otherwise negative, then the biological reinforcer will not condition the social world in the normal way. (Caregivers don't *supply* sleep and sex so much as herd them into a safe time and place.) Further, if the secondary reinforcers are not available, the person will stop pursuing them; if they are available intermittently, the person might focus on them at the expense of other reinforcers. People with personality disorders (and everyone some of the time) may rather oddly find other people's obedience or approval aversive; they may organize their behavior around feeling ashamed, say, or looking sheepish at the cost of other people's approval or obedience. If others obey people trying to look sheepish, it will make them uncomfortable; if they become therapists—as many dependent personalities do, because they view the world through a lens of care and help—they won't want to run the sessions or even tell their patients where to sit, made uncomfortable by patients' readiness to follow their lead. Regarding constricted reinforcement, we can view narcissists, for example, as pursuing admiration and (nearly) only admiration, like misers whose only reinforcement is an increase to the bank account.

Both the psychoanalytic-developmental approach and the behavioral approach to understanding personality disorders emphasize the difficulties these people have with authentic intimacy, which is aversive to them. By intimacy, I don't mean an absence of boundaries. I mean something akin to ballroom dancing: people operating in close harmony, each maintaining a frame of self-support, occasionally interdependent or entirely dependent (as during dips and lifts), and operating as a team. I also mean acknowledgment that personhood is a persona—the word *person* comes from the Latin for an actor's mask or an actor's role in a play (Goffman, 1959)—that there are elements of the self kept hidden in all encounters, and that revealing some of these can lead to self-acceptance and freedom from a host of fears. The more that one's caregivers have pushed aside these aspects of the self, the harder it is to welcome them into one's identity or one's therapy.

Cognitive therapists might view a personality disorder as excessive reliance on a limited understanding of how the social world works. We can analogize this understanding to a map for negotiating new terrain, but we can also consider it a pattern of operations or an internal system depicted in early memories, fantasies, expectational patterns, and dreams. One way to think about this is to consider the *I Ching*. This book analyzes 64 social situations and explains the moves available and unavailable in each. A superstitious practice of randomly selecting one of them used the book to figure out which pattern you're in, but if you familiarize yourself with all 64 situations, you can figure out which situation you're in through pattern recognition and then apply the book's wisdom accordingly. For someone with a personality disorder, there are only two or three different kinds of situations. This can happen if, in early life, there were indeed only a few kinds of interactions, as with parents who react to their children only with pride or disappointment. When there are only a few patterns, people rely on them excessively. It can also happen because every map of the social world also defines a role for the person to play, and some families and societies construe only a very limited array of potential roles for some of its members (like the budding narcissist who can play only the roles of king or jester, or the disabled child who can play only dependent child or neglected child, or women who can play only mother or whore).

Treatment

By definition, personality disorders are hard to change, since the associated traits must be inflexible and of long standing to qualify for the label. The reasons they are hard to change provide some clues to treatment.

Very few people come for therapy because they realize they have to change. Almost everyone who is genuinely self-referred comes either because they are suffering and want it to end or because they sense a mismatch between their expectations and reality and they want *reality* to change. The therapist's initial task is to help the person frame the problem (in what is called a *focus* or a *case conceptualization*) as a psychological one related to the patient's tendencies, expectations, and self-definition. An analogy might be someone suffering from shortness of breath who lets the doctor reframe the problem in terms of diet and exercise. A prerequisite for any such reframing is a perception of the doctor as motivated by the desire to help.

People with personality disorders do not have a reliable impression of others as being there to help in this sense. (People with dependent personality disorder think everyone is there to help, but in the way a waitress helps, not in the way a cooking teacher helps.) Instead, the patient views the therapist as a character in the pattern, not as someone trying to change the pattern. The narcissist sees the therapist's reframe of the problem in psychological terms as an insult; the borderline sees it as an effort to create a vulnerability that will lead to abandonment; the obsessive-compulsive thinks the therapist is trying to mess her up. Where most therapies capitalize on an alliance with the one part of the patient that agrees with the psychological formulation, therapists treating personality disorders are on their own.

The therapist has to create a capacity for reflection in the personality-disordered patient in much the same way parents create this capacity in children. Parents (and the rest of the verbal community) make all sorts of comments about children and their circumstances. We learn to name our emotions, to discriminate fantasy from memory, and to manage our social persona from such comments. We also learn how to think about ourselves when parents reflect on our mixed motives, invite us to weigh alternatives, or welcome in private what is unacceptable in public. We learn self-reflection by being reflected upon by others. Even when the therapist reflects on the personality-disordered patient with welcoming curiosity, the patient does not experience the reflection as educational, accepting, or wise. It's like trying to learn self-reflection from a parent who constantly criticizes the child and suddenly asks, "What were you thinking when you left the door open?" The child is likely to hear "What kind of idiot are you?" and not "I wonder what was on your mind."

My best friend as a therapist is the lose-lose comment; for example, when the patient asks for an extra session and I say, "If I say yes, then I'm concerned that I would be communicating that you can't handle things; if I say no, then I might be communicating that you're on your own. I don't much like either alternative." The lose-lose comment is my default solution whenever I am in a role conflict; it's a way of retaining the therapist role without choosing a role in the conflict. It's also a way to teach metacommunication (talking about the process) and reflection, powerful aids to conflict resolution and good decision making.

With a personality-disordered patient, the therapist is always in a role conflict. The therapist wants to play the role of a wise, benign helper, and the patient insists the therapist is an admirer, a detractor, a servant, an abandoner, and so on. Reflecting on the conflict is a way to manage the conflict while ultimately maintaining a therapeutic stance. The thing to say to someone who experiences welcoming curiosity as a criticism is something like, "I'm inclined to wonder out loud about what was going through your mind when you left the door open, but I'm concerned that if I do, you'll experience me as criticizing you, and if I don't, you'll experience me as already having judged you." The therapist can often achieve the same goals by just wondering and then noting the patient's response as a sign that the therapist was criticizing, implying that the therapist had some other motive. The main thing is the constant awareness that the patient doesn't experience the therapist as a therapist.

People with personality disorders don't often self-refer, and when they do, it's to fix the world, not themselves. Instead, someone else—perhaps a probation officer, a spouse, or an employer—insists that they come to therapy. Because they lack self-reflection, they don't see the problem, but their treatment of other people as stage props in their own dramas irritates those people. Others usually avoid them, attack them, or suppress their own agendas around them, depending on the situation and the type of relationship. It certainly makes sense in some cases to include other members of the system, especially the family, although the personality disorder is likely to prove so intractable that the goal of systemic therapy is likely to revolve around living with the person more productively rather than changing him or her. (This may be the goal of much family therapy, changing, in Minuchin's phrase, the dance rather than the dancers.) In individual therapy, the personality-disordered patient relates to someone who gently insists on being the other person in the room and helps the patient adjust accordingly.

To the extent that *personality disorder* is code for *attachment disorder*, the underlying problem is a fear of intimacy, and the treatment is what I call *intimacy exposure*. This approach also applies if you conceptualize personality disorder as an aversion to oneself. If all the bad things that ever happened to you occurred in the rain, you would hate it when it rained. In fact, all the bad things that ever happened to you did happen while you were being you, or in your own presence, and we can usefully construe much pathology as self-avoidance and self-hate. Therapy helps people relax their masks and defensive postures and constricted roles, to become comfortable with themselves, just as someone with a fear of dogs needs not-too-precipitous, incremental exposure to dogs. By maintaining a tight frame; a welcoming, curious attitude; reflection instead of attack, avoidance, or surrender; and an attitude of discovery, intimacy gradually increases in the relationship and patients learn that they don't need their own avoidance techniques, that the self is not as toxic as they expected.

Inevitably, by dint of the therapist's humanity, emotional availability, and interpersonal engagement, the therapist imagines or enacts just the kind of thing the patient expects. Therapists may catch themselves feeling like flirting, demeaning, or judging (or whatever the reciprocal role is to the patient's entrenched role), or they *actually* flirt, demean, or judge. Therapists who are committed to viewing themselves as benign have trouble with these crucial moments, because they recapture their sense of beneficence at the expense of connection and honesty. Instead, therapists need to see themselves as being in the business of making messes and cleaning them up, just as good parents are not alarmed by their less-than-ideal reactions but instead take them in stride and reflect on them. In the stage of feelings or fantasies that breach the therapist role, good therapists say something like, "It occurs to me that a lot of people in my shoes might feel an impulse to admire you at this moment." After having acted out the role, it's something like, "You perceived me as admiring you and this made you feel contempt for me." Feeling and enacting the reciprocal role to the patient's, along with reparative moves, are the start of psychotherapy, not its demise, because they signal the therapist's entering into the patient's pattern of relating and not just hovering over it.

AUTISM

One of the biological disorders that therapists ought to know a little about is autism, mainly to recognize it enough to adjust to reasonably achievable goals or, in some situations, to obtain an expert opinion. It's a condition that changes things that typically operate as social reinforcers into aversive stimuli. When patients are intellectually disabled, as often happens with autism, therapists have to work with other providers in any event, so adding a specialized assessment will not be too much of an intrusion. When autistic patients are not intellectually disabled—in what we used to call *Asperger syndrome*—therapists can work with patients to develop an understanding of whether the aversion to affection, intimacy, and touch is biologically hardwired to the point of having to adjust therapy goals and procedures: Even sitting in a room with the therapist may be too alarming to allow for therapy to occur. When patients seem immune to therapist's relational skills, it might be autism, and the dyad might need expert assessment to distinguish it from other conditions that *can* benefit from intimacy exposure rather than education on coping with differences and skill acquisition.

SUBSTANCE ABUSE

Substance abuse is one of those solutions to life problems that becomes a problem itself. In my schema, it's a *C*-solution, an effort to make unpleasant feelings go away—the hallmark of bad therapy—rather than an effort to change response tendencies so they comport better with reality. Substance abuse in that sense is like medication, relaxation techniques, soothing therapy, and *The Matrix*'s blue pill (the one that sends the person back to dreamland). In fact, nearly every problematic pattern of behavior was at one time a solution (Watzlawick et al., 1974), but with substance abuse, it can be a way of life and, like sleep deprivation, the therapist may need to address it first. What it is a solution *to* is often either a sense of pointlessness (existential angst) or disappointment in oneself. What drug or alcohol abuse avoids is an important question, and relevant information is often available in the therapy session because the patient may avoid the same things there.

For many people, those whom 12-step programs address, the problem drink is the first drink, and the case formulation should focus on the psychology of the moment that occurs. For many of these people, it is not the drink itself that is so important but the context that sets drinking in motion, whether it be a decision not to tell the spouse about a work setback, the entry into a grocery store also known to sell liquor, or not setting the alarm the night before when, historically, cocaine usage always follows oversleeping. For others, the problem drink is the third drink, say, and the moment of interest shifts accordingly. This also applies to overeating, where for some people it's the second helping and for others it's the first Oreo that demands the therapist's attention.

Therapists need to know enough to suspect substance abuse as an alternative explanation for notable behaviors rather than relying on psychological variables. Like nonsuicidal self-injury, it can awaken feelings of triumph in patients, who then refuse to report their problematic drug and alcohol usage. Excessive or depleted energy and attention, along with forsaken responsibilities, ought to be signals of interest. Substance use is often the explanation when people don't seem to earn as much money as their intelligence would lead one to expect. Excessive wealth can also lead to substance abuse, often to insulate the person from ordinariness that the wealth seems to contradict.

Substance abuse leads to intoxication and passing out. I'm usually curious about which part of the person gets drunk or high and which part passes out. Substances can quiet the needy self or the embarrassing self, or perhaps they calm down the abusive self or the judging self. A psychological approach to substance abuse would undertake a resolution of conflict between the selves.

Perhaps it's a small point, but I would like to reserve the term *addiction* for behaviors that are maintained not just by their effects but also by the fact that there are physiological costs to giving them up. When people use heroin or drink after becoming dependent, the physical pain of discontinuing helps maintain the behavior. It's more than the frustration of extinction; it's as if the soda machine refused to provide a soda (extinction) *and* it shocked you if you tried to stop inserting quarters. Habits like promiscuous sex and gambling can be painful to give up, since that incurs the irritation of extinction and also having to face whatever all the sex and gambling were helping the person avoid. However, they are not addictions in the sense of also avoiding withdrawal symptoms. Certain advantages accrue to calling them addictions, like those associated with calling alcoholism a *disease*, mainly to drive home the seriousness of the situation. As with the disease terminology, however, calling sex and gambling *addictions* has become an excuse, instead.

Chapter Four

Knowing Something about Yourself

Why do you see the speck in your neighbor's eye, but do not notice the log in your own eye?—Matthew 7:3

Therapy is a relationship between two people, and the more you know about the two people involved, the more you will be able to intervene effectively.

PSYCHOLOGICAL MINDEDNESS

There are many definitions of *psychological mindedness* available through a web search, and these include a capacity for self-reflection, interest in and knowledge about feelings, insight into one's motives, and so on. None of the definitions I found seemed all that *psychological* to me. To me, psychological mindedness is the capacity to examine yourself with the accuracy, intelligence, curiosity, empathy, and humor with which good parents view their children. Psychological mindedness means seeing yourself the way good therapists see patients, the way great novelists see their characters. Read *Middlemarch*, *War and Peace*, *Anna Karenina*, and the Shakespeare tragedies not just to learn about people from great psychologists but to learn how to relate to disparate characters with acceptance and empathy.

Psychological mindedness, then, is the capacity to see oneself as a multi-character entity, like a family or a business or a nation. It's the idea that Huxley (1956) expressed by writing, "Nor am I the captain of my soul. I am only its noisiest passenger" (pp. 68–69). It's the idea that when we speak of ourselves, we are no more spokesperson for the whole self than the secretary of state is for all the United States. *Officially*, we may be in that role, but there are always aspects of the self that we would prefer that others did not notice. The unitary self is fostered by families intent on denying aspects of children that don't fit the narrative and by language that insists that the referent of the pronoun *I* comprises the entire self. *We* would be more accurate, or even better would be *much of me*. The unitary self is a fiction, a claim of certainty. Like a proud dictator who claims to get 100 percent of the vote in a "free" election, the unitary self demands silence from the rest of the self and from others when making proclamations about what it is. The myth of the unitary self pressures people to act like swaggering tinhorn dictators vis-à-vis the rest of themselves. It makes it humiliating to say, "I'm not sure what I think" or "I'm in conflict about what to do." This is what led Jung to call symptoms the guerrilla warfare of the psyche.

What's psychological about my definition—self-knowledge and self-acceptance, essentially—is that it rejects the unitary self and views the individual not as indivisible but as a collection of selves, figures, internalized objects, and response repertoires. Therapists are wise to consider a trait like extraversion or assertiveness, or a symptom like depression or anxiety, as a multicharacter effect. An extreme extravert might be someone in whom, as only one possibility, one self is constantly accusing the other, "Nobody likes you," and the accused self must constantly prove this false. An assertive person may be one who constantly amazes herself with her own brilliance or one who is constantly proving to herself that she is not a sissy.

Psychological mindedness was a concept originally used to distinguish patients likely to benefit from therapy from those with whom it would be a longer haul. The assumption was that the therapist was already psychologically minded. Nowadays, that assumption is unwarranted. I suppose a lot of people have always wanted to be therapists because of their experiences as caregivers or diplomats in their own families or as patients themselves, but it is a recent development in clinical training to cater to the claims of righteousness in the former and daintiness in the latter at the cost of circumspection. The American Psychological Association recently downgraded "self-reflection" from being its own competency and folded it in under "professionalism," signaling diminishment of its importance to those doing clinical work, even though in my opinion it's the most important thing of all.

Psychological mindedness is a worldview, not a technique. A woman takes a stressful job and gains 20 pounds. Is that story going to be about the physiology of cortisol, the politics of feminism, or the anthropology of status? Is it forbidden even to consider whether weight gain is a problem because it can sound like fat-shaming? To be psychologically (versus politically, medically, and so on) minded is to wonder whether the weight gain is a problem for her, whether what *she* thinks about it is the best source of information on that question, and what the function might be of consuming more calories than she expends. It certainly seems relevant to know what she weighed when she started the job—a 20-pound weight gain might reflect a reliance on a well-established neurotic relationship with food, a determination to get physically fit to prepare for stress, or a new habit that moved her from her desired weight to overweight. The therapist who already knows what the problem is—the male gaze, the amygdala, the desire to fit in with other female executives—is doing her a disservice.

When Hollywood stars go haywire, it's often said that they believed their own publicity. We are all tempted by the same trap. We all put on a public face, usually inspired by one we wore in our family—or its opposite. Then we claim that this is our real face, and finally we claim it even to ourselves. Self-knowledge requires us to question what we claim about ourselves, just as self-knowledge garnered through therapy requires exploration of patients' claims of who they are. It's a very fragile, testy world that views questions as accusations (J. Goodwin, personal communication, 2017), and legion are the therapists who balk at asking patients to explore their self-descriptions because to do so seems assaultive. Good therapists understand that they have to fix the patient's idiosyncratic reaction to therapy before they can fix the patient's idiosyncratic reaction to life events. The patient says my attention makes him feel "repulsive," and I want to know what picture or movie is running in his head when he says that word. Another therapist tells me I should accept his self-description and empathize, even though I don't yet know what I would be empathizing with. It's hard to imagine that other therapist questioning her own claims of being attentive and caring if she won't question the patient's claims.

The opposite of psychological mindedness, then, is self-righteousness, the claim to be without sin or stigma, the claim that the socially desirable part of the self that has the microphone is both in charge and speaks for the whole self. In my view, we can boil down 23 volumes of Freud to this: We are not the ultimate authority on ourselves. Self-righteousness was evident in the one-star Yelp review in which the only complaint was that the reviewer discovered there would be a two-hour wait on a Saturday evening. Her emotions told her she'd been disappointed, so the restaurant must have disappointed her. Bateson (1972a) says that even a dog distinguishes a kick from being tripped over, but not dogs that base their reactions solely on their emotions. Self-righteous are the therapists who are certain that the conflicts that arise between them and their patients are the fault of the patients—or the patients' mothers, who didn't raise them right. Self-righteous are the students or the researchers who manage their conflicts about not being experts by getting angry at the faculty members and clinicians who remind him that they have much to learn. They act as if the teacher or the expert is a dangerous animal, because they feel as if their lives are at stake, never dreaming that the only dangerous animal in the situation is their own voracious and insatiable—and all-too-human—appetite for looking perfect.

Not every healthy person is psychologically minded, but every personality-disordered person is not. That's because psychological mindedness is not like political or medical mindedness in that it requires a warm relationship with oneself, not just with a psychological frame. Psychotherapy with a psychologically minded therapist is one way to become more psychologically minded, just as reading Eliot, Tolstoy, and Shakespeare is, but only if you produce your embarrassing selves with your therapist and only if you allow yourself to identify with selfish and troubled Anna and Karenin and not just with happy and healthy Kitty and Levin.

Of course, everyone's psychological mindedness fails them at times. We all occasionally get into a complex, a situation in which we fail to observe ourselves with the warm affection we typically monitor ourselves with. At these moments, we behave neurotically, as if the childish impulses are running the show and the better angels are asleep. Everyone is a diva sometimes, and it is a great irony of interpersonal relating that just at the moment when we are convinced that we are the princess, we are actually the pea, the irritant that ruins it for everyone else.

There was a time in psychology circles when claims of being above neurotic conflict and unconscious motivation were greeted with ridicule ,as if the person were claiming to be Jesus or Buddha. Of course, patients couldn't call their therapists out on that sort of nonsense, so people who secretly thought they were godly or special would act, primarily with patients, as if they did not have a personal psychology. Much contemporary thinking is a reaction to that stance, as is the whole point of this chapter, a reminder that there are two people in an individual therapy (which we ought to call *dyadic therapy*). Sometimes, there's an overreaction, like when therapists renounce an authoritative stance so as not to appear authoritarian.

Returning to the spiral staircase of chapter 1, you can see how you'd have to be psychologically minded even to approach the stairs, much less climb them. You'd have to be able to appraise yourself as okay for now but have much to learn, like a parent teaching a child how to use a camera or a coach teaching soccer, gently insisting on practice with affectionate confidence. Unless you are truly gifted—and one of the saddest and greatest things about being a therapist is that no one is truly gifted at establishing and maintaining relationships—you have to learn to love the rehearsals, the practices, and not just the accolades of performance, and that requires an internal parent or teacher or coach with whom you can enjoy the successes in rehearsals—and, more importantly, to accept the flubs. The most important word in the English language is *oops*. In therapy "practice," it's almost all rehearsal and almost never performance. Indeed, much of the craft of technique is to create a play space, a rehearsal space, distinct from the dreadful seriousness elsewhere. Another point about the spiral staircase is that in many ways, it doesn't really go upward for perspective but downward for depth, to face and embrace the parts of ourselves and our patients not shown in public.

COGNITIVE BIAS

Because therapists are people, they are subject to the laws of behavior. Psychological mindedness means applying the curriculum to themselves, including the concepts of confirmation bias, fundamental attribution error, and self-serving ways of thinking. There is a rich tradition of this in psychotherapy. Freud's specimen dream was a dream of his own, Ellis first practiced rational-emotive therapy on himself, and Skinner (who majored in literature) was more interested in accounting for the behavior of the psychologist than the behavior of the rat.

Important cognitive biases in therapy involve the Dunning-Kruger effect (Kruger & Dunning, 1999) and earned dogmatism (Ottati et al., 2015), mentioned in chapter 1. The *Dunning-Kruger effect* refers to the tendency of experts to underestimate their expertise and nonexperts to overestimate theirs. The colleagues I hold in highest esteem—genuine master clinicians—are constantly befuddled by the complexity of clinical situations even as they tend to recognize clinical patterns quickly and fluidly. My colleague Lavita Nadkarni and I once proposed that students should not receive graduate degrees unless faculty had heard them say "I don't know" at least ten times in public. *Earned dogmatism* refers to the tendency of nonexperts to especially overestimate their expertise if they have completed easy tasks. People who take an easy quiz on world capitals then rank their geography expertise higher than do people who took a difficult quiz. It is so named because experts tend to be dogmatic, having spent a lot of time making up their minds. As the curriculum gets easier and easier in order to appeal to the dainty feelings of students and to compete for tuition, students get more and more dogmatic.

The greatest cognitive bias is in the direction of things one has already said and done. *Cognitive dissonance* refers to the discomfort of holding conflicting ideas, which usually leads to trashing one in order to relieve the conflict. If you think you're smart (or are worried that you're not), it's hard to also think you might be wrong. Saving face also comes into play once you say an idea out loud. The result is therapists who think every idea they float must be a good one. Nowadays, as already noted, therapists obsess about whether they are all good rather than all-knowing. This makes it very difficult for many therapists to consider whether they have made a mistake or whether something they did might be downright harmful. They spout drivel like, "If he's still coming for therapy, he must be getting something out of it," even if the patient in question is a self-abusive depressive whose judgment about what's good for him they question in every other situation. You can be a good therapist and make mistakes, even bad mistakes; good therapists learn from them.

The *fundamental attribution error* or *actor-observer effect* (Jones & Nisbett, 1971) refers to the tendency to ascribe our own conduct to situational variables and others' conduct to character. I cut someone off in traffic because I really have to be somewhere; others do it because they're jerks. Therapists get annoyed because patients can be irritating; patients get annoyed because their mothers didn't raise them right. The use of a different vocabulary for patients often disguises the fundamental attribution error. Therapists are influential; patients are manipulative. Therapists seek people because they are gregarious; patients are dependent on the opinions of others.

It's easier to deploy self-serving cognitive biases in therapy than elsewhere because of the power differential—there's no one to call the therapist out on it. As noted above, outside of the power to affect another person's physical circumstance, the greatest social power is the authority to define what's going on in a situation, analogous to victors writing history. Therapists' expertise compared to their patients in defining situations gives them the upper hand. "I am trying to help you but you won't let me" is a common subtext; the patient is unlikely to say, "Well, you're not very good at it." This is especially true when they can both blame the patient's parents. Also, as noted above, what I call *therapeutic privilege* is the luxury of not having to think about the patient's definition of the situation when the therapist doesn't have to. My point, for now, is that a little humility is in order, because we are all of us human.

STIMULUS VALUE

We expend a great deal of energy socially in the service of ignoring what people look like. This tactful courtesy is especially demanded and especially taxing when the way one looks discredits the performance one is trying to pull off. I'm not talking about fat-shaming, remarking on a disability or disfigurement, mentioning race when the person is merely trying to perform the role of a good person or ordinary citizen. I'm talking about the drop-dead gorgeous student bravely broaching the topic of her looks only to have the plain but borderline student mention how flustered *her* patients are by *her* looks. I'm talking about holding yourself out as a therapist in a body that is obviously decades younger than the patient's. I'm talking about being a man trying to induce a woman to tell me her relevant sexual fantasies or a white guy trying to get a black girl to tell me what her home is like. It won't go well if I ignore my being a man or being white.

One of the most consistently status-lowering things that can happen is to get caught having a body. Much of what passes for politeness involves disguising this basic fact—presumably, as mentioned above in discussing status, because children can't hide their physicality, but also probably because having a body means you are going to die someday, and it's a visible sign of imperfection. You can tell when children have to pee, when they're hungry, and when they're sleepy. One of the main ways people elevate their own status is to comment on the other people's bodies, whether it's obvious, as in men's catcalls at passing women, or subtle, as in expressions of concern for older people. And yet we notice bodies without fail. A therapy that continues the charade of ignoring each person's stimulus value is not really intimate.

A 12-year-old victim of incest by her stepfather entered her overweight therapist's office and saw candy wrappers in the wastebasket. She said, "You shouldn't eat candy; you're fat." The therapist said, "That hurt my feelings"—which is fine, assuming this was information about the therapist's reaction and not a reproach. Sharing reactions to patients does not make the relationship into a social one, as disclosing autobiographical facts does. I might have preferred a grander effort to explore the girl's concern, but at least the therapist did not pretend she wasn't overweight, and she demonstrated by her willingness to articulate her reaction that the dyad could discuss it. Notice that she did not say that the girl was wrong to speak up, and if the girl took the reaction as a reproach, the therapist could have wondered why the girl took the information about her reaction as corrective (again assuming that it was not in fact a reproach).

Now, to train a psychologically minded lens on this example of stimulus value, there are parallels between the presenting problem—trying to manage the stigma and the emotions related to incest so as to live a normal life—and what happened in the office. The statement about the candy and the therapist's weight signals two major themes of this therapy. The girl is extremely suspicious of any sign of impulsivity in authority figures (such as eating candy), so the therapist will have to manage her own impulses without completely denying she has them. The girl does not know how to relate to her own stigma, and the therapist can show her that stigmatization can lead to emotional interaction rather than humiliation.

WHETHER THE THEORY APPLIES IN THE OFFICE

Many therapists act as if the therapy office is in a separate universe in which their theories of human behavior do not apply. They listen to stories about the patient's narcissistic mother with no sense at all that the patient might have tailored the stories for the occasion. This is even true of behaviorists, who supposedly think that behavior, including storytelling, is occasioned by its immediate environment. Psychoanalysts at least acknowledge that the patient *expects* narcissistic mothering from the therapist, if not that the therapist has reminded the patient of narcissistic mothering. Behaviorists often think they are getting good information about the reinforcement contingencies that operated during the patient's childhood.

The strange thing is that these same therapists have often been in therapy themselves. They rarely brought up as patients the things their therapists did that annoyed them, but they believe their own patients would not hesitate to speak up. They actively hid or disguised their own embarrassing thoughts, but they think their own patients are telling them everything. They ended therapy with relief, knowing they got through it without ever telling their therapists about the time they—well, finish this sentence yourself. How do we know all this about their therapies? Because these things are true of every therapy: It's a function of being human; there's always a backstage (Goffman, 1974). The big lie in therapy is not in holding back some things but in pretending that the parties are holding nothing back.

It's arrogant to have a theory of human behavior that does not apply to yourself, whether because you think it is humiliating to be a patient, because you think you are that special, or simply because you can get away with it. Behavior therapy should itself be behavioral, systemic therapy systemic, and so on (Karson, 2008). Behaviorists should examine patients' behaviors in the office in functional relation to their occasioning environment. Psychodynamic therapists should wonder about the impact on the situation of their own unconscious motivations, relational paradigms, and organizing principles. Cognitive behaviorists should examine the schemas of both parties operating in the session. Systems therapists should consider the system in the room and its structural ambiguities and available roles. Existentialists should wonder how to make the most of the session and of the therapy, even knowing that both will end.

Undoubtedly, there are gastroenterologists who don't get colonoscopies, estate lawyers who don't have wills, and financial consultants awash in debt. These lapses raise questions about whether they really believe their own recommendations. With therapists it goes even further, because when therapists exempt themselves from their own theories, they are not just undermining their credibility, they are actively doing something wrong to their patients. The therapist's superiority denigrates the patient as the source of all conflict, and it robs the patient of learning how to collaborate around conflict resolution. Just as with patients, the more a therapist knows herself, the more she will accept herself with affection, and the more she does that, the less tempted she will be to fall for her own publicity.

Chapter Five

Knowing Something about Conflict

Some people run from a possible fight; some people figure they can never win.—Billy Joel

CONFLICT RESOLUTION

Two people can't interact for more than a few minutes without running into a conflict—incompatible goals—however minor. Freud would have said the same about *one* person. Conflict, in the form of goals or wishes that are not consistent with the demands of reality or other people's agendas, is what brings people to therapy, and it is at the heart of what happens in the therapy office. A restated version of old clinical wisdom is that therapists should not alleviate conflicts that arise in therapy in order to get on with the business of therapy, but instead that addressing the conflicts that arise in therapy *is* the business of therapy. The idea is to address them in a way that will generalize to other conflicts that arise in patients' lives.

Psychological problems (as opposed to mental illnesses) are efforts to resolve conflict. Of course, a lot of emotional suffering is the result of adversity, so I want to remind you again of Freud's distinction between neurotic suffering (the stuff of therapy: bad coping strategies, including especially treating yourself badly) and common unhappiness. The problems therapists deal with are former efforts to resolve conflict that have become passé, that no longer work once the patient leaves home, say; or that were short-term solutions that became a way of life, like avoiding certain situations or emotions; or that served as compromises, when the patient no longer needs them. These efforts are *defense mechanisms* (all of which one can easily translate into other theoretical languages) in which the person is defending a conception of him- or herself and those he or she holds dear or depends on.

Self-concept as a source of conflict is at the heart of Wilmot and Hocker's (2007) scheme, which asserts the advantages of dividing the incompatible goals that define conflict into four categories: topic, relational, identity, and process goals. *Topic* goals are the concrete, geographic things at stake in the conflict: where we will go for dinner, what kind of kitchen we will end up with, money, sex, and who gets the last piece of pizza. *Relational* goals involve the definition of our relationship, equivalent to pressures to define the relationship communicated in systems theory's command function. Are we equals? Lovers? Friends or acquaintances? Best friends? You can often clarify relational goal conflicts by exploring the ground rules or frame of the relationship, for example, that friends take turns initiating contact. This can lead one friend to think the other friend is acting superior by not initiating, as if the second friend is trying to impose a leader-follower relationship. They can discuss what their relationship is, but they can also get somewhere by discussing the rule. They may realize that even in egalitarian friendships, the more extraverted person initiates contact disproportionately. *Identity* goals are analogous to face and status, how we want others to see us. Am I a sucker if I accept the offer? Am I a real man if I explore my own feelings? Am I a good person if I charge you for a session you missed? Am I a dependent subordinate if I initiate contact disproportionately? *Process* goals have to do with the way we want to go about resolving a conflict. One person wants to talk it over; the other wants to pretend it isn't happening.

Process goals are generally minor issues, but the parties must address them first. If one person prefers to resolve conflict through avoidance and the other through discussion, even a minor conflict over, say, emptying the dishwasher can become a casus belli. One spouse interprets the other's lack of interest in discussing the problem as a lack of interest in the marriage; the other interprets the discussion as a lack of satisfaction with the guilty spouse in general. If they both preferred avoidance or both preferred discussion, the dishwasher would remain a minor bump in the road.

Understanding conflicts around process goals can spare people a lot of trouble. I am tempted to enter political discussions until I realize that the other person is interested not in a meeting of minds but in overpowering me. One friend is extremely knowledgeable about politics, and I enjoy talking things over with him because we both know that he is an expert and I am a student in these conversations. Some people bring up white privilege or male privilege in conversation to seize power or to make me feel bad. I can't see why I'd want to pursue those conversations. Others bring up my privilege the way a loving spouse would tell me I have toothpaste on my face, a friendly reminder that I have misbehaved. When there's a mismatch in process goals—whether the parties prefer to resolve the conflict through domination, submission, avoidance, or mutual discovery, among others—it's generally better to reflect on the mismatch than to pursue the topic without dealing with the process conflict: "I can't tell if you're cross-examining me or trying to get a better sense of what I think."

In therapy it is essential for therapists to monitor whether they are on the same page as their patients. No real work can get done when the participation is at cross purposes. Also, as noted above, getting on the same page is often the real work, as difficulties with collaboration cause or aggravate many of the patient's life problems. Therapists cannot explore the meaning of a symptom if the patient experiences the exploration as a way of withholding relief. Therapists cannot usefully offer intimacy if the patient experiences it as an intrusion or as a reflection of the therapist's neediness.

Conflicts often get out of hand because they tap into identity goals. One road to happiness is to trade identity goals for topic goals, to get your needs met in exchange for making people feel better about themselves. This applies only when you don't have relational intimacy goals with the people in question; in therapy and love, preservation of relational goals needs a more cards-on-the-table approach.

Wilmot and Hocker (2007) distinguish subgoals and try to meet as many of them as possible. Our desires usually come bundled in packages with labels on them: We want to eat at Steve's Snappin' Dogs, or we want to go to Paris, or we want to have a room of our own. Conflicts then devolve into a contest between one package or the other. Instead, we can open the package and take out the components. Inside Steve's might be a Chicago Dog, or al fresco dining, or tater tots, or the retro experience. Each of these might be available at another establishment that appeals to our dining partner. The idea is not to find a compromise, such as taking turns, but to find an option that meets the largest number of subgoals inside the two packages.

Now let's get psychological about it. Like many children, I always wanted to fly. One day, I was putting the shingles on the tool shed I had built in the backyard, and I felt my spirits soar. I realized I was flying—as long as I was willing to open the package that said "flying" on the label and examine its components. I had elevated myself off the ground by dint of my own industry and initiative. This is what is meant by cherishing what you can get, even though I only stumbled on it accidentally. It's what Nietzsche meant by *amor fati*: If you can truly embrace your fate, it's the same as getting your way—just be careful not to settle too soon. If this sounds like the psychoanalytic idea of *sublimation*—gratification of impulses in a revised, more acceptable form—that's exactly right.

What's psychological about this example is the idea that metaphorically, a part of me was flying. To see that is to acknowledge that we are not just the face we show to the world, we're a community of behavioral response repertoires or selves or internalized selfobjects or Jungian figures. We are not in control of even the things we do, a frightening thought existentially and one that is contrary to virtually every culture and language. When people must take responsibility for themselves, it's easier if they repudiate many of the selves within their skins. So peering beyond the label on the package of goals to find another way to fly is akin to looking past the spokesperson of the self to internal agendas. I levitated on my tool shed, but not magically or supernaturally.

Many or maybe all symptoms are *compromise formations* (Freud, 1923/1961): efforts at conflict resolution between conflicting agendas. Watzlawick et al. (1974) give the example of sitting on a plane next to a boring passenger. You decide to pretend you are asleep at some point so as not to be trapped. (This was before headphones.) The conflict occurs only if you hate to think of yourself as the kind of person who would blow someone off like that. You resolve the conflict by actually falling asleep. The parallel to other symptoms is in the achievement of so-called secondary gain (*so-called* because it is typically the primary reason for the symptom) while fooling even yourself about your authenticity. Someone is anxious because he doesn't know what to do in a situation and others comfort him, a situation he is quite familiar and comfortable with. He hates to think he is the kind of person who would pretend to be anxious to get comfort, so he actually gets anxious.

RUPTURE AND REPAIR

The overarching lesson about conflict in therapy is that it is better to approach conflict than to avoid it. Avoidance can outlast a conflict, and it can protect oneself from strife at the cost of whatever the conflict was about, but it can never lead to resolution. Sure, if some jerk cuts you off in traffic, avoid the conflict; I'm talking about situations where the relationship is worth preserving, and that is always the case when the conflict is with yourself.

Therapists teach conflict approaching in a few ways. They establish a local culture in which the dyad picks at threads and slows things down to examine curious moments. All talk therapy claims that talking things over is good for people, even if they come for therapy only to seek relief and to get their associates to stop bugging them. Therapists address their own conflicts, usually in the form of the lose-lose statement, when something happens that elicits incompatible goals: "I'm worried that if I ask about the abuse, you'll experience me as intrusive, and if I don't ask about it, you'll experience me as uninterested." Therapists, though, mainly teach patients to approach conflict in the way they manage conflicts that arise between them.

The process of *rupture and repair*—or, as I prefer to call it, making messes and cleaning them up—always happens in therapy, simply because no one is perfect, the relationship demands a lot of the therapist, and each patient is different. Experience and wisdom can prepare therapists for repairing relationships, but no amount of experience and wisdom can put them in a position to understand patients before they even meet them and try relating to them. Self psychology holds that self-organization derives from parental attunement and psychological growth derives from parental misattunement, because it is the rupture in empathy that signals the need to find a different way to relate.

Students who are so uncomfortable with making mistakes that they can't examine them cannot become competent therapists. They can't become competent at any other complex task, either: They will read only books they have mastered, cook only things with simple recipes, and never throw an interception (which they achieve only by never throwing a pass). These are typically students who have been overly praised and react with excessive frustration to extinction, or they are students who have been so harshly criticized that they cannot examine their mistakes without being vicious to themselves. The latter say, "Why do they have to be called *mistakes*?" The search for a nicer term often signals the harshness with which they treat themselves.

Mistakes or ruptures or messes are inevitable if therapists are to get involved with patients, but shrugging as if to say that these things are inevitable diminishes the relationship. If you have a flat tire on the way to meet a friend, it's not going to impede the relational goals of friendship to shrug it off or even ask for sympathy yourself. If it happens on the way to a job interview, the relational goals require you to act reliable and take responsibility for not having left earlier or not having already downloaded the ride-sharing app to your phone so you could get a lift promptly. Whether to treat the inevitable messes in therapy as mistakes, then, is really a question about what kind of relationship therapy is and what its interpersonal goals and implicit rules are. The unavoidable (and at the same time desirable) power differential in therapy requires the therapist to take responsibility for messes that occur in therapy, much as a parent takes responsibility even when it unpredictably rains on a picnic. It's also an attitude that encourages patients to take responsibility for, or at least explore, their own contributions to messes. Humans are more likely to examine the specks in their eyes if others look for logs in their own.

Another thought that might soften any sting in calling our missteps *mistakes* has to do with the responsibilities of the parties. In the kind of therapy this book is about—talking regularly to change response tendencies—the patient has only a few responsibilities; the therapist has many. In a typical moment, the patient has virtually none, while the therapist must listen on different levels, manage the frame of the relationship, attend to the working alliance, apply the patient's reports or observable behaviors to the goals through the lens of the case conceptualization, and say things that make the patient feel understood not too shallowly and not disconcertingly deeply. With all these responsibilities operating, the therapist is bound to make mistakes—but they're still mistakes.

APOLOGY

Once therapists accept their commission of mistakes, their first impulse is often to apologize. Saying you are sorry about something is typically a social move maintained by its effect on other people, which is that it gets them to stop complaining and to set aside their emotional reactions. In conflict resolution terms, apology lowers one's status in exchange for reestablishing relationship goals, possibly because many infractions that require an apology are themselves status moves of the sort that put the perpetrator's agenda ahead of other people's. There's nothing wrong with apologizing as a social lubricant, but it can only maintain closeness, not build it. The idea in therapy is to use the messes made by the therapist to deepen the relationship, not to pave them over with a "Sorry."

A productive apology resolves conflict when one party is at fault. Often both parties are at fault, and both must apologize to preserve the relational goals. Notice that if one party has an identity goal of never being in the wrong, resolution is impossible unless the other party admires or obeys that person. A good apology is like a good case formulation in that it examines and explains problematic behavior and sets a path for changing it. It has four essential parts (more or less following Madanes, 1990): damage assessment, what the apologizer did wrong, why he did it, and what's different now.

The most important element of a real apology is the damage assessment. Until the apologizer has heard the full extent of the harm done, the apology functions to avoid this information. You also wouldn't know what you were apologizing *for*, and the process of assessing the damage itself restores a relational goal of caring about the other person's experience. Resolution requires loosening or untying (the etymology of *solve*), and the main thing that needs to be unknotted in therapy is the patient's narrative. Next, the apologizer must name the behavior that was hurtful, rather than provide a generic sense of responsibility. "I should have left earlier" shows you mean business compared to "I'm sorry I was late." The same goes for "I yawned" compared to "I'm just a little tired." The next steps are not always appropriate to the therapy relationship, since they involve a level of disclosure that typically contradicts therapy's relational goals. This also happens when parents apologize to children, but therapists and parents can at least communicate a general idea of why they misbehaved and a sense that they are working to change those circumstances: "I may have been taking advantage of your resilience instead of providing you a place where you don't have to be resilient." Just saying this implies that it will stop, that things are different now.

An exercise I recommend in the termination process—whether ending the therapy is organic or the product of external circumstances—is to reflect on the broadest ways in which the therapist might have mishandled the therapy.

My inspiration was the father explaining at the end of *Ordinary People* why he never got on his son's case: "You were always so hard on yourself, I never had the heart." I think this kind of retrospection can be liberating. Two people deeply in love after 20 years of marriage can still say to each other things like, "It took me so long to feel I could rely on you; I wish I hadn't tested you so much at the beginning." This is analogous to apologizing as a form of conflict resolution preventatively, sparked by an occasion for retrospection rather than by an injury. Whether to share the idea with a patient is another matter.

INVITATIONAL RHETORIC

Rhetoric is the art or science of effective speech, where *effective* has traditionally meant persuasive, or getting one's way. Foss and Griffin (1995) reframed all rhetoric as domineering and coined the term *invitational rhetoric* for a more collaborative sense of efficacy. Invitational rhetoric "assumes two primary rhetorical forms. One is offering perspectives . . . ; the second is the creation of external conditions that allow and encourage others to present their perspectives" (p. 7). The goal is not to persuade but to share and understand. Undoubtedly, the day after Foss and Griffin presented this useful idea, dominant people appropriated it to disguise their persuasive agendas. There is nothing wrong with persuasion when the participants have to make a decision, the terms of the debate are clear, and the subject is of the sort that may have a genuinely right or wrong answer. Most subjects discussed in therapy (not to mention other social collaborations) are not of this sort. I should add a caveat that Foss and Griffin are especially concerned with keeping hierarchies, hegemonies, and marginalizations from arising in situations that don't need them, whereas in therapy (and parenting and supervision), hierarchies are inevitable and desirable, so I'm really talking about making therapy as invitational as possible. "The creation of external conditions that allow and encourage [patients] to present their perspectives" is the purpose of a therapeutic frame. Here, let's explore the technique of offering perspectives in therapy as a form of conflict resolution.

Just as it's hard to know how to conduct a marriage if you grew up around unhappily married people, it's hard to know how to conduct a therapy if therapists never had a good therapy themselves. The big lesson from invitational rhetoric is that the therapist should *offer* ideas rather than press them, identifying them as a perspective rather than as the way things are. This approach may also encourage the offering of ideas by therapists who are too cautious because they fear making pronouncements.

Invitational rhetoric capitalizes on the systemic idea of homeostasis in the same way reflecting teams do (Andersen, 1987). Family therapists noticed that if they pushed for change, the system maintained its equilibrium by pushing back. Most people have noticed that when they suggest that a friend leave an unsatisfying relationship, the friend recounts all the good things about the partner. Some therapists will take advantage of this by counseling stasis while expecting change as a rebellion against the counsel, or by prescribing the symptom to induce a countermeasure (Madanes, 1981, for example). The reflecting team tries to influence a family by offering ideas not to the family but to each other in the family's presence. In the posture of overhearing ideas, the family is not compelled to refute them. Foss and Griffin might say that the reflecting team is invitational rather than domineering, and the family responds accordingly, sharing rather than defending or complying.

COGNITIVE DISSONANCE

Internal conflict creates cognitive dissonance, a discomfort often solved by trashing or ignoring one of the ideas or values in the conflict. Trashing or ignoring an agenda avoids but does not resolve conflict. The neglected agenda will return in dreams, ill-considered expressions of it on the side, compromise symptoms, a sense of being unfulfilled, and so forth. Further squashing of the hidden agenda won't work; finding a place for it will. Sometimes that place is therapy, which teaches the patient the skill of honoring more of the whole self in tightly framed contexts. Sometimes, to the patient's surprise, the marginalized agenda will become the primary agenda, as in patients who realize that their anxiety is not the enemy and is telling them something about how to live their lives more productively. Their symptoms aren't bugs, they're features. Sometimes, merely acknowledging the marginalized agenda satisfies it, like an angry employee or citizen who simply wants an opportunity to be heard.

Therapists are constantly in values conflicts. There are those between patients' and therapists' definitions of how to live a good life. There are those between therapists' ideas of behaving well and the mutual goals of the therapy, for example, when the dyad agrees to work on uncovering the patient's true agendas toward the end of finding more satisfying employment and discover that the process is threatening the patient's marriage or sexual orientation, while the therapist disagrees with divorce or gay sex. And there are conflicts between the values and rules that facilitate therapy and those of social and professional relationships.

One reason it is so hard for therapists to end on time (or stop nodding and cooing) is that ending on time conflicts with the value of implementing social tact in ending encounters. You see this when people committed to niceness get unsolicited sales calls or strangers approach them on the street for a handout. They want the other person to observe reciprocal niceties and end the encounter. They listen to the whole plea without interrupting and then say, “I’m on my way to a dental appointment,” expecting the aggressor to get the message. Nice people become therapists at increasing rates, partly because it has become a stereotypical caring (versus changing) profession and partly because they got to be nice in the first place by developing skills around suppressing conflict, so now they seek out new and more challenging conflicts to suppress.

The traditional way of resolving the conflict between niceness and effective therapy is to tie therapy skills to some higher form of niceness—call it *kindness* or *responsibility*. In the long run, it’s kinder and more responsible to secure the therapeutic frame, to discipline your children, and so on. I have no major problems with this strategy, but it does still trash the value of aggression; I compromise, as noted, by talking about *virtuous* aggression. Therapists may need to promote the value of aggression more, well, aggressively, when working with patients who twist themselves in knots about their own aggression.

Chapter Six

Knowing Something about the Working Alliance and Case Formulation

Psychoanalytic understanding is making sense together.—Donna Orange

THE COMMON FACTORS

In 1936, Rosenzweig argued in a brief paper that therapies of the sort this book is about may register successes because of factors common to all of them, not for the reasons advanced by their separate theoretical rationales. Research since then seems to bear him out, and the American Psychological Association's (2012) statement recognizing the efficacy of psychotherapy emphasizes the common factors. In an influential paper, Bordin (1979) reduced the common factors to only three: mutual goals, relevant tasks, and relational bonds. This economy of expression allows therapists to actually use the idea in sessions, since only one of three things can be going wrong.

An original set of common factors involved patient strengths, including resilience, hope, industry, and fortunate circumstances. Shedler (personal communication, 2010) has pointed out how Bordin's triad still includes these factors implicitly, since it is healthy and well-situated patients who are most capable of setting goals, engaging in therapy tasks, and developing relational bonds.

THE WORKING ALLIANCE

Shedler also noted that the *working alliance* has morphed in the literature into the *therapeutic alliance*, a term that ought to mean the same thing but functionally omits the crucial idea that the therapist and patient are working on something together. One question that good supervisors keep in mind, and that therapists eventually internalize, is whether at any given moment the therapist is *working*. Therapists often coast, both in sessions and with respect to climbing the spiral staircase; these therapists cannot serve as patients' role models for change. Another crucial question is whether the patient is on board.

Bordin posits the working alliance as the place to look when anything goes wrong in therapy—also in parenting, supervision, or teaching. There may be a breach in the sense of purpose normally generated by the therapist and patient sharing mutual goals, in a sense that engaging in the tasks of therapy will result in those goals, or in the relational bonds expected to develop between collaborators. The big idea is that if something's off—and of course only a therapist versed in what productive therapy looks and feels like can tell when something's off—there are only three places to look. The dyad may not be working toward the same purpose, like two rowers heading to different places on a lake. The dyad may not be engaging in the tasks of therapy because they don't seem to lead to the goal, like two rowers going in circles because they don't see the need to coordinate their movements or like rowers who spend so much energy wishing they could fly that they don't see the relevance of rowing. Or the dyad may be off relationally, rowing half-heartedly, perhaps because one member is feeling unappreciated, resentful, disappointed, or something else. I often wonder whether sports teams fail at times because some of the players really want the demeaning coach or their arrogant or lazy teammates to lose.

The concept of the working alliance insists that therapy is something the therapist and patient do together. The most common supervision problem is a therapist trying to figure out what is going on and what to do about it. "If only there were someone else in the room who could assist you," I say. Just as process goals must be addressed first in conflicts, problems in mutuality of purpose must be addressed in therapy. And the sense of collaboration, again, is not just a requirement for effective therapy—it *is* (when carefully framed) effective therapy. It energizes patients to do their parts, and the hindrances that arise that interfere with collaboration are (in a carefully framed relationship) those that arise in other settings as well.

Physical therapists treat some injuries with direct intervention, but they treat many injuries by prescribing exercises, analogous to music lessons in which the teacher has taught the technique and the student's job is to practice it. Clear, shared, realistic goals; an understanding of the relevance of the exercise or practice to achieving those goals; and carefully framed relational bonds are what induce the patient or student to exercise or practice.

MUTUAL GOALS

The drift toward gentleness and downright fragility in therapists is nowhere more apparent than in goal setting, which requires a certain amount of virtuous aggression. Some will say that setting goals at all is a mean thing to do, because it makes patients feel that they are not perfect as they are. But patients are *not* perfect as they are, and to suggest otherwise is to heap on them the burden of living up to such claims. Some say that the patient alone sets the goals, that for therapists to have an agenda is oppressive. When I press them, these therapists agree that they will not work with an 80-pound adult women on shedding a few more pounds. To leave the goals to the patient is to assume that the patient already knows what's wrong with his or her life, when we have every reason to believe that his or her thinking on this matter is distorted, affected by the psychological patterns that make what's wrong, wrong. One example is the woman who sought therapy for help with managing her resentment about her husband's amazing job opportunity in another state. The therapist conducted the whole therapy—successfully, in his estimation—without ever wondering whether the husband ought to take the job. Was the patient sacrificing her own well-being to money and careerism? Had the husband taken a job that was too demanding for the marriage to get the attention she might want? We (and more importantly, *she*) will never know, because the therapist didn't think it was his business to set goals mutually.

Some therapists avoid setting life goals, such as finding a mate or getting a rewarding job. They focus on in-therapy goals like self-understanding or psychological flexibility. Some say they don't want to make promises they can't keep, but a goal is not a promise unless you guarantee the outcome. Some are so skittish about anything that looks like failure that they avoid goals because an unmet goal is a kind of failure. How such a therapist can help others face and own their imperfections is hard to imagine. If therapy doesn't improve the patient's life, then it's an academic exercise, like learning Latin or memorizing the state capitals. Therapists who claim exorbitant success rates may be setting overly modest goals.

So there are levels of goals—life changes, behavioral and emotional changes, understanding, working through, acceptance—but they must imply actual life outcomes to generate the working alliance. Therapy should not be its own reason. In open-ended therapies, it's not uncommon for the dyad never to mention the life goals again, concentrating instead on the in-therapy goals. This will work as long as the in-therapy goals—such as removing barriers to showing oneself to the therapist or experiencing what it means for someone to "get" the patient—have been rooted in life goals. Some patients see the connection so readily that the therapist need not specify it.

Reducing anxiety and depression, managing anger, and comporting one's conduct to the demands of social norms are not good goals. These life problems frequently bring people to therapy, but using them to define the reasons for therapy exacerbates the way these problems dominate the patient's narrative. What would it profit the patient to act less anxiously or angrily? Even if depression seems enormous and something like socializing more seems trivial to someone with so many bad feelings, a goal like socializing more gives the patient something to work toward, not just something to work against. It also allows the therapist to focus on attempts to socialize, and these are the moments when depressive behavior actually gets in the way. If reducing depression itself is the goal, it consumes the therapy as it does the patient's life, when both ought to be about dating, working, friendship, and so on. Therapists should engage patients in exploring what, for example, the depressive feelings, thoughts, and expectations keep them from doing that they want to do or make them do that they don't want to do. Therapists can also focus on specific moments when the patient would have expected to enjoy, say, a crossword puzzle but didn't. Exploration of the moments that block positive steps toward life goals is an important step in developing a case formulation, and it also upends a master narrative about the pervasiveness of depression, anger, or anxiety.

I consulted with the child welfare system on a contract that left me their only option on a variety of cases—they had no way to pay anyone else. I would plead incompetence to assess the parenting of a woman from a small tribe in Ethiopia or the legal status of a girl from a remote Indonesian island who didn't know her own age, but there was no one else. In that context, a caseworker asked me to assess the psychological functioning of a six-week-old girl. I called a friend who specialized in infant mental health to ask how to do this. He asked, "What are six-week-old girls supposed to do?" I replied, "Eat, sleep, and poop?" He said, "So assess for those."

Since then, I have asked myself of every patient, whether in assessment or therapy, what the person is supposed to do. The answer always varies with age, often with culture, and occasionally with sex. The answer also varies according to my own moods, my recent experiences, and my overarching value system. I have no interest in pretending that my value system doesn't inform the work I do. Instead, I intend to subject my values to self-scrutiny (especially by reading), to the scrutiny of colleagues and friends (by articulating them), and to the scrutiny of patients and students (by letting them inform our agreements of what we are working on). Freud famously said that the goals of therapy are love and work. Winnicott added play, and Adler added doing something useful for others. I find that these are good places for me to look when I am considering my input into therapy's mutual goals.

The lesson is that you can't decide on treatment goals, whether explicit or implicit, without consulting your ideas about what people are supposed to be doing. Just as a physician is entitled to address smoking when the presenting problem is a broken bone, a therapist is entitled to address a lack of friendships, unrewarding work, or neglect of sexual needs regardless of the presenting problem. (How to do so is a matter of technique.) What are 25-year-old men supposed to do? Eighty-one-year-old women? Sixteen-year-old boys? My answers are embedded in my culture and class, but they are conversation starters, not final words.

Well, some of my ideas are the final word—not on what the patient should be working on but on what *I* am willing to work on. That question has a personal/cultural side and also a professional side. The former includes not only my assessment of what is missing from the patient's life, but also what kinds of things I am willing to help the patient achieve. The obvious cases are the previously mentioned anorexic who wants to lose more weight or the arrogant man who wants to stop feeling haunted by the damage he inflicts on others. The less obvious cases typically involve patients who want to mute, subdue, marginalize, or destroy the parts of themselves that are causing upheaval. Before I agree, for example, to work with a patient to stop her panic attacks, I want to be sure that the panic attacks are not the wise part of the system insisting that there is something wrong with the way things are going. What is personal and cultural about this is my acknowledgment that I tend to root for the rebels and not for the authorities that want to quell rebellion.

The professional problem with goal setting centers on the tendency to come for therapy with goals that are not psychological. Few and far between are the patients who start therapy by saying they are tripping over their own feet and want help changing their own behavior. (Few and far between are *therapists* who think their setbacks stem from their own behavior!) Instead, patients want a therapist to tell their spouses to be more reasonable or compliant, to sympathize with them about how unfair reality is, or to compliment them for being such stalwart tragic heroes in the face of adversity. More than anything, they want therapists to alleviate their symptoms without their having to do anything differently themselves. The therapist's job is to maintain clarity about what is and is not therapy. It doesn't have to involve challenging the patient, although some patients will laugh with self-recognition if the therapist says, "You know I'm a psychotherapist, right? You know I'm not a debate coach, political reformer, or pharmacist, right?" Generally, it's better to say, "You seem to want to describe the problem as political [or chemical, or whatever], and yet you've called a psychotherapist, so there must be some recognition that your own actions or way of seeing things has to change."

In other words, therapists must insist that the goals of therapy involve life problems whose presence stems from the patient's psychology, either directly (as in depression based on self-hate) or indirectly (as in loneliness resulting from the patient's refusal to take proactive steps to meet people). If the patient is lonely because of bad luck (outliving all her friends, for example) and is already doing everything possible to meet people, then she needs a friend, not a therapist.

Another problem that arises around goal setting is that patients frequently won't tell therapists their real goals. A star athlete feels compelled to say the goal is winning, when in fact it may be to develop other life spheres. What looks like a problem—not practicing enough—is actually the desired behavior. I already mentioned the woman who said her goal was to ride the bus when in fact the goal may have been to lose the job the bus would take her to. Many patients claim that their goal is to improve their social lives, but they actually want fans to admire them. In these cases, the therapist can agree on the goal only until the dyad clarifies it: "I wonder what an improved social life would look like." Or better: "Take us to a moment that for you represents the way a social encounter ought to be." If therapists leave goal setting to patients, the perfectionistic part of the patient is most likely to speak.

Patients also have a tendency to start with a minor, more socially acceptable problem before getting to the bigger issue, as a way of testing the waters. I call this the *Snowden effect* after the *Catch-22* (Heller, 1961) character: Yossarian successfully patches up Snowden's minor leg injury only then to open Snowden's flak jacket and find that he is mortally wounded. Patients will tell you they are depressed but not that they are cutting themselves, that they are sexually unsatisfied but not that they are seeing prostitutes, or that they are having trouble keeping up with their housework but not that they have adopted 45 stray dogs.

Goals are not set in stone. If the patient or therapist stops doing what either is expected to do, then they must consider whether the rationale for engaging in therapy *tasks* is strong enough. They also must consider whether they have set the right *goals*, which would also explain the lapses in task engagement. One reason therapists often don't like doing good therapy is that it is hard. The therapist might prefer more successes, a common feeling in sports as well, where the answer is to enjoy the small successes and focus less on the overall picture. A good season doesn't have to mean an undefeated season or even a championship. A consultation group can help therapists applaud their moments of restraint or their ending sessions on time or the delectable moments when patients relate differently to themselves. The therapist may have a secret goal of socializing with people who really appreciate her—an understandable need that she should meet outside of therapy—and again, consultation can help. Patients often turn to therapy for nontherapeutic goals, such as socializing with the therapist or feeling sexy with someone who, even if he never says yes, also never says no. In that context, it is interesting to recall that *placebo* first appeared in a medical context as a pseudonym for an ineffective doctor who enlarged his practice by pleasing rather than curing patients (placebo being Latin for *I will please*). Therapists can maintain a financially—but not psychologically—successful practice by ignoring goals and pleasing patients. That may satisfy both parties; just don't call it *psychotherapy*.

In law and psychoanalysis, the principle of unconscious intentionality holds true. (*Unconscious*, as Skinner said, is not an attribute of the intention but of the person with respect to the intention.) If a consequence is substantially certain to follow from an act, then it is correct to say that the person intended it to happened (*Garratt v. Dailey*, 1956). Acceptance and commitment therapy (ACT) clinicians encourage patients to behave in accordance with their values. Often, though, the problem is not the failure to behave congruently with values but the fact that the stated values are not the actual values. Working on incongruity with a value is a misplaced effort when the dyad has neglected the first order of business—namely, to clarify or, especially, to contextualize the actual values, to determine which ones really hold sway and under which circumstances. Similarly, the behavior of therapists and patients often reveal their actual goals rather than representing departures from achieving them. At these moments, the dyad must get on the same page as to the purpose of the therapy.

Many patients cannot set goals. With them, the first part of therapy must have a goal of setting goals. This leads to developing a case formulation to explain why goals are so hard to set, a formulation that implies the way therapy can help with that. For example, the patient may construe goal setting as humiliating because, in his experience, the world laughs at those who want something they don't have. A childhood memory might depict this as a vocational plan—to be a cowboy, say—that led to ridicule. The dyad has to work on the acceptance of wanting before it can clarify what exactly the patient wants.

Similarly, some patients can set goals but can't accept a case formulation, and with them, acceptance of a psychological explanation of the problem, in pencil not in stone, must become the next order of business. Some patients cannot see the connection between therapy and the goals, and this must become the focus. Finally, some patients can go through the motions of therapy but cannot develop relational bonds with the therapist. Whatever is getting in the way of allowing these bonds to develop must become the focus. Of course, with patients who can set goals, play with a case formulation, intuit the relationship between therapy and goals, and develop and even relish relational bonds with the therapist, there's not a lot more to do except to oversee the process to its natural end of integration, self-acceptance, and initiative. This observation parallels the old psychoanalytic adage that all the patient has to do to succeed is to say whatever comes to mind, holding nothing back, but of course no patient can do that. The idea is that resolution of the barriers to free association often resolves the life problem as well.

CASE FORMULATION

A case formulation explains the life problem that brought the patient to therapy as a psychological problem and implies how therapy can help. For example, a man (I'll call him Mr. Clean) with shallow relationships and no romance worked in a hospital sterilizing instruments. He mentioned that sterilization itself is easy; the hard part is getting the sterilizing poisons *off* so the staff can use the instruments again. Our case formulation was that he had sterilized his impulses and emotions, but his methods, analogizing intellectualization to antibacterial poisons, kept him from bringing his impulses and emotions into use again. I could promise not to overreact to his "dirty" inner life, so he could take chances with infecting me that he would be reluctant to take with others. This could lead to a different way of managing his impulses and emotions, a way that would not insulate him from people.

Depictions of troublesome patterns can derive from many sources, including childhood memories, dreams, fantasies, incidents, or events from the session. It's important to work with a depiction that the patient and therapist both accept as meaningful. Good therapists accept *any* narrative as a potentially meaningful depiction of important relational patterns; patients vary. I wrote a book on early memories (Karson, 2006b) rather than on dreams partly because I find that people are suspicious these days about whether their dreams meaningfully reflect their psychological patterns, but because they often believe that memory is accurate and that childhood affects adulthood, they believe early memories are relevant. In this case, Mr. Clean's description of his work did the trick, partly because he was an expert at sterilization and a novice at interpreting dreams, and stating the case formulation in his own purview engaged him.

A case formulation ties the life goals to the therapy plan, to the things the therapist will ask the patient to do. It is what makes relevant tasks relevant. I'll provide some more examples, but first I want to discuss some aspects of good case formulations, features that make them more useful to the therapy by inducing a sense of collaboration between the therapist and patient.

A good case formulation is explicit. Because of the power dynamics in therapy, many patients will agree to participate without any explanation of the psychology behind the problem and without any explanation of how therapy can help. These therapies typically get under way because these patients focus on whether the therapy makes them feel good during and after the session, and so does the therapist. This is not psychotherapy; it's a verbal version of massage, consolation, or even prostitution. The therapy becomes a service that avoids unpleasantness. You can't remodel your house, get into shape, learn clinical work, or resolve conflicts without some measure of unpleasantness, and the same goes for changing response tendencies.

The power imbalance in therapy makes it difficult for patients to demand an explanation. Similarly, students don't want faculty to see them as challenging or difficult, so they refrain from asking a teacher how an assignment relates to the course goals; surgery patients refrain from asking their anesthesiologists to explain how they induce unconsciousness only temporarily. An explicit case formulation helps set the cultural rhetoric of therapy as *invitational* (see chapter 5) rather than as *persuasive by appeal to authority*. Indeed, ACT teaches us that many of the patient's problems stem from deference to authoritative verbal rules. Replacing those rules with better authoritative rules may be good, but setting a tone of questioning such rules and deriving flexible, situational options is even better. Requiring deference to unstated, implicit rules is not good, and that is what typically happens when the reason for the therapy is not explicit. ACT therapists are good at making the case formulation explicit; their problem is usually one of making it unique and mutual, drawing on standard metaphors instead of using the patient's.

An explicit case formulation also sets a tone of making other things explicit. This intratherapy cultural value suits most of the ways of thinking about therapy described in chapter 1, from reworking a narrative, including what the patient has hitherto omitted, to accepting rather than marginalizing what has been unspeakable. My ongoing fantasy was that my patients' best friends would find out they were in therapy and ask them why, and then my patients would tell their best friends our case formulation.

A good case formulation is mutual. Indeed, when a patient reacts to an offered formulation with suspicions of the therapist's motives or assessments of its accuracy, as examples, the therapist can turn the reaction into grist for the mill: "I thought we were bouncing around ideas like people hitting a balloon back and forth; you act as if I'm in the Olympics and you're a judge. I wonder if you often evaluate overtures and find yourself out of synch with others." I don't recall how Mr. Clean and I arrived at our case formulation, but almost certainly he provided the metaphor and I suggested it as an analogy to his reluctance to get close to people and as a guide to what we would be doing together. It was an offer on my part, not a diagnosis; a working hypothesis, not a conclusion. It can be quite insightful and all tied up with a ribbon as long as it's offered with the wonder or delight of discovery and not even a hint of triumph. Expert chefs, claiming to have served a meal that they have prepared exactly right, don't put salt and pepper on the table. Therapy should be more like a diner, with various condiments and seasonings available. The expert chef knows exactly how to prepare everything, giving you a choice only about whether a steak is rare or medium rare. At the diner, you can say exactly how crispy you want the bacon, and the cook, not being a chef, doesn't take it as an insult to the cuisine. Collaboration requires expertise in collaborating, not expertise in the content. I'd bet that even a great chef making breakfast for her daughter cooks the eggs the way the daughter likes them.

Because they're mutual, good case formulations are revisable. After the initial stage of therapy, Mr. Clean reported various thoughts and memories that led us to consider that his entire organization around germs at work and around rationality elsewhere was a diversion from feeling weak and girlish (in a bad way) when he was sensitive or emotional. This was depicted especially aptly in a memory of his father telling him he sounded like a girl (in a bad way) because he cried when kids left him out of a kickball game. This image generated our new case formulation. He avoided intimacy to appease that paternal image, making sure he was never vulnerable enough to get his feelings hurt; by letting his sensitivities out in therapy, he might find me—rather than hard to repulse, as in the prior formulation—unlikely to repudiate or denigrate him as unmanly. Of course, I ended up compelled to do roughly that, frustrated with his excessive caution, and we had to work out together what happened between us. For now, suffice it to say that a case formulation is also a guide to potholes and abysses on the road to resolution, so at least in this instance I was prepared for my feelings of bullying and recognized more quickly than usual that we were enacting the pattern interpersonally. It also helped that I don't often feel like bullying people, so those feelings stood out as meaningful.

Good case formulations are unique. Many patients in many therapies have worked on their sense of being unmanly when having feelings, but only Mr. Clean and I worked on the specific version of that complex depicted in the memory of his dad castigating him—down to the look on his dad's face and especially the pathetic, wheedling image of himself—rather than teaching him how to kick a ball and catch one. A unique case formulation engages the patient because no one wants to be an example of something. Indeed, many of the problems that bring patients to therapy stem from the expectation that they be exemplary—in terms of culture, gender, religion, or family—instead of finding an individualized path. While it may be true that "happy families are all alike" (Tolstoy, 1965 [1873], p. 1), implying that the endpoints of the therapeutic odyssey have much in common, it is also true that "every unhappy family is unhappy in its own way" (ibid.). Specifying that "own way" suggests an interest in journeying together.

One of the great ironies of contemporary practice is that therapies are becoming less unique just as cancer treatment is becoming more individualized. The entire medical model in psychology is based on the idea that the patient's problematic behavior is a disease rather than an implementation of a different agenda, and that all instances of the disease are similar enough to warrant a generic treatment. (We visited this in chapter 3, under "Evidence-Based Practice," along with idea that all scurvy is the same and each depression is unique.) Finances and politics spur manualized therapy treatments just as oncologists are treating each cancer as one-of-a-kind (Mukherjee, 2016). Physicians grow hundreds of samples of an individual's cancer to experiment with different drug combinations on them, while therapists are committing themselves to a single, predetermined method for treating depression.

It's striking how often a supervisor or consultant can elucidate a question by asking, "What are the goals?" and "What is the case formulation?" For example, let's spiral back to the question that started this book: What do you do when a patient has something embarrassing to tell you? With Mr. Clean, a goal of romance implied that he had better learn to divulge emotionally laden information. What he didn't know was that vulnerability is what gets you invited to join the ultimate kickball game, while the performance of masculine efficacy, which he thought necessary, is an obstacle to connection. So therapist silence might still be the answer (depending on whether Mr. Clean experiences the silence as invitational), but if the therapist does reflect on Mr. Clean's dilemma, the reflection ought to be on vulnerability and masculinity rather than on whether to speak or remain silent. In other words, that angry dad inside Mr. Clean is trying to decide if it's a good idea to let the embarrassed son speak to the therapist, and the therapist should address the dad's dilemma, not the boy's. In this sense of identifying the conflict not just between the young Mr. Clean and a father figure but also in the way he treats himself when incompetent, good case formulations are both relational and intrapsychic. This paves the way for the therapist to comment, using the formulation as a lens, on how the dyad is relating to each other and on how the patient is relating to him- or herself.

Case Formulation Example: Slim

A gay man, whom I'll call Slim, came for therapy because he would get anxious about his place in a family and a society that was heteronormative and saw homosexuality as a deviation. He had lots of examples; the best one involved his father providing good arguments to his mother about why it wasn't the end of the world that their son was gay. Slim felt he would never possess his father's ability to pull off a conversation like that one, which meant that his place in the family depended on his father and not on himself. Even though he knew it was irrational, Slim attributed his father's ability in this area to his father's being straight. While he was talking about this, Slim noticed his glasses had come loose, took them off, and asked me if I had one of those little screwdrivers. I remained still and silent, so the question hung in the air. I rarely act this way in a first session, but I was pretty sure he would play along without me having to suggest exploring the moment. He laughed at himself and reflected on his dad always being the guy with the tools, a do-it-yourself handyman at home. Whether Slim had tools of his own or could only hope to borrow his father's tools became our case formulation, with the addition that his father delighted in lending Slim his tools—and that therapy could be a place to develop his own. I would have to refrain from jumping in with ideas.

I can't resist reporting how our therapy ended. After about a year and a half, he had made some notable life changes. I repeatedly erred by offering superficially helpful but functionally subordinating ideas, and then we would repair the rupture by reviewing the moments together. One day, Slim was telling me about some event with his boyfriend. As he talked, he took off his glasses and tightened the screw with his fingernail. He suddenly stopped talking, looked up at me, and said, "Fuck. I think we're done."

Case Formulation Example: Eve

As an example of an evolving case formulation, there's Eve, a woman who came for therapy after years of torturing herself whenever she sensed that someone was cool toward her. Intellectually, she pinned this need to be liked on her father's narcissism and her mother's artificiality, but experientially, all such insights evaporated in the moment, and the only thing she knew was that she had to win the person over. She would compliment women until they thought they were her close friends, and then they would shun her when she could not live up to the implied promise of connection. She would flirt with men but ultimately not sleep with them, also leading to anger or disappointment. With both sexes, when she sensed that things were sour she doubled down on compliments or flirting.

Eve may initially have been genuinely interested in therapy, but once we met she was interested only in getting my approval. By the end of the first session, she had discovered that flirting was not the right path with me, so she switched to being an excellent patient. Our preliminary case formulation involved the difficulty of distinguishing genuine and superficial closeness, depicted in a memory of a dance recital at age four when her parents attended, congratulating her as the other girls' parents did their daughters, but then left with her before the celebration, signaling that they were only discharging a duty. "Enough is enough," said her father in the memory. She would produce herself in therapy and together we would explore whether I was tolerating her or getting her. I anticipated that ending sessions on time would be difficult if she got the idea that the only way to prove I wasn't glad to see her leave was to extend the time.

Therapy looked as if it were going well, but I didn't feel anything for Eve other than a vague appreciation of her being so easy to work with. I would reflect on whether there was something missing in our relationship and, more importantly, whether there was a way to talk about it that didn't feel like an accusation. The first case formulation would work only if she authentically appeared on stage for the recital. When I brought up the issue, Eve was reminded of cheating on certain assignments in college by handing in other people's work. So we developed a pre-formulation, relevant to whether we could do psychotherapy, depicted by plagiarism and spelled out as the confusion between participation to get the grade or to get the feedback for an education. Eventually, we equated anything she said to me while focused on my reaction as grade oriented and anything she said while lost in thought as educationally oriented. After working for months on making her participation genuine, we could then revert back to the original question of whether I was merely tolerating her.

As noted, case formulations also frequently specify what might go wrong. With many patients it helps to spell this out as a way of inoculating the patient against the inevitable mistake. I might have told Eve that it seems inevitable that I would one day want a session to end (like the parents' impatience for the recital to end), and we need to prepare ourselves to explore the moment together rather than to conclude that she has discovered a terrible secret about me. I might have told Slim that it would not be surprising if I myself took him too easily in stride (like the father's reaction to his coming out) to the point of making him wonder if I really had heard what he was saying. As noted under "Rupture and Repair" in chapter 5, this is not a failing of therapy but a consequence of therapists' immersing themselves in patients' patterns. Replication of problematic patterns—with awareness that it has happened—is often not the end of therapy but its beginning.

RELEVANT TASKS

People will do things that connect to desired outcomes. This whole book is an effort to link certain therapist behaviors to patient improvement, rather than patient satisfaction, so that readers will do what's recommended. Tying tasks to goals is a good habit to get into. I don't "take a history" or otherwise conduct an intake interview at the outset because the only goal I can tie it to is the unwanted goals of evoking a professional frame and nailing down an unproductive narrative before trying to modify it.

Another reason not to take a history is that the procedure can make the patient feel as if the therapist sees her as a victim of her history. For example, when a therapist asks a patient about any abuse history, the therapist may then use a revelation of abuse as an explanation for, say, problems with sexual intimacy. This feels to many patients as if the therapist is imposing a supposition on them. Instead, in discussing problems with sexual intimacy, the therapist can express curiosity about what actually occurs to the patient on the brink of sex. If at that moment the patient reports a memory of abuse, then it is clear that expectations based on or depicted in the memory are getting in the way. This leads to an alliance about the interference of the abuse rather than the patient's feeling trapped by the history.

For assessments, I still get an autobiography, and I tell the person why I am asking each question: "The way our parents raised us affects the way we raise our kids, so I'm going to ask you now about your parents and the kind of job they did." In therapy, I disclose the things the state requires me to disclose, but I tell the patient why. After we agree to work together, I say something like, "The state of Colorado regulates psychotherapy, and one of the rules is that I have to tell you what some of the other regulations are."

The classic psychoanalytic task is to say whatever comes to mind, holding nothing back. Therapists can supplement this by suggesting that especially valuable are stories from the week, dreams, and childhood memories that come to mind while in session, or fleeting fantasies that occur spontaneously. The idea is to get to the bottom of things, to get to the specific personal meanings that occur in the space between situations and reactions. When ego psychologists say to patients, regarding why something happened, "I don't know either, but I know how to find out," they're saying that the meaning of events is different for each patient, and that the associative method reveals that meaning.

Like the working alliance, which originally referred to the partnership between the psychoanalyst and the observing self of the patient, free association has escaped its psychoanalytic roots. Now it is also the task most relevant to revealing automatic thoughts, depicting schemas, exposing oneself to the therapist, exposing oneself to oneself, and so on for every way of thinking about therapy discussed in chapter 1. When the patient speaks to reveal what's going on in her mind, the working alliance is in good repair. When she speaks to hide what's going on in her mind, or to implement some other way of relating (such as befriending, dominating, or pleasing the therapist), there is a rupture in the alliance. Again, the places to look to resolve a rupture are whether the goals are shared and psychological, whether the tasks of therapy are linked to those goals, and whether collaborative relational bonds have developed.

The inverse of goals implying tasks—that tasks imply goals—is also true. All the things that the patient actually does in therapy are relevant to some goal, especially the identity and relational goals mentioned in chapter 5. Whenever the patient does something that doesn't seem like the sort of thing that promotes the mutual therapy goals, the patient is promoting some relational or identity goal. Instead of thinking of the labile patient as borderline, the therapist can think of him as not a bad patient (or husband or employee) but as a very good disrupter of convention and mocker of intimacy. The coy patient is promoting a goal of being mined rather than invited. The boring patient is promoting a goal of disconnection. If the dyad has at least a superficial understanding of the therapy goals and their psychological nature, the therapist can refer back to the agreed-upon goals when the patient's idiosyncratic engagement in other tasks promotes incompatible personal goals.

This is also why it's so important for therapists to stay in character. Therapy is a daunting business, requiring the patient to question her life narrative, to present herself warts and all, and to take ownership of her disreputable identity elements. She will make many offers to do almost anything else than undertake this terrible odyssey, and the therapist must remain alert to what else she is up to.

RELATIONAL BONDS

The tyranny of niceness in the therapy world has distorted this aspect of the working alliance. Good therapists do not "build rapport" before getting on with it. Therapists who take that approach find themselves in pleasant relationships whose culture is antithetical to therapeutic work. Asking a patient with whom one has "built rapport" to tell you what is really on her mind when she gets overly emotional is like asking the wedding guest seated next to you to tell you the worst thing she's ever done. Instead, the dyad must build rapport by *doing* the work of therapy, not in preparing for it. Therapists typically hesitate to get on with it because they don't know what to say when a therapeutic statement falls flat. "We seem to have really different expectations about what we're doing together" can open a window into that issue, instead of cultivating the patient's prior approval with rapport building.

Different therapies will require different relational bonds, but virtually all therapies require enough trust in the therapist's agenda and competence to speak honestly about one's situation. Few therapies develop strong enough bonds for the patient to complain about annoying things the therapist does. A recent movement asks patients to fill out a feedback form at the end of or after every session. Not surprisingly, this strengthens the relational bonds in the therapy, as the patient is often surprised to learn that the therapist is interested in how it went. The form avoids the power imbalance; it's like the suggestion box I bring to every class I teach, allowing students to complain about me, make suggestions, or note microinsensitivities anonymously. In therapy these forms are an improvement over not seeking or receiving feedback, but they inadvertently communicate that the dyad must avoid its power imbalance and that intimacy cannot survive complaints. A very strong therapeutic bond would incorporate complaints, much as real-time feedback improves sex. The difference is that in sex, the complainer is the final authority on what works, whereas therapy complaints are entries to dialogue.

Patients often appreciate but rarely enjoy good therapy, analogous to a dental patient not enjoying a procedure. The patient must trust the dentist enough to describe the problem and then open his mouth. Relational bonds between patient and dentist may not deepen if the patient tells the dentist that her tardiness or dumb jokes make him uneasy. If a dental patient reports a sharp pain, he expects the dentist to explain whether that is par for the course, an indication of a problem, or a sign of an error. If a patient complains about the kind of things good therapists do—the tasks of the therapist relevant to their mutual goals—such as ending on time or not responding to flirting, the therapist has to strengthen the link between those tasks and the goals. Focusing on the sense the patient is making of those behaviors accomplishes this, resolving the complaint within the therapeutic frame. If the patient complains about something stupid the therapist said—or any nontherapeutic behavior—the therapist must take the feedback and adjust to it. Mutual adjustment within the relational frame produces relational bonds of the sort the frame requires.

When something doesn't seem right in therapy, the therapist can explore relational bonding. Typically, this is done by applying the therapist's theory of psychology to the moments of rupture. The behaviorist wonders what the function might be of the patient's refusals to comply or of expressions of dependency. The cognitive behaviorist wonders what schemas are operating in the session. The systems therapist wonders about the functioning of the therapy system, its ambiguities and patterns. The psychodynamic therapist wonders about transference and countertransference paradigms, about how the patient is experiencing the therapist at those moments and vice versa.

It's hard for beginning therapists to know what therapeutic bonds are supposed to feel like. If they're lucky, they've felt this in their lives, but rarely have they done so from a position of authority. They may have had strong working relationships with parents, teachers, friends, bosses, or co-workers. In supervision, I sometimes sound like a broken record, asking if therapist and patient are on the same page, asking if the therapist is working *on* the patient or *with* the patient, asking if the supervisees experience me as working *on* them or *with* them. When I see a working bond developing or the therapist capitalizing on one, I point it out and invite the supervisee to reflect on or savor that moment.

It's also helpful to label the type of bond that's developing, to help the trainee distinguish it from a therapeutic bond. It might be social, advisory, spiritual, sibling, romantic, educational, or intellectual, as examples. Therapy success depends primarily on the strength of the working alliance, but it must be an alliance around therapeutic work and not around some easier or less psychological enterprise.

Chapter Seven

Knowing Something about the Therapeutic Frame

There is a smile of love, and there is a smile of deceit, and there is a smile of smiles in which these two smiles meet.—William Blake

RELATIONSHIPS HAVE FRAMES

Every relationship has implicit ground rules that serve the participants' goals, furthering their agendas about what kind of relationship they want or expect. Relational-goal conflicts, as discussed in chapter 5, are conflicts about what kind of relationship the parties are in; the dyad can usefully consider these as disagreements about the ground rules of the relationship, since these define the type of relationship. For example, marriages vary in the implicit rules that dictate the extent to which the partners keep each other up to date about the daily vagaries of work. You could say that there are newsfeed marriages, headline marriages, and emergency alert marriages, but sometimes it's hard to tell what kind of marriage the spouses really want, because they may come from cultures that make emergency-only communication about work seem estranged or newsfeed communication seem enmeshed. A therapist who wants to know what kind of marriage a couple has on this score can get a lot more information by probing the implicit rule about sharing work details than by asking the couple what kind of marriage they want to have or think they have. If the therapist tries asking about the general description, two very different couples might both report that they construe their marriage to be a true life partnership. Instead, therapists will learn more about their couples if they can determine whether they tell each other only about major conflicts at work, whether they also discuss puzzling relational problems they are having with colleagues, or whether they go so far as to mention that the coffee room ran out of skim milk. This is an example of the more general directive to get examples. What goes for therapists and couples goes for supervisors and therapy dyads, and they cannot discern the kind of therapy they are doing by stating the theoretical orientation; one must know the actual ground rules.

Implicit and explicit rules define all sorts of relationships, including those between friends, colleagues, and even restaurant servers and diners. Implicit rules are contingencies of reinforcement, an articulation of what happens when someone does this or that. We call a list of rules that govern or describe behavior in a geographic location a culture; we call a list of rules that govern or describe behavior in a situation a frame. Psychotherapy is designed to elicit the patients' framing errors (Goffman, 1974), their characteristic attempts to define situations in ways that conflict with other people's definitions and lead to disadvantageous conduct. The histrionic patient may frame the closeness of therapy as sexual; the narcissist may frame the conversation as either admiring or derogatory rather than exploratory. Whether these are framing errors or preferences is a conflict that therapists are likely to find themselves going back and forth on as they climb the spiral staircase. Eventually, therapists are likely to drop this distinction in favor of the one between "something we are working on," "something we are not working on but should," and "something we need not work on." In that context, the term *errors* excites work on changing them, since errors are those things that need correction.

An important rule in any interaction concerns the amount of information you are supposed to consider about other people. The classic example is not noticing a stutter. Another widespread social rule is that you don't tell people what you are really thinking: not about the seasoning on the meals they prepare, not about the wild sexual and aggressive thoughts that go through your head, and not about the ugly secrets from your past. This rule facilitates most social interactions (that is, it fosters the goals in almost all relationships), but it leaves people hungry for intimacy if they don't have any friends, lovers, or family members who really get them. One reason widowers have so much a harder time of it than widows in our culture is that when the wife in a straight marriage dies, the widower has often lost his only intimate relationship (Christakis & Fowler, 2009). The corollary of the rules against intimate disclosure and noticing things is that society generally forbids people from commenting on the behavior of other adults if the comment identifies aspects of the self behind the social mask.

The set of rules that govern a relationship are like the frame of a painting or the stage in a theater; the frame of a painting tells you the kind of thing it is, the sort of attitude—aesthetic in the case of a painting—that you should adopt in relating to it, and what's in the painting and what's not. An artistic frame also facilitates what Dewey (1934) called *engrossment* and Hegel called *absorption*, since the audience takes elements inside the artistic frame on their own terms; a weak frame is like seeing backstage during a theater production. The artist selects a picture frame after the painting is complete, so a relational frame is really more like the frame that the artist stretches the canvas on before painting; its size and structure depend on what sort of painting the artist is undertaking in response to different artistic agendas and the needs of the patron or the audience. The frame needn't be the same for every therapy. Instead, therapists should manage any changes in the frame thoughtfully, knowing that tight frames enhance engrossment and that the frame of every therapy will need to distinguish it from social and professional relationships that inhibit authenticity and intimacy.

Many forms of individual therapy depend on access to thoughts, wishes, and memories normally kept behind the social mask. Good therapy also authorizes the therapist to comment on the patient's behavior. A therapeutic frame facilitates the two relational goals of authentic disclosure and illuminating comment. Much is known about which rules lead to authentic disclosure and illuminating comment and which inhibit them (discussed below). The social rules against authentic disclosure and illuminating comment are so pervasive that the frame of therapy must set it apart from all other types of social relating. As noted, therapy itself is such a demanding journey that patients will jump at the chance to be social rather than therapeutic. Refreshments, chitchat, and "supportive" comments are social. Therapy must also be distinct from professional relationships—learned in relation to doctors—where only directly relevant disclosure and advice are authorized, a form of relating that is desirable at the beginning of therapy and necessary until the therapist offers a therapy contract and case formulation that the patient accepts. The therapist wants to be neither social nor professional, and yet the therapist and the patient can easily see themselves as two people trying to have a conversation (social) and the therapy is indeed ultimately a professional service. These are the Scylla and Charybdis of therapeutic relating, and maintaining a therapeutic frame requires an extraordinary effort because it is so easy to drift into social or professional relating. Teaching many therapists what a therapeutic relationship feels like is like teaching an only child how to act like a sibling, and therapists who have never experienced a therapeutic frame find it hard to believe that such a thing exists.

THERAPEUTIC FRAMES ARE FIRM

Some therapists and some patients balk at the word *firm* because it is the opposite of flexible, and they think flexibility is somehow inherently good or, at least, nice. *Firm* is also the opposite of weak, unreliable, and arbitrary. Therapists should apply the ground rules firmly, but warmly and with curiosity about their impact, to reduce the amount of caprice and superstition in the situation. For example, the only way to keep the patient from speculating as to why the therapist ended a session at that particular moment is to end them on time. Sometimes the ground rules are unhelpful (but much less often than needy patients and delicate therapists would have us think); if so, therapists should change rather than bend them. If a patient can't reflect on a rule, or seems likely to overreact to it, the therapist can discuss it before applying it (usually by acknowledging that the therapist is in a lose-lose situation). When patients want to talk about the therapist's personal history with depression, anxiety, or drug abuse, it sounds authoritarian to say, "We're here to talk about you, not about me." It sounds teacherly to say, "Therapy works best if . . . " It's not just setting the stage for therapy but actually doing therapy to say, "I'm concerned that if I answer that question, we're going to veer off into a social way of relating we won't be able to get out of, but I'm concerned that if I don't answer the question, you'll decide you can't work with me." The therapist might follow this with a suggestion that the patient inform the therapist when the patient feels misunderstood instead of deciding beforehand that the therapist can or cannot understand the patient.

Firm application of rules also frees the therapist to be entirely curious about the patient's experience. Many therapists can't effectively explore a request to modify the frame because they are spending a lot of mental energy on whether they are going to agree to do it. Any possibility of breaking the rule will distract the therapist with thoughts about whether to do so. A therapist who already knows that there will be no hugging, for example, can explore the topic with his or her full attention.

Besides facilitating authenticity and the integration of what is marginalized, the frame of therapy is, as noted above, designed to enhance the patient's engrossment in the experience, inviting into the therapy the patient's real self or "inner child." After all, if the relationship with the therapist—lasting for only an hour or maybe two a week—is to counterbalance all the problematic relationships in the patient's history, it had better be an important relationship. Engagement in the process enhances this needed importance. Tight frames can engross people in even trivial experiences, such as board games, quiz shows, and sporting events; when the matter at hand is the patient's most personal self, a tight frame can empower the therapy enormously.

Goffman (1974) construes almost all psychologically based pathology as a framing problem on the part of the patient. An obvious example of a framing problem would be to mistake an overheard play rehearsal for real life; you think a couple are having a fight because you are using the wrong frame to contextualize what you are hearing. A man who can't commit to his romantic partner may be framing the relationship as a trap, or as an end to sexual validation, or as a contest implying that he is not amazing enough to get someone better. Histrionic people (and many additional men, for a different reason) tend to impose a sexual frame on nonsexual encounters, and some narcissists frame interactions as if they are occurring between royalty and their subjects when most people would say they are occurring between, say, restaurant patrons and waitstaff. Many therapists frame the therapy not as if it is an encounter between a person seeking change and a change agent but as if it is an encounter between a rescuer and a stray puppy. (It's easier to rescue animals than to do therapy, but it's harder for the patient to be a lost puppy than to be a noble individual seeking self-improvement.)

We all develop framing devices from our exposure to different relationships in childhood. A therapist speaks (or refrains from speaking) as a therapist speaks to a patient (and not as a health-care professional speaks to a patient and not as one friend speaks to another), but the patient misconstrues the speech by framing it according to some familiar expectation. This is called *transference* when the pattern is imposed by the patient and *countertransference* when imposed by the therapist, although the term *relational drift* emphasizes the phenomenon's cocreated nature. Only an ambiguous yet predictable therapeutic frame can both evoke and highlight these framing errors and address them in real time; otherwise, the dyad just talks about the problem.

We can analogize the frame of therapy to the ground rules in a movie theater. There may someday be a movie that is better with the house lights on, but the vast majority of movies benefit from turning them down so the audience can get engrossed. The theater should be set up so as to enable audience members to see the screen; the movie should start on time; the speaker volume should be within a certain decibel range; the audience should turn off their cell phones; the curtains should part; the audience should have some idea of how long the movie will last so they don't start worrying about parking tickets and dinner reservations. These ground rules enhance absorption in the movie, partly because they frame the movie tightly and partly because their implementation communicates that the management is competent and that the audience is in good hands.

No movie patron has ever left his or her seat at the beginning of a show and sought a manager to express gratitude for turning down the house lights or opening the curtain. Instead, patrons seek out management to complain about any deviation in the frame, because a deviation dominates the patron's experience of the moment and interferes with engrossment. Similarly, therapy patients don't sit there appreciating the fact that therapists designed their offices so as not to intrude themselves unnecessarily into the space; instead, patients wonder why the therapist is wearing an outfit that calls attention to itself.

Because of what I called *therapeutic privilege* in chapter 2, it is very difficult for therapists to find out what patients make of frame deviations.

Asking them is like asking students if the professor's not knowing how to run the PowerPoint projector annoys them. What are patients going to say, knowing the power therapists have to define them as disturbed? It's also like asking children if letting them stay up late is good for them. There are indeed ways to get this information, which amount to listening to metaphorical representations of the deviation (Langs, 1978) or establishing a textured and multifaceted dialogue around the patient's reactions to the therapist (Buirski, 2005). The point for now is that the ground rules of therapy developed not from a theoretical hypothesis but from an understanding over the years and decades of which ground rules facilitate therapeutic progress. These are just a starting point, and any particular therapist-patient dyad may develop different rules based on analysis of what works in their relationship. Still, all such analyses are suspect when the suggested rule change makes things easier or immediately more gratifying for either party. It is a truism of psychology that immediate reinforcers are more powerful than deferred ones, and therapists must constantly be on guard against pleasing themselves and their clients in the moment at the cost of deferred rewards (like changing response tendencies, life narratives, and relational paradigms).

Another reason good therapeutic frames are firm has to do with de-hypnotization. Erickson (Haley, 1973) noted that hypnotization is a useful treatment tool, but most patients are already hypnotized and have to be de-hypnotized. He meant that they are locked into a frame and can't switch perspectives. You hypnotize someone by evoking a hypnotic frame. The way you de-hypnotize someone is to revert to a social or professional frame: raising the lighting, speaking normally rather than soothingly, and expecting a collegial rather than submissive posture. You promote a useful frame by sustaining it and not evoking an alternative frame. If the de-hypnotizing professional keeps slipping into the rhythms of hypnosis, the patient might not completely wake up. A lax or weak therapeutic frame will not effectively distinguish itself from the social or idiosyncratic frame from which it needs to be different.

Much of the trouble patients face involves their tendency to define situations idiosyncratically, putting themselves in the familiar roles they already know how to perform. These roles, though, may not be available under actual conditions. An off-key musician will be easier to spot if the entire orchestra is tuned to a single key. The patient's idiosyncratic framing will stand out for exploration and understanding if the therapy is firmly framed.

THERAPY RULES ARE AN EMBRACE, NOT A CAGE

Fortunately, the very worst moment in my entire life lasted less than one second. I was observing the birth of my first child, his head having crowned.

Suddenly, there was his whole head, a deep dusky blue. I had gone to classes and read books, but I was utterly unprepared for his color. Later, I learned that it is quite common among healthy babies to come out blue and change with the first breath, but at the time, my world went inside out, while panic in an abyss of loss consumed me. In less than a second, I noticed something remarkable that I think provides a valuable lesson for therapists. I noticed that the doctor's hands weren't moving any faster than they had been. Quicker than words, I knew that this meant that all was okay, despite what I could see and all that I thought I knew. I instantly relaxed.

The frame of therapy, like a reliable bedtime, communicates to patients and children that therapists and parents can take in stride whatever they are going through. Whether a session ends in tears, laughter, reflection, or anger, it ends on time, communicating that all is equally welcome and all equally merits attention. When therapists are as ambiguous as possible to facilitate the patient's display of idiosyncratic expectations of relationships, they don't indulge the patient's thirst for personal information about them. Instead, they communicate that the patient's curiosity need not upset the pace and content of what they are doing together. When patients ask for their advice, they interpret the function of the request, often in the context of the patient's frustration with the lack of results. This should lead therapists to reconsider whether the working alliance needs repair; but they don't indulge the request with a tantalizing morsel of personal history to distract the dyad from the lack of progress or lack of agreement about what it is they are doing together.

Many problems that patients bring to therapy have to do with difficulties reconciling themselves with reality. A vast number of mating concerns have to do with the fact that you can generally mate only with someone who possesses about as much social capital as you have. This is a law of nature that many people find oppressive. Many weight-loss problems have to do with an implicit protest against the laws of thermodynamics (calories in and calories out). Many people live a life that challenges the proposition that they will get older and that there are only so many hours in a day, and their constant emotional bruising as they bump up against reality brings them to therapy. Flexibility in the frame of the therapy inadvertently communicates that they don't need to adjust to reality or to its existential quandaries after all; it communicates that reality will adjust to them.

In ballroom dancing, the frame is the shape maintained by the dancers' bodies as they interact with each other. Dancers, like lovers and therapy dyads, must not dominate each other or lean on each other, the occasional lift notwithstanding. Instead they must collaborate, each in his or her own role. It is the frame of the dance that allows them to maintain their autonomy and their interdependence simultaneously. This is what a therapeutic frame means: an embrace rather than a cage.

What follows is a host of rules, but these are all, as it were, written in pencil. The best policy is to have no policy, to make decisions based on the meaning of events. On the other hand, these rules will provide a starting place that generally facilitates the goals and processes of successful therapy.

PRIVACY

Assume that you are thinking of doing something bad. It's probably too hard to imagine that you are thinking seriously of shooting up an elementary school, but I will say that the public health problem is not just identifying and providing services to potential mass killers; it's how to provide services that would actually induce a shooter to share his thoughts. Imagine you are considering embezzlement, undermining a coworker, or cheating on your spouse. You would benefit from the chance to reflect if you shared this with someone, but with whom? Your reputation with that person, and with anyone they told, could be damaged forever.

The same consideration applies to more normal troubles, such as anxiety and depression. These problems are easy to divulge to a therapist, and the therapist prompts the patient for good examples. The patient reports truthfully that she often experiences intense anxiety when the phone rings. Now the therapist wants to know what goes through her mind when the phone starts ringing. The patient knows perfectly well that the therapist's question makes her think of her pregnant sister miscarrying, but she either thinks that this cannot be the problem—she loves her sister—or she thinks that she will disgust the therapist if she reports this image. Instead, she makes up something sensible (but false) about bad news she once got over the phone, wasting months of therapy on the wrong focus but saving face. What would the therapist and the therapy space have to be like to induce her to report what actually occurs to her?

We develop one set of explicit guidelines for producing honesty and authenticity in the abstract and quite another de facto set when immediate feelings are at stake. Out of love or fear, patients generally want to make their therapists feel good and their parents look innocent. (With demoralizing frequency, the way to make the therapist feel good is to make the parents look guilty.) An abstract set of guidelines, such as those I am about to provide, has much to recommend it, because prearranged rules escape the patient's desire to make the therapist feel good about the relationship provided (not to mention the *therapist's* desire to feel good about it). Many therapists, starting with Freud, agree that certain practices are desirable and then proceed to ignore them. So the question is, "What ought the frame to be?" and not, "How can I justify the frame I provide?" It is, "What's keeping me from living up to the highest standards of practice?" and not, "Oh, I don't think there's any harm in it."

An important component of the therapeutic frame, known since 1915 or so, is privacy: What happens in therapy stays in therapy. Patients would be more likely to divulge their sordid plans or their embarrassing thoughts to someone incapable of repeating the information—on a crashing airplane, say. They would not then benefit from the relational acceptance offered by therapy, but it's easy to see how guarantees of privacy can facilitate honesty. Therapists used to call this *confidentiality*, but that term now refers to legalisms so that nowadays therapists think they are providing privacy if the law requires or patients consent to all the intrusions on privacy.

As much as possible, the therapy relationship should be out of time, out of place—a special world of its own that intersects only through resonance with the rest of life, like a great novel or play. The patient should have an ironclad sense that nothing leaves the room. The therapist undermines that sense by writing progress notes and promising to report threats and child abuse, even though the law requires therapists to implement these intrusions. The therapist further undermines privacy by doing anything that ties the therapy province to the rest of life (after establishing the goals and case formulation), which reduces the patient's willingness to take off the social mask and examine the psychology of the situation. Offenses include gossip and newsy talk as well as casual status-enhancing or entertaining disclosures to the therapist's friends or spouse. These may not get back to the patient in particular, but they create a cultural awareness that therapists are not as discreet as they pretend to be. Gossipy therapists will have a harder time distinguishing themselves from this cultural expectation than therapists who never gossip. Offenses also include mentioning other patients in sessions, providing a public waiting room, and diagnosing the patient to obtain insurance. The latter two may be unavoidable, but they are still offenses against privacy.

Most patients are struggling with collisions between the way their families raised them and the way things are, between their loyalty to schemas and their schemas' poor utility. The solution is not to provide schemas that are correct but to provide schemas that are not arbitrary, self-serving, unquestioned, or unhealthy. Therapists further this solution by treating their own rules (the frame) as subject to examination, not because the therapist feels uncomfortable about upholding them but because the therapist is genuinely curious about the patient's reaction to them. Indeed, the patient's reactions are often a window into his or her peculiar patterns of responding in other situations.

All therapists should ask themselves if they told their own therapists everything—and if not, why not? All therapists, instead of imitating their own therapists, should try to rectify the frame elements that they know from personal experience put a damper on honesty and authenticity.

ANONYMITY

A woman I'd seen in therapy for a few months sat down and wished me a happy birthday. This was before Google, even before personal computers. "How on earth . . . ?" I blurted out. She said, "You're wearing new pants that you would never buy." So the point of anonymity is not to pretend that patients see therapists as blank screens. They would know us, after a few months of intimacy, as well as anyone, if only they hadn't been trained their whole lives to tactfully ignore their knowledge of others, if only the power differential in therapy didn't put them at risk for seeing our foibles.

Anonymity is the opposite of self-disclosure. It is a rule against purposely sharing personal information, and its purpose is mystification (Goffman, 1959) or idealization (Kohut, 1971). The work of therapy speeds up in proportion to the patient's experience of the therapist as fundamentally benign, fundamentally sound, and fundamentally willing to set aside any personal agendas in exchange for a fee. Virtually any fact from personal history discredits this performance. Therapists can't even specify what college they went to without fostering a narrative of what they are doing in the other chair that undermines the patient's needed experience: Harvard and a handful of other colleges communicate an overachiever who cannot relate to the typical patient's experience; anything short of Harvard is a disappointment.

In the new-age world, a would-be guru is discredited by having a personal history; this is one reason they often change their names. Therapists are sort of pretending to be gurus for an hour at a time—only "sort of" because the pretense is open; therapists are stage magicians, not false prophets who claim to really do magic. Their biggest errors on this score are either failing to let the mystification develop or believing their own hype once it does. Indeed, it's not uncommon to see a self-disclosing therapist—usually done in the name of egalitarianism—assume an air of superiority over nondisclosing therapists, who are abstemiously stifling themselves for the benefit of their patients. Reik (1948) told the story of a German actor who refused the part of Prospero in *The Tempest*, arguing that to play the role one needed not only to be a great actor but also a great man. "And what great man would become an actor?" asked the German. Reik thought that a therapist should also be a great man or woman, but what person of greatness would become a therapist? Surely the answer to this conundrum is to train therapists to be willing to let their patients think them great or wonderful or uncommonly perceptive without really believing it themselves.

Therapists need a developmental model like my spiral staircase to think about anonymity productively. They need to be open to the idea that anonymous therapists aren't all trying to become real-life gurus, that they are not acting superior to their patients. They need to be open to the idea that they may think differently about the topic as the years go by. The best argument for anonymity lies in close inspection of what the patient does after a self-disclosure. As with most frame violations, the patient typically expresses conscious relief and pleasure, followed by unconscious concerns. These produce a diversion into a social frame as well as metaphorical communication (discussed in chapter 9) about the self-disclosing therapist's motivation and reliability.

NEUTRALITY

Neutrality doesn't mean the therapist is emotionless, passive, or uninterested. It means the therapist has no agendas other than those stated or implied by the therapy contract. Many people, including a large percentage of therapists, don't really know what it means to be nonjudgmental because they don't really know what it means to be unjudged. Growing up human involves receiving an inordinate number of messages about whether our conduct is desirable or undesirable. For many of us, it is only during rare moments of utter engrossment—in dreams, say, or at the climax of a thriller—that we turn off our internal monitor of what is okay and not okay. The point of meditation is to observe oneself without that filter, but isn't that really a poor imitation of the real thing—the real thing being *another* person who sees you, who gets you, and still does not judge? Every other way we have of treating ourselves we learned from others, and so should acceptance be learned from others, to make it truly human and relational.

Neutrality spares therapists that awkward moment when they have been nodding and cooing in sympathy and suddenly the patient blurts out into that shower of approval a confession, maybe about the guilty thought of inheritance that actually consumed them on the news of a parent's death, the desperate fantasy of sexual conquest that actually underlies their agreeable performance of the role of patient, or any other statement that the therapist would like to greet with quiet curiosity. At these moments, the therapist's sudden silence connotes disapproval because it is the end of cooing and nodding. A therapy organized around approving therapists and appreciative patients invariably becomes one that excludes the ugly and sordid aspects of the self that need acceptance.

An existential theme underlying every therapy is the adjustment to a world that is, in fact, random. God did not make it rain on your birthday to punish you, and acceptance into graduate school had much to do with luck, not just industry. A consoling, approving therapist communicates that relationships should offer retreat from reality, as opposed to discovering a useful, even restorative way of living in a context of randomness. A play about Grand Canyon (Goodwin, 2016) put it thus: "To take in the glorious indifference of a universe that requires of me nothing. No apology. No flattery. No praise, pretense, or supplication. Yet which stirs in me reverence, gratitude, and a sense of belonging to everything."

Even with suicidal patients, neutrality is important. It's awkward and uncomfortable to put the therapeutic, accepting stance ahead of the social, facilitative stance in even the best of circumstances. I once talked an unusually fit young man into not answering his patient's initial "How are you?" He appeared after the session in my office holding the arm of his chair, which he had ripped off in the tension of remaining silent, telling me that it might take several more tries before he got used to it. With suicidal patients, it can feel quite callous to say, as sometimes recommended (Kernberg, Selzer, Koenigsberg, Carr, & Appelbaum, 1989), that one is responsible for protecting the therapy and that the reason for hospitalizing the patient is that the therapy cannot proceed if the patient has died. If you think of suicide as a multicharacter event (see "Suicide" in chapter 2), the need for neutrality becomes clear. Instead of imagining a unitary patient who hates herself and needs support, imagine a mother who has always hated her daughter for being the cherished object of the father's affection, for being playful, or for being thin. Feeling eclipsed, the mother indulges her rage and holds a gun to her daughter's head. This is not the moment to tell the girl how likable, appealing, and wonderful she is; you're likely to get her killed.

TIME

Start on time and end on time. Give yourself a window of thirty seconds, and repeatedly glance at the clock halfway through the window. Radio hosts learn to signal that the end is nigh, and so can therapists. As noted above, all frame elements are designed to distinguish therapy from a social or professional encounter, but nothing does the job as well as ending on time. Even lawyers just charge more for going over. The peculiarity of starting and ending on time merely because the dyad has agreed to do so signals not only that the usual social rules of interaction don't apply, but also that the therapist is reliable. Patients need therapists to be not only loving but also strong, and time management denotes strength. And it's not rude, just as not answering a question isn't rude, because politeness is a function of local cultural norms, and the therapist's job is to establish the local culture as a therapeutic one.

Putting the clock behind the patient allows the patient to get engrossed and leaves the responsibilities of situation consciousness to the therapist. Stigma makes people situation conscious (Goffman, 1963), and removing the burden of monitoring the situation is another way of communicating that the therapy is a place where the patient cannot be stigmatized.

As already noted, ending on time communicates the therapist's ability to take the patient in stride. Whether the patient has just wrapped up an interesting story or is in the middle of one, whether the patient is crying or angry, the therapist behaves the same. This consistency defines a holding environment (Winnicott, 1972) where the hold is both tender and firm.

In therapy, professional distance should be embedded in charging a fee and in ending sessions on time. The most important thing about ending on time is that it gets therapists what regular bedtimes get parents. It's a lot easier to be empathic, curious, and accepting when you know when it will stop. Ending on time is thus closely related to paying attention for the entire 50-minute session.

Lastly, I want to mention what famed Norwegian psychologist Magne Raundalen said to me when I complained about therapists not ending on time. He said such therapists ask children to visit terrible events and frightening emotions and then don't let them leave. "It's torture," he said.

PLACE

The location of therapy ought to promote the working alliance and the other elements of the frame. The office should not be so well decorated as to contradict goals of improving relationships over lust for money, for example. It should not be so humble or stark as to contradict goals of self-care or enjoying one's environment. It should be soundproofed to promote privacy and devoid of personal artifacts to promote anonymity and neutrality. The location should be consistent week after week, if only to quell the patient's preoccupation with each new space and questions about whether the therapist is powerful enough to command his or her own place of business. Ideally, there is a private waiting area for the patient and a separate way out of the consulting room, but therapists can manage many imperfections by acknowledging them and their effects.

"Place" also concerns what to do when the dyad encounters each other outside of therapy. Therapists learn the head bob, acknowledging the patient but not initiating interaction. On occasions when someone might inquire how they know each other, therapists learn to make a discreet but knowing eye contact instead of the head bob. Any approach will work better if the dyad shares an understanding that missteps are discussed and resolved.

The therapy location should not be in or attached to the therapist's home, for anonymity and privacy reasons listed above. That last sentence will provoke disagreement from practitioners who work at home. If you engage with them in thinking about the issue, be sure to consider whether they are arguing from convenience or from objective concern about how to structure a therapy. All of therapy is an inconvenience to therapists, who forgo self-expression, opinions, cancelling for more appealing events, and any kind of personal impulsivity that could get into the news or local gossip mills. In exchange, they get a fee. Their situation is not unlike old-time bankers who needed a reputation for sobriety and solidity to induce deposits.

FEE

As noted, the fee compensates therapists not only for their time but also for abstinence from social reinforcement and scheduling conveniences. Therapists must charge enough to make them glad that they have carved the time out of their schedule. That implies that the fee might be lower when setting up a practice and higher for early morning or evening appointments. Therapists are entitled to set fees according to how enjoyable the patient seems, although a fee that is too low will backfire when patients organize their thinking around it, wondering what's in it for the therapist. Higher up the staircase, the enjoyable patients are simply the ones who pay on time and don't call between sessions. In my view, therapists should never raise the fee, because the patient is not in a position to negotiate fairly once invested in a relationship with a particular therapist. It's not like a dental patient who can pick up with a new dentist where she left off. I did raise a fee once. I had set a low fee for a graduate student who eventually married someone of remarkable wealth. She told me keeping the old fee was ridiculous. I'm still not sure it was the right decision, because it is impossible to think about it independent of the reward of getting the extra money.

As with the design of the office, there is an ideal way to collect fees, but therapists need not pursue it at all costs. The ideal is to tell patients that it is their responsibility to keep track of the number of sessions in any given month and to bring a check on the first session of each month for all the sessions of the previous month. This method foregrounds the fee periodically but not every session. It communicates trust within the professional frame, which is a requirement for trust within the therapeutic frame. It avoids the sense of greed or dependency implied by payment at every session. It is not quite as private as demanding cash, but cash raises other questions, especially concerning the therapist's compliance with tax laws. A monthly check is as private (and more personal) than any other form of noncash payment. The convenience of billing a credit card is probably not going to overly intrude on the therapy. When therapists accept credit cards and keep the patient's number on file, it's silly to wait a month to bill it.

A check may not be for the expected amount, at which time the dyad can review the decision whether to charge or not. The therapist should bring the disputed check to the next session and leave it in plain sight to evoke conscious thoughts and unconscious associations to the conflict. I once brought a check to 12 consecutive sessions while the patient and I made sense of charging or not charging for a session she had missed, meanwhile collecting three new monthly fees from her. The question of charging her was central to our case formulation, which circled around her confusion about her father's motives when getting close to her. With a credit card, the onus would have been on her to bring up the fact that I had charged for a session she thought I shouldn't have charged for, and it's not clear to me that she would have.

Therapy is free. Therapists charge only for their time, but they charge enough to make them want to provide therapy for free while they are with the patient. I don't think therapists should charge for every single phone call, but for some suicidal patients or with some patients who repeatedly test the boundaries of the relationship, there will be many phone calls. Charging for the time spent on the phone, prorated, is generally a good idea once the calls get to be annoying. It makes the extratherapy contact a part of therapy, and it compensates the therapist for the intrusion.

Frame management often sounds harsh in a social frame, but that's true of every professional relationship if viewed as a deficient friendship. That said, if the patient has a financial setback and can no longer pay the fee, the only way to maintain a therapeutic frame is to suspend or stop the therapy. If the patient is desperate or if the setback seems likely to last, the patient may need a referral to a more affordable alternative, such as a mental health center or training clinic. Some fees, though, are so high to begin with that the therapist may actually feel well compensated at half the previous rate. However, it's hard to see how the patient can bring her annoying behaviors and stigmatized identity elements into the relationship when the relationship is framed as the therapist doing the patient a favor. Adoptive and foster children have the same problem when parents expect gratitude.

TERMINATION

No element of the therapeutic frame besides the fee and ending on time more clearly distinguishes it from social relationships than termination. Therapy is a relationship that ends when the dyad achieves its goals; unlike social relationships, the dyad does not continue meeting for intrinsic rewards of companionship, friendship, or sexualization. A therapy relationship that won't or doesn't terminate is defining the relationship as a life benefit rather than as a path to changing response tendencies, to changing the patient's psychology. That said, the decision to terminate must be the patient's, except for the fairly unusual situations where the therapist does not reasonably believe he or she can help the patient or the patient violates the frame in a way that makes it impossible or very difficult for the therapist to get back into character. The latter might include failure to pay the fee, putting the therapist in fear for his or her personal or family safety, or filing a licensure complaint or a lawsuit, as examples. Otherwise, the therapist ideally tells the patient at the outset of treatment that the therapist intends to make sessions available for as long as the patient wants them. This balances the power differential in the professional frame—the relationship is up to the patient—while maintaining the desirable power imbalance in the therapeutic frame, where the therapist needs the power to change the patient. If the patient were to refuse to terminate once meeting the goals, the therapist would make sure to stay in character, insisting on joint exploration of the reasons and articulation of new goals or a new case formulation. Of course, before reaching a therapy agreement at the outset, the therapist is free to decline to get involved, as long the reasons do not violate the patient's civil rights. Refusal to agree even provisionally on a psychological case formulation is the main reason this happens.

In my own work, termination has often come rapidly. The patient realizes that we have lost our focus because we have resolved the conflict expressed in the case formulation, and it's time to stop. There's no period of reflecting on our work or putting our relationship in good order, because that's what we've been doing all along. Sometimes, they are surprised and relieved to discover that I meant what I said at the beginning, and I am not going to try to talk them into staying. The decision to terminate invokes the professional frame and suspends the therapeutic frame, just as a report of child abuse or a threat of suicide or a severe weight loss does. The way therapists manage termination validates or belies the authenticity of the therapy relationship. It puts the finishing touch on the seductive patient's discovery of what it is like to relate to someone who isn't seducible (when the therapist does not pursue), on the dependent patient's learning what it is like to meet his own needs at the expense of others' needs (when the therapist doesn't whine), on the tap-dancing patient's newfound belief that it may be possible after all to be intimate but not trapped (when the therapist does not insist), and so on.

If there is any contact after therapy, the therapist must stay in character. Therapists who befriend or date former patients are dangerous and should not practice therapy. It's not just that they mess up their therapies by screening patients for friendship or romance, but also that they demonstrate that they are not looking for equal partners in friendship and romance, and this says a lot about how much they believe their own guru hype in the therapy relationship. If the reason therapists maintain a therapy frame is because of virtue, then they must face Shaw's definition of virtue as "insufficient temptation." They are like parents who don't have sex with their children because the children aren't attractive enough or because it would be bad for the children. Therapists should be like parents who don't have sex with their children because the relationship is of a sort that is not sexy, not because the parent is able to resist temptation. If therapists do it right, evoking the patient's aching inner self in a power differential designed to induce growth through intimacy and vulnerability, only the most narcissistic of them will want to be friends or lovers afterward. Again, less narcissistic people want friendships and romances to start on more equal footing.

FRAME MANAGEMENT

Frame management is also a technique issue, addressed in the next chapter. Here, the issue is that frame management is *part* of the therapeutic frame. In many relationships, the dyad maintains the frame out of mutual interest, and conflicts arise when either party makes a framing error or when either party is dissatisfied with the frame, with the kind of friendship or romance they find themselves in. One spouse wants more companionship (doing stuff together), say, or one of two friends would like it to be a romance. The parties might learn to live with the conflict, or they might find a compromise—or even, in cases rare outside therapy, find a resolution as discussed in chapter 5. Monitoring relational rules and approaching conflict are not essential aspects of the roles of friend or spouse, but they are essential aspects of the therapist role.

My approach to couples therapy is largely to teach them frame management. They talk about this issue or that and I listen for frame deviations in their relationship. These usually take the form of a communication whose command function (see "Systems Theory" in chapter 3) invites a definition of the relationship that strikes me as being in conflict with the way functional couples relate to each other. For example, one partner may say something that sounds to me like a parent speaking to a child or an employee speaking to a boss. I call a time-out, and we discuss whether such a communication does comport with their frame and, if so, what the implications are for their relationship that it includes this kind of talk. Maybe they need to change their definition of what a marriage is. If not—if they agree with me that the statement was in conflict with their relationship goals—we give the speaker a chance to communicate the same content, but as one spouse speaks to another.

This is often how I supervise, too. I watch a video or listen to process notes and stop the action when the patient or therapist says or does something that I don't think patients or therapists, respectively, say or do. If it's the therapist, we discuss the implications for therapy of including this kind of thing. Usually, it's social or professional rather than therapeutic, and the implication is that it blocks intimacy, especially by strengthening the desire to maintain a social mask. If it's the patient who has violated the frame, the therapist must learn techniques, discussed in the next chapter, for managing the situation. These amount to exploring the departure as a therapist would and not reacting as a character in the patient's drama would.

THE BUDDY SYSTEM

It's hard enough to maintain a solid therapeutic frame without worrying about financial hits. Once, when I worked in a public clinic, the staff staged an "intervention," confronting me with the fact that half my intakes did not return for a second session. I responded by pointing out that my caseload was full of patients working in therapy on psychological difficulties, and as a result, I was actually interested in therapy and spent a lot of my free time reading literature, philosophy, history, and therapy books—climbing (I would have said, if I'd had the metaphor then) the spiral staircase. They all had become adept at retaining patients, but they spent their free time planning their vacations. I suggested that a firmer therapy frame would make them happier and ensure more productive therapies. The truth is that I was able to be a purist partly because I was on a salary, and there was no shortage of potential patients trying to get into our low-cost clinic. I was also a purist in my private practice, but that may have been partly because I had the full-time job to take away the financial sting from losing patients. Typically, though, the kind of patient who calls a private practitioner is often readier to accept a psychological framing of life problems; people often attend training centers and public clinics not just because they are cheaper, but also because they are avoiding someone with enough experience and power to change them.

In case you're wondering about whether I could have done more for patients with whom I couldn't develop a therapy contract, the answer is yes—but I didn't know how to do it at the time. Dialectical behavior therapy was originally designed to help unsuitable patients work with their therapists, and I could have offered (with a different clinician) some sort of psychoeducation and case management to anyone who couldn't collaborate with me on identifying and working on psychological barriers to life goals. Another possibility would have been to make setting goals the first goal, as noted in the previous chapter, or to make the original case formulation about why it was so hard to agree on a psychological frame.

When income is at stake, it's harder for therapists to maintain a solid frame. For this reason, I recommend a buddy system for therapists in private practice. The buddy sees patients whom one ought to refer out but whose fees one doesn't want to lose, and over the long the run the buddy ought to refer a similar number to the therapist. These cases include relatives and close friends of current and former patients, couples with a partner already treated individually or vice versa, the therapist's neighbors, and so on. The buddy could also provide ancillary treatments, as recommended for trauma patients (see "Trauma" in chapter 3) and others.

Chapter Eight

Knowing Something about Technique

> *If one were properly to perform a difficult and subtle act, he should first inspect the end to be achieved and then . . . he should forget it completely and concentrate solely on the means, [so as not to] be moved to false action by anxiety or hurry or fear.*—John Steinbeck, *East of Eden*

Technique is what therapists actually do during sessions. In this chapter, we'll explore how to do therapy, reserving for chapter 9 the argument for how we know these methods are optimal. It might seem more logical to present the rationale first, but in my experience the spiral staircase passes through practical levels and defers the rationale. The rationale is quite simple—what happens after therapists act one way or another tells them if it was a good idea—and it requires therapists to start somewhere before they can get feedback, so this chapter provides a good starting approach. The staircase levels can be described by the questions therapists ask themselves during sessions about what to do, as discussed in chapter 1 under "Owning the Staircase." The trail starts with things any therapist would say to any patient and ends with things that only this therapist would say to only this patient.

THE PURPOSE OF TECHNIQUE

It's useful to consider what therapists are up to in therapy sessions before thinking about how they should proceed. The purpose of technique is to further the goals of therapy by implementing the restorative relationship implied by the case formulation. If the implied relationship is one of acceptance, say, then technique should elicit production of the parts of the marginalized parts of the self. If it's using bumps on the road to collaboration as a window into collaborative difficulties, then technique should occasion such bumps. If it's intimacy exposure, then technique should foster intimacy.

Certain key elements of the therapy relationship make it more effective than reading self-help blogs (partly because many therapy patients are people who have already read and did not get enough out of popular psychology). These elements appear throughout the book, so I'm only listing them here. The therapy should be ambiguous enough to occasion problematic psychological patterns so the dyad can work on them in real time. This means inducing the patient to take off the social mask as much as possible. The cure for exploitation is a power differential that does not exploit, not the absence of a power differential. So the therapy must preserve the therapist's power, notably the authority to comment on what is going on. The therapy must avoid social and professional frames, because the former will stigmatize socially inappropriate thoughts and feelings and the latter will stigmatize professionally inappropriate expectations of mutuality and collaboration. Friends don't want to hear your hostile fantasies about them and lawyers don't want to consider that you might know as much about the subject of the consultation as they do.

SILENCE

The purpose of silence in therapy is to speed up access to the patient's private thoughts and fantasies about life events and therapy moments. The vast majority of therapists have trouble keeping still at the outset of training and never learn to do it. The presence of the other person evokes a lifetime of training to accept and validate the other person's persona, whereas the whole point of therapy is to question, together, whether the public persona is suitable to the person's humanity and to various situations. Curiosity about what the patient's persona leaves out ought to be akin to a physician asking a patient to disrobe or a dentist asking a patient to open wide, but therapists overly reactive to patients' embarrassment want to avoid discomfiting them. Silence also seems withholding to many therapists when it actually provides a rare opportunity for patients to get to know themselves, to share their reactions without fear of judgment. Silence provides interpersonal (versus intrapsychic) meditation, where the therapist notices the patient's flow of thoughts without judgment, withdrawal, or pursuit.

Therapists can't master silent stillness if they feel incompetent to manage patients' reactions to it. Ideally, patients experience therapists' silences as warm invitations to explore situations by letting their thoughts roam freely and reporting them without censorship. Therapists help them get there by first making sure that this is their genuine intent and then by establishing that attitude interpersonally. Therapists slow down patients and focus on specific moments, whether in the patients' narratives or in the therapy interaction. They say things that attempt to intensify the focus on context and narrative without distracting the patient: "Let's look more closely at that moment." "Paint me a picture of how you imagine yourself in that situation." "Give me some examples." "I wonder if that situation reminds you of anything—a childhood memory, perhaps, or a dream, or something else." "I don't know what it means, either, but I know how to find out: Let's see where your thoughts go from here." "Tell me more about that." "Then what happened?" Silence should come to mean all these things; it should mean "Keep going; I'll come up with something." Unfortunately, a generation of therapists used silence as barrier, not an invitation, and many therapists now characterize their approach as "active," meaning, "I won't just sit there." Therapists who know how to be silent don't refuse to speak; instead, they speak whenever speaking is called for.

When therapists remain silent, they must be prepared for patients to react with some sort of idiosyncratic perception of them. They may appear injured or rebuked, they may stutter and hide their awkwardness, or they may plow on ahead as if they are used to being on their own. They may complain outright. Whatever they do, therapists must use these moments to elucidate problematic patterns and to acculturate patients to therapy: "You reacted to my silence as if I were challenging you to do this by yourself" or something else that is accurate and, if possible, related to the case formulation. For example, a depressed patient who believes that her own needs should always be secondary, illustrated by a memory of bringing tea to comfort her exhausted mother, might react to silence by letting the therapist off the hook. She might fill up the space with pseudotherapeutic observations about herself, complimenting (i.e., bringing tea to) the therapist for providing her with the opportunity. The therapist might say, "It struck me that you reacted to my silence like the girl in the tea memory."

As always, a great deal of therapeutic work involves identifying the patient's idiosyncratic reaction to the therapy, whether to the therapist's silence, the frame, the case formulation, or seeking help. The big idea in every clinical theory is that the patient will react in character, and these reactions bring problems into the relationship where they can be worked on. Often the real problem is not the life problem but the lens through which the life problem is perceived. Everyone gets ill, but some view illness through a lens of weakness versus strength. Everyone makes mistakes, but some view all behavior through a lens of right or wrong. When patients won't play with a case formulation but instead grade it for correctness, they are showing their evaluative lens. When patients won't accept silence but instead feel abandoned, they are showing their dependency lens. Therapists can maintain a therapeutic frame only if they are prepared to respond to the patient's repudiations of it therapeutically—with acceptance, curiosity, empathy, and interpretation.

Sometimes, of course, the reaction to silence is not the same pattern as the one in the case formulation, and therapists must be prepared for this as well: "I wonder why my silence just then didn't seem like an invitation to explore your thoughts." As with process goals in conflict resolution, the dyad must often resolve reactions to therapy before the real work can begin, like a medical patient ashamed of undressing but whose physical problem is unrelated to that shame. More typically, as noted, resolution of the reactions to therapy *is* the real work. Higher up the spiral staircase, these all become *we* statements: "I wonder how we got to a place where my silence feels like the depressed mom in the tea memory." "We seem to be reenacting the tea ceremony." Or, even higher up the staircase: "Mmm, tea."

We can consider therapy, as noted in chapter 1, a place to include what has been marginalized. The problems with encouraging, nodding, cooing, and clucking are many, but they amount to marginalizing content that does not fit cooing. Patients need to tell someone who will greet the information with welcoming curiosity that their jealousy of their spouse is based on breaking into the spouse's e-mail account (or that they felt oddly gleeful at a friend's misfortune or that they wiped snot on the hotel carpet at a conference on narcissism, or something equally socially unacceptable but psychologically meaningful). You lose the chance to explore what was going on with them when they hacked the e-mails, and you confine yourself to pseudotherapy when you talk about the spouse's flirtatiousness but not the patient's misconduct. Nowhere is this truer than in trauma reactions, where the horror is often a response to what patients themselves did or thought (Van der Kolk, 2015). All signs of a social frame induce patients to hide their bad behavior. More specifically, cooing imposes a "you poor dear" frame on the proceedings. Patients get the message that they are to whine and the therapist's job is to comfort. Approval communicates the potential for disapproval, which is inhibiting. Worst of all, cooing stops abruptly when patients report misconduct, violent fantasies, or grandiose beliefs, and then silence, even welcoming silence, connotes disapproval.

LITERATURE VERSUS JOURNALISM

Technique should not be naive about the reliability of memory and the accuracy of patients' narratives. Too often, therapists treat what patients say as journalism, essentially correct renditions of what actually happened. The problem with this attitude is that it is both ill informed and unnecessary. Eyewitness testimony is notoriously inaccurate, for both minor and major events, even among functional adults reporting on events of recent occurrence. If you can't rely on an adult telling you what happened yesterday, how can you even consider relying on the report of an incident decades old and experienced at the time by a child?

The journalistic approach misunderstands memory, the behavior of remembering. Memory is something we do, not something we have (Karson, 2006b). Even perception is not a passive process but a behavior. Seeing a dog in the presence of a dog is something people *do*, not something that happens passively. Seeing something is not the same thing as registering photons on the retina, which *is* a passive process. History and context will affect the behavior of seeing, like all behavior. People with histories only with large dogs might not see *dogs* on their first exposure to small dogs. People who are fearful might see teeth instead of a wagging tail. Seeing things as they are is rewarded by occasioning more effective action. Once people learn to see a dog in the presence of a dog, it is possible for them to see a dog when no dog is present. This is called *remembering*. It's no different from learning to type when a keyboard is present and then emitting typing behavior without a keyboard. Each time the behavior of remembering is emitted, it will be influenced by context. If seeing dogs is sinful, for example, and met with reproach, people will visualize some other animal. Thus, childhood memories tell us hardly anything about what happened as children; they tell us how people organize their autobiographies and master narratives.

The journalistic approach is unnecessary. It's hard to imagine a scenario where the factual accuracy of a recollection is relevant to therapy. Indeed, pinning things down makes them harder to change, and that goes double for a master narrative. Whether the patient's father was actually alcoholic or undemonstrative or overbearing is nowhere near as important as the patient's experience of him. In fact, therapists are fond of saying that patients are thus-and-so because their parents were this-and-that, but it is at least as likely, and more useful, to consider that their depictions of their parents reflect their own personalities. Narcissists think their parents were weak or glorious much more reliably than weak or glorious parents produce narcissists. Therapists never need to say things like, "Why are you dating someone so mean?" They can say instead, "You've made him sound so mean, and yet you're still dating him."

It's quite common for patients to say they can't recall what they were thinking on relevant occasions such as hacking the spouse's e-mails or feeling unexpected anxiety. I quite happily inform them that while it *might* be interesting and useful to remember what they were thinking, it's *undoubtedly* interesting and useful for them to make something up. What they invent is bound to be psychologically meaningful, whereas the vicissitudes of realistic situational factors will constrain mere recollection. For the same reason, dreams are excellent depictions of psychological patterns because they are unconstrained by reality. Recollections are like movies on a budget, using available actors and sets. Dreams have no such limitations. On this topic, I'll also mention that I have told patients who "can't recall" what was on their minds that I'd be happy to guess if they won't, but I only guess sex, anger, or death.

To me, psychotherapy is not a branch of medicine or applied psychology; it's applied literature. Literature provides access to private events—the inner workings of the imagination—enabling readers and audience members to expand their experience beyond their own heads and the handful of people they might get close to in life. Therapy is a career for people who like stories and relationships, although too often clinics are populated by helpers and former patients enacting patterns of their own. My main point here is that when patients speak, it's more likely to be great literature than reliable journalism, with apt metaphors suited to the occasion. There are endless numbers of quotations asserting that fiction is truth, and I agree with them.

When therapists start wondering about the actual state of affairs in the patient's life, it's often a sign that they are not doing therapy anymore. They ask colleagues about custody law when a patient is going through a divorce, or about building codes when the patient is having trouble getting a renovation approved. They start advocating for the patient vis-à-vis the world rather than advocating for the marginalized aspects of the patient's selfhood vis-à-vis the rest of the patient and the therapy dyad. Psychotherapy doesn't directly solve patients' problems or directly meet their needs; instead, psychotherapy removes psychological barriers and changes psychological patterns that interfere with finding solutions, getting needs met, or reconciling with reality. The only reality the therapist needs to have an opinion about is the one in the therapy office—the one the therapist has direct access to.

GETTING EXAMPLES

In addition to the misalliances that I have called *social* and *professional*, relating in the therapeutic frame gets sidetracked by what I call the *philosophical mode*. This sounds like therapy to many people. It involves talking about the patient's psychology, but doing so in headlines, as it were, rather than in stories. The dyad can spend an entire session discussing the relationship between depression and unexpressed anger, or between vulnerability and emotional closeness, without exploring a single specific incident. It's as if they were writing a paper on depression rather than treating it.

The solution is to get specific examples. Therapists should institute this orientation at the very start of therapy when trying to get a grasp on the presenting problem. They must maintain it with a constant interest in examples. In many ways, I think this alone can lead to therapeutic change, since few people get a chance to report specific incidents for constructive commentary. Useful examples for presenting problems include the first recalled instance, the latest, the worst it ever got, and the best example (in the sense of the example that best captures the problem or pattern). In addition, it's useful to get a good counterexample—a moment when the patient would have expected to feel anxious or depressed or enraged but did not—for ideas about what may keep the problem from occurring.

How to get examples varies with the dyad and the therapist's developmental level. It's fine to ask for examples while indicating that the specific context will help with understanding the meaning of the thing. The dyad can decide jointly which example they should spend time on understanding more deeply. The old standby "Let's see where your thoughts go from here" works if the dyad knows that specific examples are the grist for the therapy mill, but by then, silence will serve just as well. Later, therapists can interpret the lack of examples as an avoidance and wonder whether there is something about the office or the relationship that is making the patient evasive.

COMMUNICATIVE FIELDS

There are four kinds of communication in therapy: journalism (with all its deficiencies), poetry, theater, and avoidance (cf. Langs, 1978). Journalism evokes a professional or social frame, depending on what the patient reports, and these frames eventually become avoidant because the former blocks rather than welcomes problematic patterns while the latter promotes social masks and social tact rather than intimacy. Still, in even the purest therapy relationship, patients sometimes report salient facts, journalistically but constructively, as if describing the still life or model they will then paint interpretively.

Poetry

By *poetry*, I mean metaphorical or even allegorical speech. The female therapist offers an idea she's quite pleased with and the male patient looks confused. The therapist skips over the process question of whether they're on the same page and instead carefully explains the idea. Soon thereafter, the patient remembers a story about a father who spent extra time preparing a meal that his son did not like, so the father lost his temper and forced the son to eat it. It doesn't matter whether the patient presented the story as an invention on the spur of the moment, as a childhood memory of his own father, as something that had happened to a friend, as a dream he'd had the night before, or as a movie he'd seen on TV. The story expresses the patient's experience of being force-fed what the authority figure is proud of better than any label (such as "I feel constrained by your impatience with me") could possibly do.

Since behavior is a function of its occasioning environment, and since speech is behavior, a lot more of speech than we may like to believe reflects the speaker's experience of the immediate environment. Therapists' preference for casting themselves in the role of trusted adviser rather than the villain in the piece is self-serving. Of course they'd rather think of themselves as the sympathetic ear to whom the patient could tell such a miserable story than to think of themselves as brutally force-feeding the patient some idea they are inordinately proud of. Buirski (2005) describes the alternatives as the *innocent analyst* or the *implicated analyst*. As painful as it is for therapists to accept their implication in what occurs to patients while in their presence, it's better than the alternative. The alternative is a claim that the therapist did *not* influence the patient's speech behavior, but the whole point of the relationship is to influence the patient's behavior. Further, even when the communication turns out to be journalistic, it's good for the relationship if the therapist shows a willingness to be implicated, to wear one of the hats that the patient has trouble integrating into the sense of self. Ironically, the more innocent the therapist in fact, the easier it is to accept implication.

A poetic lens can lead to a productive reflection on how the patient force-feeds *himself*. The dyad can take any memory or dream—or really, any event—as an allegory, the different characters representing different aspects of the person. The father might represent the desire for excellence or the part of the patient that is embarrassed by his rather childish abilities or exhausted by his childish needs, with the childlike qualities represented by the son. If the therapist demonstrates that it is not repugnant to identify with either of those aspects of the self, the patient will be more open to wearing both hats. A good way to do this is for the therapist to try on those same hats—in this case, the father's and the son's—to see how they fit. Also in support of leaning toward implication rather than innocence is the idea that if therapists are willing to look at their own contributions to difficult moments, patients are more likely to look at theirs. Would-be innocent therapists are like narcissistic spouses who want the other person to wallow in fault. Even when it is actually the spouse's fault, accusations are not as conducive to the partner's taking responsibility as genuine reflections on one's own contributions are.

Metaphor is especially suitable for expressing things under threat of punishment or under a system of disapproval. This was Asimov's (1969) theory of why Jesus taught in parables (plausible deniability of what Jesus was really saying) and Freud's theory of why dream images are symbolic (when the straight dope would be intolerable). However, people also favor metaphor over reportage because metaphor can communicate more accurately, especially when it comes to feelings. Much of our emotional vocabulary comes from metaphor: anger and anxiety, for example, both come from a word meaning "strangle," the difference being who is doing the strangling. As noted in chapter 3 under "Emotion," we learn the names of emotions when people observe the situation we're in and supply the name of the feeling. The implied question in therapy might be, "What was it like for you when you were depressed at that moment?" A list of adjectives is limited in utility by the uncertainty around the extent to which the dyad shares their meanings, but also by the lack of information in a title as compared to a good story. "I was sad" is nowhere near as informative as "For some reason what came into my head was a news story I read yesterday about a guy who went on a long trip to India and died on the first day, but his mother didn't find out until a year later when he didn't return. I keep thinking about what it would be like to look back on a year of work accomplishments and coffee dates and fine dining, knowing now that your kid had been dead all that time."

In my view, all humans are great poets when it comes to capturing a moment or symbolizing themselves. What distinguishes us from actual poets is that we symbolize moments of idiosyncratic versus widespread interest, and good poets put the symbols into language that others can relate to as well. A dream is like a note you left to yourself in a context you've forgotten: "Call MT." "Who the heck is MT?" you wonder. A good poem makes the context clear, so the listener knows what the speaker is talking about. If therapists honor the poetry in speech, patients will censor themselves less, provide those missing contexts by divulging what the symbols remind them of, and speak the unspeakable. "Heard melodies are sweet," said Keats, "but those unheard are sweeter."

Theater

By *theater*, I mean expression in therapy by acting things out rather than by painting a picture of them in words. To understand the concept, let's revisit the force-feeding story. That might have emerged primarily from a problematic pattern of the therapist (who may feel her good ideas are chronically unappreciated), of the patient (who may have a complex around depending on authority figures), or of the dyad (some interaction between their two psychologies). Perhaps this patient, whenever he senses that someone is trying to feed him, wrinkles his nose and otherwise communicates displeasure. This leads to many people calling him ungrateful, enough for him to maintain his experience of feeders as pushy. Suppose the story was a memory from his own childhood. The journalistic therapist sees it as evidence that his father was narcissistic, more concerned about his fancy meal than about his son's well-being. The literary therapist thinks the problem is the living pattern, not the decades-old behavior of the patient's father. Perhaps the patient has come for therapy because of depression, and the case formulation is that he doesn't know how to take care of himself. He either forces himself to have fun, which ruins it, or he doesn't try at all. This memory depicts the case formulation for the dyad. Now, suitably prepared, when the therapist offers her big idea and the patient seems not to get it, she realizes she's about to force-feed him. A small bit of theater has been staged in the therapy—her pride in what she has to offer, and his distaste for it—to give them a chance to change the pattern from within.

I want the therapist to do, at that moment, an analogue of what she would want the father in the memory to do (Karson, 2006b). It has to be something he might actually do; you can't tell people to just be different. For example, I want the father in the story to say, "Well, if you get hungry later, it's easy enough to warm it up." I don't mind him saying, "When you're older, your palate will be more sophisticated and you'll like these subtle flavors," especially if the kid knows he's yanking his chain, but that's too complex to translate into something the therapist can do. The therapist equivalent of the former might be, "You don't seem that interested right now in my idea," implying that the idea can be heated up later.

To review, patients (and therapists, once they learn how to listen to their own imaginations) are reminded of narratives that shed poetic light on whatever patterns are operating in the therapy. The dyad also theatrically enacts problematic patterns that arise in the intimate power differential of therapy. With the former, the therapist brings the patient to a point where the dyad can interpret the narrative. With the latter, the therapist can also head toward interpretation, or the therapist can operate from within the pattern and act accordingly.

Theater also describes pressures on the therapist to change the frame. Often, these pressures are *projective identifications*, referring to the defense mechanism, a way of protecting one's narrative by exporting aspects of the self that don't fit it. People who can't see themselves as angry drive slowly in the left lane and make others angry and often find themselves the least angry person in sight, supporting their narrative. It's tempting for therapists to think of internal pressures as "put into them" by patients, and thinking this way can even be useful if the therapist's reaction is not to shove back but to reflect. In this sense, therapists are *containers* (Winnicott, 1972; Ogden, 1981). "It occurs to me that a lot of people might find that behavior frustrating," if meant to collaborate, can be a good thing to say. "I think you're showing me what it's like to feel ignored" can also be useful, if genuinely meant as a discussion opener, but reflecting on the situation as a bit of theater is often even more engaging. "I wonder how we got to a place where I'm trying to push an idea on you" allows that the moment was cocreated. "We seem to be slipping into force-feeding" also works, especially if "force-feeding" is a key phrase in the case conceptualization. Higher up the staircase, the therapist might clutch her throat and make gagging sounds. (Higher up the staircase, the dyad has its own language and its private jokes.)

It's often difficult to distinguish theater from poetry, because poetry is often produced to have an effect on the listener and drama is often enacted to make a point. Skinner (1957) distinguished *tacts* from *mands*. Tacts are verbal behaviors designed to report information that improves contact with the environment: "We're out of detergent." Mands have an immediate command effect on the listener: "Duck!" People learn to disguise their mands as tacts because other people often balk at obeying. "We're out of detergent" is a tact at the store, but it's a disguised mand when it really means, "Go buy some." "I read that these gas fireplaces are inefficient" might really mean, "Please get me a blanket." In therapy, theater means mands, verbal behavior designed to get the therapist to directly meet the patient's needs, and poetry means tacts, verbal behavior designed to provide the information needed to resolve problematic relational patterns.

Avoidance

Barriered speech (Langs, 1978) diverts attention from something else, or it avoids connection or vulnerability. Most social exchanges, including chitchat of the "how was your week" and "what a storm" varieties, fit this description, although then the barrier is in the entire misalliance rather than in the specific speech acts. Journalistic speech almost always settles into prepackaged stories, which are the hallmark of barriers in therapy, signs that the patient's speech is not affected by or uniquely tailored to the therapist. Most people prefer barriered speech, because it facilitates the performance of a social role to script it. Many social gatherings, even warm and friendly ones, comprise recitations of stories not overly tailored to the specific audience and certainly not inhibited by the fact that the speaker's spouse has already heard the exact same speech.

Though barriers function as avoidance, therapists often wisely treat them as poetry or theater. They can treat them as poetry when avoidant metaphors creep into the speech. A patient, fed up with my barely hidden judgments about his love life, told me in mind-numbing detail about all his lovers, as if I were Kinsey doing research and not his therapist. He carefully and obsessively organized the entire litany around the use of condoms, which he repeatedly described as providing safety at the cost of satisfaction. I eventually wondered aloud if there were a layer of plastic between us, dulling our emotions but keeping us safe. Therapists can also treat barriered communication as a piece of theater whose agenda is to keep therapy from happening. As always, therapists ought first to consider what signals they have sent to suggest that blocking therapy is a good idea, including all the frame deviations they have introduced and any way they might have communicated that they are superior beings with whom any conflicts are the patient's (or the patient's mother's) fault: "You don't seem that emotionally invested in what you're talking about right now." "I wonder how we drifted from therapy into a catalog of science fiction movies." Once I told a woman that she was obsessing about a shoebox full of shells to keep from relating to me. She said, "You idiot. I'm telling you my deepest secret, the one I've never told another living soul." Oops. We talked about why I couldn't tell the difference.

WHAT TO SAY WHEN YOU HAVE TO SAY SOMETHING

Often therapists realize it's their turn to talk, but they don't know what to say. In a therapy where the dyad has reliably established silence as a welcoming communication, it's a good choice, but then it wouldn't be a situation where the therapist thinks it's his or her turn to talk. Some people default to "Let's see where your thoughts go from here" or "How are you feeling right now?" but these seem like copouts to me. The former and its ilk suggest you don't know what to say, and the latter and its ilk (including "You seem sad") change the topic, suggesting that the prior speech has all been wasted. "This is an awkward moment" and "I get it that you want something from me right now" are not avoidant of the relationship or the moment, but they avoid the themes that the dyad has expressed so far in the session. It's a bit like professions of love in a marriage to disperse conflict about who will do the dishes.

When it's the therapist's turn to talk, the default speech should be a summary of what just transpired. It may be replaying the theme (Langs, 1978) or providing a precis (Bruhn, 1990; Karson, 2006b) of the story the patient just told, or it may be a synopsis of what just transpired in the room. The overt intent is to keep the situation status quo, acknowledging that it's the therapist's turn to talk but not wanting to add anything new for the patient to react to. The covert intent is to demonstrate that the therapist has been listening and to spin the story to be summarized in a way that furthers the purposes of the therapy. Therapists accomplish the latter agenda by highlighting potential elements of the synopsis that also occur in the case formulation and its connection to the therapy relationship.

For example, imagine that the patient with the force-feeding memory has agreed that many of his problems relate to the way he polishes his adult self at the expense of his child self, and that it makes his adult self angry, as depicted in the memory, when the child self expresses dissatisfaction with all this polishing. He has also agreed that therapy is a place for the adult self to get to know the child self and a place for the child self to learn to be treated differently via interacting with the therapist. He has also agreed that the child self will appear for that purpose through saying whatever comes to mind, holding nothing back. One day, he tells the therapist a long story from work that week, which I will condense for space reasons before summarizing the story as I might in therapy. The patient is a team leader of system analysts at a major bank. A subordinate made a mistake, and the patient publicly rebuked her while fixing the mistake himself; his boss told him that he should have turned it into a teaching moment. The boss also said about the public nature of the rebuke, "I don't care what you do in the privacy of your own unit, but when word gets around the proverbial water cooler, that doesn't work for me."

The patient pauses after bringing this story to a conclusion, and it's clearly the therapist's turn to say something. There are a number of good summaries the therapist could offer, depending on what she wants to emphasize. Suppose, for example, that the therapist recently signed or is considering signing an insurance form that would reimburse the patient by his health insurance but requires that she provide a diagnosis. The therapist might reasonably suspect that the work story is poetry on that topic. (This is especially true if the frame is otherwise clear enough for the breach to stand out, and even more so if the therapist's technique has been good enough to hold in abeyance the decision about whether to complete the form until they both felt they understood what it might mean.) Her summary of the story might then highlight its confidentiality aspect. She might say, "So, you're telling me about how a minor conflict escalated because it wasn't kept private." The therapist already thinks she knows what the story is about (because she values privacy and sees the insurance form as a breach of it) and summarizes it to spin it in that direction.

Now suppose there is no insurance form. The therapist may appreciate Horney's concerns with perfectionism and the real self. She might say, "It sounds as if the shame of the unappreciated work led to a quick remedy rather than to a more lasting, relational one." Perhaps this will remind the patient of something that happened in therapy that he perceived as quickly remedied at the expense of relating. You can see how this resonates with the case conceptualization, where the father is interpreted as having a perfectionistic agenda in his meal preparation and as feeling shame about his work going unappreciated. Suppose the therapist is relational, assuming that the patient is unconsciously communicating about the therapy, or behavioral, assuming that the patient's speech was occasioned by the immediate environment, of which the therapist herself is the most salient feature. She might say, "You experienced the mistake that emerged as something you had to handle on your own, and then the person over you experienced the organizational issue as something that *she* had to handle on *her* own." Perhaps this will lead to a discussion of something that happened to make the patient think that the therapist feels as if she is on her own and not collaborating with him. Incidentally, these comments are not followed with interrogation about what feature of the relationship might have prompted the story; they are followed with invitational silence, largely because the patient is more likely to accept some feature of the relationship as significant if it comes from the patient. The patient might say, "For some reason, I flashed on that moment when you were so proud of understanding that memory of my dad" or "What have you decided about the insurance form?"

So the therapist can shape the summary of what the patient just said or of what just happened to meet the ends of the therapeutic agenda in the context of the case formulation. This is no different from the tendency of historians (both personal and professional historians) to summarize events to foster a master narrative, except that the therapist does it consciously to promote the therapy goals and the therapist's concept of health.

Of particular concern is deciding which specifics to retain in a summary and which to make more generic. For example, food is unlikely to be directly relevant to the therapy relationship, unless, for example, the patient offered the therapist something to eat and she declined, thinking that frame management required her to decline rather than to explore the meaning of the offer. So the therapist should probably summarize the force-feeding memory's setting as caretaking or nurturing, which are likely to apply both to the memory itself and to the therapy relationship, rather than as cooking or feeding. In the work story synopsis, the therapist is superordinate to the patient (in the therapy frame, not in the professional or social frame), but she is not his boss. The summary may be more useful transversally (Langs, 1978)—as a comment both on the story and implicitly about the therapy—if the therapist converts *your boss* (which applies only to the story) to *the person over you* (which applies both to the story and to the therapy), as I did in the precis above.

Summarizing stories to make a point or to invite a way to think about what happened is a skill that takes a lot of practice. I recommend my own training method, which was to summarize every story I heard outside of therapy—every commercial, every TV episode, every newspaper article—out loud if possible, until I'd done it thousands of times. There are some situations where you are not authorized to speak, but if you don't do this aloud, you will trail off in your imagination and not really develop the skill. It takes thousands of trials before you can get to the point of summarizing fluently, and it takes thousands more to generalize symbols to make them more transversal. Another good reason for therapists to free themselves from nodding, cooing, and talking is that they can then concentrate on molding their summaries while patients are telling stories.

ATTUNEMENT

Whatever the therapist's theoretical orientation, two big truths about emotions seem unavoidable to me: (1) Acceptance and integration of emotions is a step toward health, just as any system can operate more efficiently and effectively if it accepts what it is; and (2) emotions are sometimes precious and sometimes annoying to other people. This, in a social animal like humans, leads to marginalization and stigmatization of people's annoying emotions to make groups more immediately functional. *Attunement* refers to a collection of techniques that make patients feel that their therapists *get* them. The psychological embrace leads to self-acceptance, which in turn, depending on the theoretical language, leads to more efficient problem solving, resiliency, reduced anxiety about revealing oneself, and so on.

While I have no doubt about the advantages of attuning to patients' emotions, my hesitations about attunement as a technique are twofold. First, as noted in chapter 3, descriptions of emotions should usually provide the context and not a label. This is how we learn the labels originally, from family members who observe what happened to us and teach us the name of the feeling, either directly or by using it in conversation. Many families routinely misname emotions as a way to marginalize them—telling angry girls they're tired, for example. If therapists express their attunement with the label, it not only treats all anger or all disappointment the same, but it runs the risk of using a label the patient has not learned to apply correctly. Summarizing the story is a better way of expressing attunement, especially when the summary captures the emotional tone of the story.

Second, it's not always clear which emotion the therapist should express attunement to. As noted throughout this book, clinicians can usefully think of patients as two (or more) interconnected selves, a neglected child and a defensive parent trying to justify the life he or she has led, for example. If the therapist expresses attunement to the inner parent's frustration around striving for excellence only to garner complaints, the child self may feel rebuked for wanting to get his or her needs met. If the therapist expresses attunement to the inner child's feelings of neglect, the parent self may feel rebuked for not meeting those needs and then go to even greater lengths in preparing the next meal. Many therapists think attunement refers to the emotions that patients are most aware of, but effective attunement keeps the whole system of the patient's psychology in mind.

PROCESS OVER CONTENT

Emphasizing process over content is a way of stressing therapy over problem solving. Some friends—let's call them *men*—treat life problems as puzzles to solve. This leaves the troubled friend with good ideas but feeling as lonely as before the conversation. Some friends—let's call them *women*—commiserate well but leave it at that. Therapists are supposed to collaborate on sharing the emotional experience, of course, but for the purpose of coming to a psychological resolution. An example will illustrate the difference between a psychological resolution and solving a puzzle. A woman reports that her boyfriend, with whom she is in love, socked her. This is a simple life puzzle: She should leave the relationship, at least for the time being, and collect her thoughts. The *psychological* resolution won't come until she stops beating herself up for whatever decision she makes. Her individual therapist must be genuinely indifferent to the choice she makes about returning to the relationship if psychotherapy around self-beating is to occur (unless she is in danger, and then protecting the therapy requires keeping the patient alive, as in suicidality). For one thing, pushing for separation backfires, as it homeostatically awakens in her all the positive aspects of the relationship. For another, the press to decide overrides the agenda of exploring how she treats herself. In this respect, the therapist's attitude is *aesthetic*, defined as an appreciation of an object or event without having to do anything about it (Fry, 1920). When you frame a scribble, you are asking the viewer to appreciate it as a work of art, expressing some meaning. When the scribble is left near the phone, it's just a doodle asking to be thrown away. The therapeutic frame is designed to enhance the focus on process and not on reacting.

I may have shocked some readers by saying that battery is not really the business of the individual therapist. I remind them that—as with trauma, suicidality, cancer, and eating disorders—other professionals may need to be involved to leave the psychotherapy to do its thing, which, again, is to change psychological patterns that interfere with life goals. Here, the battered woman's couples therapist may want to require some graded changes on the batterer's part or even require termination of the relationship. Many domestic violence professionals rebel at the thought of couples therapy, but that's because they assume a couples therapist will work on reunification or relationship maintenance. Like a family therapist with an abusive parent, a good couples therapist, if properly authorized and empowered by contract or court order, might not even allow the couple to contact each other until they've made some changes.

NOTE TAKING AND RECORD KEEPING

The importance of process over content, and literature over journalism, makes in-session note taking a simple question to answer: Don't do it. It evokes a professional relationship rather than a therapeutic one. It ossifies a narrative the relationship is designed to change. (*Analysis* comes from the Greek, ανάλυση, meaning "loosen up.") Why put down in black and white what needs changing?

Therapists should write progress notes as if for a potential lawsuit or board complaint. No one ever got sued or grieved for forgetting the details of a genogram, although this is partly because there is no need for a patient ever to discover that the therapist has forgotten that he or she had two siblings and not three. Patients can discover this sort of forgetfulness only if the therapist is doing journalism, giving advice, or making content rather than process comments. Progress notes should represent the therapist's knowledge and concern about suicidality, potential for violence, and frame deviations, and they should reflect the therapist's thoughtful responses to these. This includes documenting consultation on dangerous situations and on any patient's efforts to reframe the therapy that go beyond sitting in the chair and fantasizing.

Sometimes insurance companies inspect progress notes to make sure that what they're paying for is actually occurring. The insurer may have some format that therapists have to abide by, including diagnosis. As with other intrusions, it may be that, all things considered, it's a good idea to do therapy under these circumstances, but it's never a good idea to pretend that the circumstances don't compromise privacy and neutrality.

FRAME MANAGEMENT TECHNIQUES

Good therapists want to understand before acting. Whenever the therapist proposes a frame deviation, he or she should find another way to meet the need expressed in the proposed deviation. Whenever a patient proposes a frame deviation, the therapist should "put a pin it" and assume that the patient's flow of associations will provide some guidance to what the alternatives mean. If the dyad has a strong alliance around discussing reactions openly, they can also just talk it over. Just as not having to react overtly to art occasions an aesthetic attitude, therapists who know they won't be engaging in the frame deviation enhance therapeutic processing. Therapists tend to reproach patients for suggesting things that tempt them or make them feel guilty for refusing; therapists work more productively when they manage their temptations and guilt on their own.

Sometimes therapists complain that this focus on exploring frame deviations, including all relational drifts, can get the therapy bogged down in frame management. Process-oriented therapies seem to discuss endlessly whether patients have to pay for missed sessions or whether therapists can say where they went to college. They want to get on to the question of whether patients should quit their jobs or how to lose weight, but frame deviations and relational drifts are a feature of therapy, not a bug. The creation of an ambiguous power differential occasions the expression of problematic ways of relating to oneself, and frame deviations represent patients' efforts to turn the therapy into something else. Managing the frame relationally *is* psychotherapy, not its prelude.

The other main method of managing the frame is the lose-lose comment (Karson, 2008), also discussed in chapter 3 under "Personality Disorders."

The patient brings up an important topic after the therapist says, "It's time to stop." The therapist might say, "If I invite you to tell me more about that, I'm concerned that I will be communicating that this topic is too big to be contained by the parameters of our relationship. If I end the session now, I am concerned that I will be communicating a lack of interest in the topic. I don't like either option." Since the session has ended, the therapist might add, "Since the session has ended, I'm going to opt for the choice of waiting until next time under the assumption that we can talk about this then."

The lose-lose comment, as I have said, is the therapist's best friend. It can get therapists out of all sorts of sticky situations. It is therapeutic in the sense of teaching metacommunication as a conflict resolution strategy and in the sense of inviting discussion about what is happening. It's there when patients talk about suicide. Toward the end of a session, the therapist might say, "I want to get a clearer picture of how you were seeing yourself at that moment, but I also want to check on your safety." I mention the end of the session because too often therapists take off the therapy hat the moment the patient mentions suicide. There is often plenty of time to do therapy—slow things down (Peebles, 2012) and make sense together (Buirski & Haglund, 2001)—and later in the session raise the question of real-life safety (if it's still relevant).

COMMENTING

The frame of therapy is designed to facilitate commentary on the patient's behavior, a behavior usually reserved for professionals and for parents of young children. It is the flip side of the patient's removing the social mask; social tact requires us not to comment on other people's partly hidden selves, and evoking a social frame with chitchat and self-disclosure inhibits the therapist from commentary. Commentary teaches patients how to relate to themselves, but it also indirectly imports the lessons the therapist has learned about life and psychology. Therapists need never comment on the patient's life versus what the therapist can observe. There's an important difference between saying, "Your father is an alcoholic; stop accepting his calls after dinnertime" and saying, "You make your father sound like an alcoholic and yet you say you still accept his calls after he starts drinking." There's a fine but distinct line between the professional role of giving advice and the therapy role of commenting on the story. Even my go-to habit of summarizing stories comments on what the patient said, not on the event itself.

Here's another example of a pointed comment. There are a lot of patients who don't know how to tell how other people feel about them, so either they assume the worst or the best and miss interpersonal opportunities or they fail to monitor themselves. As always, it's best to discuss specific examples, but often the therapist will realize that the patient is not looking at other people's faces, where such information resides, and neither are they observing their own fantasies, where their default expectations reside. Therapists don't have to tell patients that the important information about a first date resides not only in what the potential partner was like, but in who the patient got to be or had to be in the encounter. Instead, they can comment on how patients depict themselves or on how they seem to avoid exploring their own role on the date. Therapists don't have to direct attention to other people's faces; they can comment on how little attention the patient seems to pay to other people's faces.

INTERPRETATION

I use *interpretation* to refer to a specific type of commentary. Interpretation links the narrative of a report in therapy or the drama of an exchange in therapy to its occasioning environment (something that happened in therapy). Then, it specifies the function of the narrative or enactment and invites the patient to jointly consider the implications. Interpretations have to wait until the occasioning stimulus or activating event is so obvious that the patient won't get into an argument with the therapist about whether the patient is responding to the environment. Typically, the therapist summarizes stories and attunes to affect until the patient mentions something about the therapy that the therapist can relate the stories to. Some patients are allied enough around this process that the therapist can offer a guess instead of having to prove, as it were, that a therapy event provoked the chain of associations or the notable in-session behavior. With the typical sort of patient, the dyad explores together the meaning of material once the therapist has established its connection to the therapy; with the latter sort, which ideally includes all patients once they get the hang of it, the whole business of connecting free associations to therapy events is conducted in concert.

I worked with an engineer who refused to accept the idea that I or my office affected her speech. I've met a lot of therapists over the years who thought this way, but she was one of the few patients I've met who just wouldn't have it. She told me one day that she and her husband had recently gone fishing off a dock on a lake. After a while, she hooked a large bass, reeled it in, and held it up for her husband to admire. "Where'd you get that?" he said. She laughed at the silliness of his question. I laughed, too. "That's exactly how *I* feel," I said, "when you ask me where I get my interpretations from."

Interpretation applies clinical theory to the therapy itself. For behaviorists, it's understanding how the observed behavior—the story or drama—is functionally related to its occasioning environment. Until recently, behaviorists seemed the least interested of all psychologists in the metaphorical meaning of patients' narratives, even though their theory—also known as *functional contextualism*—binds them to this conclusion. Systems theorists get there by tying the communication of a member of a system to the rest of the system. If the therapy is not the relevant system for in-therapy communication, then the therapist is not going to be able to affect the patient. Psychodynamic therapists are so open to metaphor that they don't really need a rationale, but they can see that they intend the relationship to be important and that the patient expresses reactions symbolically. Self-psychologists and cognitive behaviorists expect patients to respond to events in therapy according to their organizing principles or core beliefs, respectively, implying that exploration of narratives can elucidate those principles and beliefs. Responding symbolically to our surroundings is a central part of being human, so it's not surprising that any decent clinical theory can account for the phenomenon. To use it, though, therapists have to be genuinely curious about their patients' reactions to them, instead of relying on the privilege of assuming that everything is just dandy with the less powerful member of the system.

Freud thought the purpose of an interpretation was accuracy. He thought the patient's symbolic or hidden expression of an impulse, feeling, or fantasy in a symptom would be useless if the therapist noted what the patient was really up to. To me, the purpose of interpretation is to facilitate intimacy exposure and the other ways to think about therapy discussed in chapter 1. An interpretation, right or wrong, communicates the therapist's genuine interest in understanding the patient. It promotes a healthy way of looking at oneself, through the lens of curiosity about what one is up to instead of a judgmental lens. It implies that there are other ways to react to situations by considering other discriminative stimuli in them or other ways of defining them. And yes, it can provide insight, putting patients on alert about their own response tendencies, which can lead to second thoughts before behaving overtly.

Therapists don't get many opportunities to practice making interpretations in rehearsal spaces. These kinds of comments are generally socially inappropriate, since they undermine the performance of freedom and dignity that most social encounters insist on. Naturally, therapists are hesitant to make such comments to patients, fearful not only of their own ineptness but also because society has told them all their lives that it is demeaning to comment on other people's behaviors. Just as the difference between interrogation and curiosity is a matter of framing, an interpretation can be a great gift when the recipient is in an intimate frame like therapy. This is another of those matters that people balk at as therapists but cherish as patients. Therapists in training are often alarmed at the idea of telling patients what they really think is wrong with them, but they readily acknowledge that they would have loved it if their own therapists had provided a unique case formulation. For these reasons, I try to make my psychotherapy seminar into a place in which trainees rehearse interpretations. After some time working together, we give each other all the information needed to make interpretations, including a genogram, an autobiography, a statement of values, and a few early memories. I go first to model a level of self-disclosure that is truly personal but not quite embarrassing. Next we observe each other's behaviors in supervision or in sessions and offer interpretations about the patterns that were operating at the moment. Then we discuss whether the trainee made the interpretation in the spirit of elucidation, as opposed, say, to one-upping the recipient, and we try to specify which qualities in the comment departed from or furthered the ideal.

BRIEF TREATMENT

Ideally, therapy is open-ended and termination is up to the patient, but logistical and financial exigencies often preclude this. Therapists should adapt therapy under time constraints accordingly. Often this means not doing the kind of therapy this book is about, which has to do with working on response tendencies rather than on controlling activating stimuli (as in avoiding threats) or managing problematic responses (as with medication or relaxation). When therapists are not in a position to make promises about continuing availability, they should not offer open-ended therapy. These include therapists working in certain clinics or overseas at disaster sites and those working with children in the foster care system, because insurance limits the number of visits, overseas trips end, and foster children move. In these cases, therapists are well advised to build potentially lasting relationships in patients' communities or in group or family treatments.

Sometimes, therapists recommend brief treatment not because of extraneous circumstances but because the life problem is circumscribed. If the problem is limited to a relationship or system, the therapist may provide conjoint or family therapy. If the problem is limited to a particular situation, then the therapist may provide exposure therapy. Conjoint therapy retains the relational-therapy advantage of reproducing the problematic pattern in the therapy office, where the therapist can address it directly. Exposure therapy gets there by bringing the therapy to the situation—the bus stop, say, or the mall—where, again, the therapist can address it directly.

Brief therapy typically uses what happens in the office to illustrate rather than to reproduce the problematic patterns of responding. I think of psychodynamic therapy as an invitation for the patient's adult self to stay in the waiting room while the therapist works directly with the patient's child self. I think of relational therapy as an invitation for both selves to come to the sessions. In brief treatment, therapists often work only with the patient's adult self, consulting as one might do with a parent whose child is troubled.

Still relevant are the working alliance, the therapeutic frame, and techniques of slowing things down, depicting problematic moments rather than just labeling them, and so on. Worldly knowledge may be even more important in brief treatment, since one often has to take a stab at understanding what is going on with the person without having the time to create a space for self-revelation.

HOMEWORK

Homework is appropriate in brief treatment and to address skill deficits, such as those that dialectical behavior therapy addresses to prepare patients for psychotherapy. In therapy designed to change patterns of responding, homework diverts attention from the real-time evocation of those patterns in the therapy relationship. Behaviorists are especially fond of homework even though they, more than any other theoretical group, are suspicious of verbal rules and favor situation awareness and response flexibility. Homework and in-session exercises involve the therapist telling the patient what to do. Regardless of how cleverly the homework is designed to free the person from verbal rules, the practice inadvertently strengthens the reliance on the therapist's rules. Even if the therapist's rules are better than the patient's, they are still rules and always ultimately clunky. Homework thus has the paradoxical effect one finds in commands such as, "Be spontaneous!" "Stop following rules!" Therapists can achieve the same ends nonparadoxically by exploring what happens in sessions that keeps patients from looking at the problem instead of the manual—at what keeps them from being spontaneous.

THINGS TO SAY IN FIRST SESSIONS

On the path to discovering their own way to implement the ideas in this book, supervisees have occasionally expressed interest in mine. These are the things I typically say when the initial consultation heads toward relational therapy. They don't have to be rote just because they were memorized.

Have a seat (indicating where). *What can I help you with?* We begin in a professional rather than a therapeutic frame, so I am going to guide the discussion. I try to engage the patient in clarifying the problem, articulating life (versus in-therapy) goals, and developing a tentative case formulation by exploring imagery and associations related to specific examples of what goes wrong when the patient takes steps to achieve life goals. For example, we discuss what happens when she almost opens on online dating account; perhaps she reports a memory of her mother telling her she's not very pretty. I make an interpretation about what's happened in therapy already that illustrates the case formulation, especially some way that a problematic pattern has already emerged between us, and I note that resolving the pattern between us would go a long way to resolving it when it interferes with goals. For example, I might point to her hesitance in acknowledging what's in her head when she thinks of dating and suggest that she expects me to find her inner self to be ugly. If she could bring the girl from the memory here, she might discover a different, nonevaluative way to look at her, and the girl might find a different, unevaluated way to show up. The patient may look relieved that I have implicitly accepted that girl uncritically.

So that's basically what therapy is. I think I can help you. Is it something you want to pursue?

It turns out that the state regulates psychotherapy, and one of the rules is that I have to tell you some of the other rules. Everything you tell me is private and stays between us, with a few exceptions. If you tell me about any child abuse or abuse of an elderly person, I have to report it to the proper authorities. If you seem imminently in danger of seriously injuring yourself or someone else, I may be required to take steps to prevent it.

Does this time work for you as a regular time? Okay, then, our time will be [Wednesdays at 3] for 50 minutes.

My fee is [X] dollars a session. On the first session of any month, bring me a check for all the sessions in the previous month.

For relational therapy to make sense, some aspect of the case formulation involves relationships, self-knowledge, or some other connection between the case formulation and our meeting and talking. *We're the sum of all the relationships we've ever been in, so for me to help you, our relationship is going to have to be an important one. It turns out that our relationship can become important just by your revealing yourself in it.* Or: *For us to learn about you, to get to know you, you'll have to produce your inner self here, and the best way to do that is to say whatever comes to mind, holding nothing back.* Or I provide some other way of making free association relevant to the case formulation.

So you'll be responsible for showing up on time, keeping track of and paying for sessions, and saying whatever comes to mind while you're here, holding nothing back. Especially useful are stories from your week, stray thoughts, dreams, and childhood memories as they occur to you. I'll be responsible for everything else. I intend to make sessions available to you for as long as you want to keep coming here. Let's see where your thoughts go from here.

And then, at the 50-minute mark, *It's time to stop.*

I encourage students to give themselves several sessions to cover all this ground. When they do, they have to note toward the end of the initial consultation that the dyad needs more time to decide if therapy is right for the person. Before ending the first session, the therapist should mention the state's regulation of therapy and discusse the mandatory disclosures and the fee, even though it's out of order (since the case formulation is still pending).

MANDATED THERAPY

The therapist must adjust the technique when the patient has been mandated to attend therapy. At the school where I teach, we require our master's students in forensic psychology to attend 10 sessions of therapy, partly to experience therapy from the other side, partly to experience *mandated* therapy from the other side (since it's a forensic program), and partly because everyone has something to work on. Then they write a paper about the experience—a paper about the therapist's technique, not about the student's psychology. It's alarming to read about how many of the therapists don't even try to do therapy. They slip into supervision, gossip, and friendly conversation. It takes enormous strength to maintain a therapy frame even when patients want one, and even more when they don't.

Therapists doing mandated treatment must insist on a psychological goal and case formulation. They must be willing to shrug and say, "If we can't find something psychological to work on, I won't be able to help you fulfill your requirement." That requirement might be a report of completion of therapy to a judge for substance abusers and sex offenders, or to the faculty for our students. They must be willing to say, "If we can't find a psychological reason for your neglect of your children [or whatever the underlying issue is], then I won't be able to help you: I'm a therapist." With startling frequency, when I ask therapists in the child welfare system what they are working on with their patients, they tell me they're working on the parent's "trauma" of having the children removed or the children's "trauma" of being removed. Only a handful have ever said that they are working on the behavior that led to the removal or the behavior that is interfering with postplacement adjustment.

When patients won't discuss their actual life problems or the psychology that accounts for them, therapists are entitled to offer their own observations: "I wonder if your stubborn approach to meeting this requirement says something about your relationship to authority in general." "You won't tell me about any problems, but perhaps you are showing me one. Your approach here has been—I'm sorry, but there's no other word for it—rather whiney. I suspect that's a familiar pattern for you." "Your denial of having any psychological struggles sounds perfectionistic to me. Perhaps you are supposed to be some sort of superhero or even an angel."

Many patients are mandated to attend therapy, although the mandate is usually a social rather than a legal or programmatic threat. A mistreated wife might insist that her husband get help, or a depressed man might lose the sympathy of his friends after years of moping. Even one part of the patient may mandate therapy for another part. A perfectionist wants the therapist to deal with the inadequacies that the patient washes his or her hands of. As noted in chapter 1, Minuchin's formula for who should attend applies here. Therapy must include the person who wants to change, the person who can change, and the person who has to change, although it can *start* with only the one who has to change (I. Ioannou, personal communication, 2017). Mandated individual therapy makes sense only if the therapist can develop a case formulation that makes it clear that the patient has to change.

Chapter Nine

Knowing Something about Feedback

How could you fail to perceive that I was not speaking about bread?
—Matthew 16:11

METAPHOR AS FEEDBACK

It's hard to get good feedback across a power differential. I ask students how they would fire a therapist, and a lot of them admit they would report success and gratitude: "I really appreciate all you've done for me, and if I ever need help again, I'll call you." This would help them avoid the therapist's expected pressure to keep coming. So how are the therapists to know they've blown it?

Much the same problem arises after every single thing therapists say or do. If therapists ask patients what they thought of the last idea, the last comment, the last "mm-hmm," patients find themselves in a tricky situation. Do they really want to critique the work of someone who has the power to define them as chronically unsatisfied? And if they do offer a critique, will they get it right? Ask most children what their parents are doing well and you are likely to hear about staying up late, eating sweets, and skipping school.

A recent trend we already visited in chapter 6, under "Relational Bonds," asks patients to fill out a questionnaire about the session right after it ends. Some clinicians think this enhances the working alliance and provides useful information. The question is, Compared to what? The vast majority of therapists either don't seek feedback at all or they don't look beyond the surface approval they get when they do. These questionnaires often prompt therapists to talk with patients about the therapy, but why not do that without the questionnaire, since it sends a message that feedback has to start outside the session?

Therapists must seek feedback on various levels. They need information on how the therapy is going overall, on which standing features of the relationship need improvement, and on the utility of the last thing they said or did. Overall feedback is hard to get because of patients' complicated motivations, which include pleasing the therapist, justifying the investment of time and money, fears of the therapist's reactions, and avoidance of painful or unpleasant aspects of the process. Therapists often say that patients must be getting something out of it or they wouldn't keep coming—but what they get out of it might be a pleasant social or even quasi-sexual encounter, a firming-up of an unproductive narrative about how unfair life is, or a sense of utility in providing for someone even needier than they are. Once the dyad enters a misalliance of these sorts, the last thing the therapist wants to do is to seek and absorb honest feedback.

One useful source of information is the therapist's direct observation of the patient. Therapists are entitled to use cheerfulness in depressed patients and calm in anxious ones as signs of how the therapy is going, even though patients can act depressed or cheerful, anxious or calm, to further a nontherapeutic agenda. Indeed, one old cognitive behavioral strategy was to have depressed patients set a watch alarm at random times of the day and note how they were feeling at the moment. This often demonstrated that patients weren't as depressed as they thought, and that in fact their depressive narrative—not depression as a thing that people *have*—was the problem. The therapy office can induce a patient to act depressed partly because it is the natural location for that narrative, but also because therapists often develop a "you poor dear" complementary role that sustains it. Still, if a narcissist regularly talks empathically about other people's agendas, or if a histrionic patient stops sexualizing the therapy, the therapist may consider that as evidence of being on the right track, especially if the evidence is not under the conscious control of the patient.

Therapists have to find another way—besides compliments—to keep score, but the problem in therapy is that there is not widespread agreement on what constitutes success after the therapist says something. Everyone can agree on whether an infielder caught the ball, whether a bit of software code crashed, or whether the soup needs salt. It's not so easy to get everyone to agree on whether an unsuccessful infielder used bad technique or suffered a bad hop, whether a code crash signals a problem with coding or with protective systems to test code before deploying it, or whether the soup needs more garlic. Therapists frequently report with pride things that I think were mistakes, and I have done things that I was proud of—especially maintaining the therapy frame by, for example, not offering condolences—that alarmed others. (Instead of expressing consolation, I am likely to express curiosity about what happened.)

The ideal feedback avoids any of the patient's agendas besides getting better. Also, there should be a clear link between the feedback and what it was feedback *on*. When Minuchin hooked up juvenile diabetics to blood monitors during family therapy sessions, the monitors were presumably not responsive to the patients' conscious agendas and were probably reacting to what was happening in the moment. Even so, it wasn't possible to say exactly which statement by which family member was producing a change in blood chemistry, and indeed, Minuchin's point was to demonstrate that family dynamics in general affect diabetes rather than to shape the family's behavior with feedback from the monitor. Most therapists are so active that it's often hard to tell which speech or action patients are responding to. The ultimate feedback on whether to nod, for example, would come from comparing patients' reactions to two different therapists whose only difference was nodding—but nodding tends to come with a lot of other cues that evoke a social frame, and at any rate, therapists wouldn't agree on what the feedback meant.

There is an answer to this problem, but many therapists don't like it. In my admittedly snobbish view, many therapists are running fast-food franchises, and when you tell them that there is objective evidence that restaurants with cooks and fresh ingredients serve better food—better tasting and better nutritionally—they smirk and point at all the business they're doing. Something happens to the diners who stop going out for fast food in favor of home cooking or restaurants (to the extent that it's not just snobbery), or to people who grow up to prefer more complicated and less sweet desserts. Whatever that something is also happens to therapists—a process of making distinctions and seeking complexities. You can't improve your cooking if you can't taste the difference between good and excellent, and you certainly can't improve it if you are content to serve and consume fast food. Some will say this is elitist, not just snobbish, but I disagree. I'm not talking about haute cuisine versus McDonald's; I'm talking about mediocre, overcooked, soggy hot dogs versus tasty ones. I'm also talking about the therapist acquiring an appreciation for fine distinctions, not about what the patient can afford.

The answer to the feedback problem is to realize that therapists are already constantly getting feedback on every step they take. It's right there, but the therapist has to want to hear it. Therapists act and patients react. These reactions are either in or out of character—that is, they are the kinds of things that we expect patients to do or say in a therapeutic frame or they are evoking some other frame. Any time a patient evokes some other frame, the easy, privileged course for therapists is to call it *transference* and blame it on the patient's parents. The hard thing to do is to consider whether the thing the therapist did was itself evoking another frame. Therapists can answer this only if they can distinguish therapy frames from other frames, but in the long run, therapists may notice that their asking questions about family history or their expressing sympathy tends to evoke a professional frame or a dependent demeanor. Then they can stop doing those things—assuming they are interested in doing therapy, which is hard, and not in providing consolation and gossip, which is easy.

Even within a therapeutic frame, patients' reactions to therapists' acts will contain information about those acts, especially if the therapeutic frame defines the patient's role as free associating—letting the mind roam freely and reporting what occurs to the patient. All the other arguments for free association—discovering who one is, presenting marginalized selves for empathy and attunement, intimacy exposure, self-exposure, and reparenting—pale in comparison to this one. Free association provides feedback on what the therapist has said or done. If you are willing to work hard enough, there is only one skill you really need to become a good bowler: letting go of the ball. Hard work and innovative experimentation will lead to improvement because the pins will tell you everything you need to know about your technique. The therapy analogue of letting go of the ball is for the therapist to stop and listen after talking to assess the impact of what the therapist just said, and the analogue to knocking down pins is feedback on technique in the form of metaphorical communication. Therapists who experiment in a quest for positive metaphors will eventually become excellent clinicians.

The idea is to improve the responsiveness of therapeutic technique by making it contingency shaped rather than rule governed. The former kind of learning is trial and error. The person makes more mistakes, but in the end the person responds to terrain rather than to maps, and finer distinctions are possible. "Season to taste" produces better cooking in the long run than requiring an exact amount of salt and pepper, as long as the cook's behavior evolved under appropriate contingencies of what tastes good. The ideal is Chuang-tzu's Cook Ting, who after 19 years of butchering had not sharpened his knife. He said that an average cook goes through a knife in a month, because he hacks. A good cook goes through a knife in a year, because he cuts. Cook Ting let the ox's body rather than an *idea* about the ox's anatomy control the knife, and this meant he never cut through tough parts or hacked at them. The problem for therapists is specifying which reactions from patients constitute encouraging feedback. Praise from supervisors and praise from patients distracts therapists from this process.

Bateson (1972a) discussed the interpretation of patients' metaphors as commentary on technique, and Langs (1978) made it the centerpiece of a psychoanalytic approach. Behaviorists—which according to some (Hayes, Follette, & Linehan, 2004) ought to include cognitive behaviorists—should be even more inclined than systems theorists and psychoanalysts to consider patients' speech acts as verbal behavior occasioned by the immediate environment, the most prominent aspect of which is, or ought to be, the last thing the therapist said. If what therapists say is not the most prominent thing in the room, therapists will have to wonder how they expect to change their patients by talking. Humanists believe that metaphor is at the heart of creative self-actualization, so treating speech as literature fosters its intrinsic goal of elevating the person. Let's treat patients as if they are all secret Shakespeares, gifted at poetry and theater, not as if they are all invalids.

The examples that follow will help illustrate this.

I supervised a man treating a woman for depression. The patient confessed a tendency to shoplift small items for the thrill it gave her. Her therapist said in friendly tones, "You have to stop doing that! You could mess up your life!" The patient agreed and said she wanted to stop. This sort of conscious management of the therapist's statement is not of much interest. If he, the therapist, can only keep quiet, we might discover how she actually interpreted his message. Now, at this point, as he was reading me his process notes, I said, "Yikes." I explained that, while there's a place in therapy for good-natured commentary on patients' conduct, after a confession the patient is likely to hear it as a rebuke. The next story the patient told was about her dad, who had grown up on a farm, killing a litter of unwanted kittens, unaware that the patient wanted to keep one of them as a pet. The therapist's comment had reminded the patient of this incident because the rebuke was like a killing, and the patient even understood unconsciously that it was not sadistic (that is, the father was depicted as dispatching rather than abusing the kittens). My supervision goal was not for the therapist to bring his behavior under the sway of my opinions about how to do therapy (and my goal in writing this book parallels that), but to bring it under the control of the patient's unintentional illumination of what the therapist's comment actually meant to her.

As to technique, the therapist could now have summarized what happened: "I told you to stop shoplifting and your mind went to a story about an authority figure unknowingly crushing a girl's impulse to keep something she wanted." With some patients, especially later in therapy, the therapist can continue with an interpretation: "I guess you experienced my comment as me crushing your desires." Or, even later in therapy, instead of the summary and the interpretation, the therapist might have said, "Oops—I should have been more aware of how sensitive the topic of shoplifting was for you."

At a case conference, a therapist with a European accent reported a patient's dream. The patient was on an ocean liner traveling to Europe when she got tangled up in some white sheets and fell overboard. I said, "You're not taking notes during the session, are you?" The therapist said she writes on a pad all through her sessions. I said, "The patient is trying to tell you that she is hindered from connecting with you because she gets tangled up in your white sheets." This therapist could have just stopped taking notes, but she assured me that her own therapist took notes and they did not interfere with the process.

A patient with cystic fibrosis told her therapist that the therapist, as a healthy woman, could never understand her. The therapist said, "You're telling me that your disease makes you different." The patient thought this over for a while. The therapist eventually said, "Where'd you go?" The patient said, "I made a new friend this week. We were working on a class project, making each other laugh. I thought he might ask me out, so I told him I have CF. He didn't know what it was, so I said it's a lung disease that will probably kill me before I'm 30. He said we'd better get cracking on the project, then." The therapist's deft management of the accusation reminded the patient of making a new friend who was indifferent to her disease.

There are two lessons here. One is the beauty of not caring—what we call *neutrality* but what really means *indifference*. It's easy to see the beauty of not caring in a phrase like, "He doesn't care that I have a disease." The other is that it is usually not necessary or desirable to interpret positive metaphors. Therapists can enjoy positive metaphors without saying, for example, "My deft management of your accusation reminded you of making a new friend." If therapists feel they must say something about good news, they can say (typically in brief treatment), "Notice how productively you manage a social encounter when you are thinking well of yourself," or (typically in relational treatment), "Take us to the moment when you realized you were going to be friends."

With a patient, Joanne, who I felt was engaged in our process, I glanced at the clock behind her and was just about to end the session. She said, "My uncle sexually abused me when I was fourteen." I said, "It's time to stop." She stared at me; I may have held my breath. She got up and left. The next week, she started the session by saying that since I wasn't going to help her with her trauma, she realized she would have to help herself. She had done a lot of reading and had decided that she had been letting the abuse control her. She needed to learn how to put it in perspective. She thought of how supportive her mother had been when Joanne had finally told her what had happened. Her abuse had freaked out her father, and their relationship became superficial. Her reading had helped her understand that the abuse had enraged her father, and also that he was confused about how to talk to her about anything overtly sexual. Then she remembered the detective, a woman who had made her feel that this was a problem they could fix. The detective was especially good at keeping her informed. The detective would call her and tell her what was going to happen at the arraignment, for example, whether Joanne needed to be there, and what the next steps were. Joanne was consciously disappointed in me, and we would work on that in an analogy to her disappointment with others who couldn't prevent the abuse. All the metaphors rewarded me for ending the session, including the spur to self-help and the image of a detective who managed the frame of their relationship adroitly.

For several months I saw a chronically depressed man, James, whose case formulation involved an image of his father constantly criticizing him, depicted most movingly in a memory of himself at age six with a crush on a girl in his class. James gave the girl a Valentine after school while waiting to get picked up, and his father saw him do it from the car. His father said, "You don't even have pubic hair yet and you're chasing girls." As James revealed his desires to me in therapy and I reacted neutrally, he began to experiment with a more fulfilling life. As his depression lifted—that is, as he stopped humiliating himself for wanting to live—our sessions turned livelier. I got to that desirable stage where I stopped thinking about what I was going to say and just said it. One day he told me about coming across his father's *Playboy* magazines in the basement when he was in high school. He looked through them but felt too weird to get turned on by the images in them, so he put them back.

Something about the delicacy of a father's secret stash made me think things over instead of blurting out, "So it's your dad who was interested in women he wasn't man enough to get." I kept silent. James thought of a memory of his mother trying to be playful. She was vacuuming and James's dad wanted to watch TV, so she sped up but also danced while doing it. James recalled his father just staring at her with annoyance. Then James talked about how little affection there was between them, how polite they were to each other. I summarized the stories around the theme of making things work, but at the cost of liveliness. The stories painted a picture of a marriage that was functional but that relegated sex to magazines. James said that our sessions used to be like that: polite. I said that a strange thing about our relationship that I didn't know what to make of was that he seemed to me to kind of resent the fact that I was livelier with his happy self than I had been when he was so depressed. I said I didn't think there was any way for me to have been lively when he was so depressed, but that didn't mean he didn't still resent it.

James mulled this over and left. The next week, he started by telling me that he had had a pain in his ear, which he had ignored until it became too distracting. He called his doctor, who looked in his ear, saw no infection, and referred him to an ear, nose, and throat specialist (ENT). James called the ENT and described the problem to the nurse, who suggested he go see his dentist. James was angry at his doctor and at the nurse for not helping him, but he called his dentist. James had a cracked tooth after all, and, as the nurse had suspected, the pain was from the tooth. James noted that he was still mad at the nurse because she could have told him her hypothesis instead of just making him feel rejected. I said, "See? So, there *was* more I could have done when you were depressed to make you feel included in the therapy." This led to a productive discussion and, not incidentally, his discovery that even his anger toward me might be welcomed and included in our relationship.

Many stories are not actually commentaries on the therapist's technique. Indeed, months can go by with patients using the contained space of therapy and the benign gaze of the therapist to welcome and integrate formerly marginalized identity elements, to consolidate a more productive master narrative, and to bask in the glow of acceptance. Naturally, patients are going to tell their therapists important events from their week and from their lives. If those events are painful, it doesn't have to mean that the patients are metaphorically saying that the therapists hurt them. It doesn't have to, but it often does. Therapists should acknowledge to themselves a tendency to lean toward the interpretation that doesn't implicate them. Also, beneficial effects accrue from assuming for the sake of exploration that the story does implicate the therapist. It's like a lover reporting that he or she has been hurt before. A partner who responds with sympathy communicates that the problem is the victim's. A partner who wonders if he or she has already done something insensitive communicates a collaboration. Only the most rigidly narcissistic patients seize on a therapist's admission of potential error and distance themselves; most people meet reflective curiosity about another person's responsibility for conflicts with reflection of their own. And even narcissists could stand to see that it does not devastate the therapist to look inward when things get ugly.

IMPROVISATION

A supervisee named Joe pointed out to me a long time ago that the skill of interpreting metaphors had a liberating effect on his technique. Most people associate it with a constricted approach to therapy, since the feedback reliably pushes therapists to clean up their acts, stay in character, and manage the frame. Joe's point was that he now had a way to evaluate whether something was a good idea or not, so he could experiment more, whereas when he was flying blind it made sense to fly cautiously. He was working with an occasionally psychotic woman who did not speak much. It's not clear that anything could have turned their relationship into a therapy relationship, but he thought he'd try taking her to a bagel shop to see if the less intimate setting would put her more at ease. The only thing she said during the snack besides ordering her bagel was, "The peasant thinks the Indian is a virgin." To her, the bagel shop was not less intimate—it was more like a date. She poetically reminded him that she was a sexual being who wondered what he was up to by taking her out for breakfast. Put differently, he would never have suggested breakfast to an attractive, functional patient, so she knew he was insulting her. If Joe hadn't had a method of evaluating its effectiveness, he never would have tried something so out-of-the-box. Joe used the episode to reflect with her on how her presentation of self garnered invalidating messages, wondering how they could change that cycle. I doubt they would have gotten there without the mistake.

When good actors improvise in a scripted play, they still show up on time and they still stay on book. (In an unscripted improvisation, they stick to the frame that emerges between them, rather than freely saying anything at all.) What they improvise is how to express their characters' emotions and agenda. Therapists, too, have enormous leeway in communicating their welcoming curiosity while staying on book—that is, maintaining the therapy frame. Good actors also improvise the way they elicit the appropriate response in the audience or, especially, in other actors. An actress playing Isabella in *Measure for Measure* asked renowned director Peter Brook how long she should wait before finally kneeling before the duke to plead for the life of the villain she thinks has killed her brother. He responded, "Until the audience can stand it no more." What he really wanted to do was to shock the audience out of their knowledge of what was going to happen and bring them back to the immediate moment. Brook's method was always to have the actors read the situation rather than to follow a rule: "The basis of the craft of the shoemaker is to make shoes that don't hurt; the basis of the theater craft consists in producing, with the audience, from very concrete elements, a relationship that works" (Brook, 1993, pp. 75–76).

An actress playing Desdemona must not just be blithely innocent; she must be blithe to the point that the actor playing Othello feels like strangling her. Therapists, similarly, must improvise to produce the desired effects in patients. Unfortunately, many therapists think the desired effect is to feel comforted rather than to feel understood. Patients constantly improvise to produce desired effects in therapists, and often those effects are idiosyncratic and a window into the patient's problems. All therapy is play therapy.

THERAPEUTIC EGOCENTRISM

The metaphorical and relational approaches assume that the therapist is important enough to affect everything the patient says or does. It seems obvious that a social animal like a human patient would take notice of the other human in the room and organize behavior around that presence. However, many therapists are not comfortable with so much attention. These are the natural-born therapists, who came to the profession to fulfill an identity as a helper, and the literati, who came to the profession because it's one of the few ways to make a living as a consumer of tales. The natural-born patients, who came to the profession to fix themselves, already assume that everything is about them.

So competent therapists are egocentric, but not excessively so. It's the difference between the therapist wondering what a patient's tardiness might say about the therapy versus being certain that it is a message to the therapist. It's the difference between therapists using their feelings as information about the relationship versus insisting that all their feelings are projective identifications from the patient, as if the therapist were a blank screen. A blank screen may sound like a humble stance, as if those therapists are not important enough to include themselves in interpretations, but it is actually a claim of superiority, a claim that they are superhuman.

Therapists who think they're less noticeable than they really are tend to hold still, confirming their narrative when others ignore them. Those who think they are more important than they really are tend to take up a lot of space, confirming their narrative when people seem to talk about their impact all the time. Therapists need conversations that can help them assess how important they are in order to distinguish what happens because of their presence and what happens independent of it. Children in general start out thinking that everything is about them, and then need to learn to tell how important they are or are not in various situations. If people disguise their narcissism by pretending to be invisible, other people often assist this performance by not calling attention to them. This is another major feature of the social frame—ignoring other people's efforts at grandstanding or at invisibility—that interferes with therapy, in which the therapist must be authorized to call attention to the patient. It's another reason to evoke a therapeutic frame that is distinct from the social frame.

HEURISTICS

Although the term *heuristic* originally referred to hands-on learning, in psychology it now means a rough-and-ready, jury-rigged estimation that guides decision making for the time being. The *availability heuristic*, for example, refers to our susceptibility to overvalue whatever occurs to us, what is most available to us (Kahneman, 2011). That's largely how advertising works; it makes a specific product come to mind when we are shopping. It influences therapists who are attempting pattern recognition when their patients' stories remind them of the movie they saw the night before.

In science, rules evolve that describe the world and guide behavior. Rational people happily follow them and extend them to novel situations. Except for those few rules that get labeled *laws of nature*, exceptions are discovered to the application of the rules. A period of confusion and competition follows, during which people return to making decisions based on immediate contingencies and heuristics. Eventually, science develops refined rules that account for the exceptions, and the cycle repeats. The law works the same way but pretends not to (Holmes, 1881), since the legal system treats laws as handed down (because their origin is in authority and not in discovery) and has to disguise the fact that the system actually largely, over time, modifies rules according to "considerations of what is expedient for the community concerned" (p. 35). Even statutes turn out to be heuristics.

Much of therapy involves patients learning that their rules of conduct are heuristics that are not written in stone. They learn this better in a frame that is itself firm where it has to be and flexible otherwise. The imposition of even rigid rules need not occur rigidly, and there ought to be plenty of time and interest for exploring what the parameters of the frame ought to be. The basic rule is not to have rules; "it depends" is the best heuristic.

Much of therapy involves mourning the utility of formerly effective rules. This has to do especially with rules handed down by people associated with love and dependency, but it is also familiar to anyone undergoing change in a cared-about system. An analogy to grammatical rules may be useful: "It's I" is still, for the time being, good grammar, but for those of us who care about the rules of language, the writing is on the wall (and that writing is misspelled); someday that phrasing will be wrong and "It's me" will be correct (along with "me and my friends went shopping"). If you feel your heart sink when former correct usage becomes an error, then you know what it's like for patients to give up old ways that once worked and no longer do.

Therapists, too, have to give up their old ways. They have to relinquish all their nodding and cooing and socializing, and then they have to relinquish their relinquishing as they discover that a firm therapeutic frame can turn out to be surprisingly flexible once its maintenance is overlearned and it's cast in heuristics such as "make sense together" or "maintain a welcoming curiosity" or "work with patients, not on them."

But wait—throughout this book, we visited various therapy situations where I prescribed what therapists ought to do. Exactly. Therapists should end every session on time until it comes so naturally to them that they can embrace exceptions—the extra minute or two spent on why it's so hard to end, the extra seconds allowing a story to conclude, the minutes needed for a sobbing patient to collect him- or herself. Once it becomes second nature to end on time, extra time will be imbued with a sense that something unusual is occurring, like the difference between families with no bedtime and those with the occasional staying up late, and that unusual occurrence itself will be certainly discussed and brought back into the therapeutic frame.

How do therapists know that their technique has become too precious? Patients tell them; patients' free associations in a preciously maintained, punctilious frame drift toward metaphorical illustrations. One patient told me a dream of having dinner with his intellectual idol. The idol served exquisite wine in exquisite glasses so delicate that a single touch would shatter the crystal. It wasn't hard for me to see that my technique had become too precious with him. Another patient recalled a story he had heard about a friend trying to talk to a monk who was so lost in prayer that the monk couldn't hear him. This made me wonder if I was so devoted to the right way to do therapy that I had lost my connection with him. A third patient told me that she couldn't find a dress that fit her at any store, that she needed something tailor-made rather than off the rack. I inferred that my excellent technique seemed premade rather than suited to her particularly.

Knowing how to listen to feedback liberates the therapist from the form. Good therapists master and apply every rule until they achieve a new normal, and then a new look at the rule comes from the new perspective of a higher ground. That's what I mean by the spiral staircase, and that brings us round to where we started.

References

Ablon, J. S., & Jones, E. E. (1998). How expert clinicians' prototypes of an ideal treatment correlate with outcome in psychodynamic and cognitive-behavioral therapy. *Psychotherapy Research*, *8*, 71–83. doi: 10.1080/10503309812331332207

Ablon, J. S., & Jones, E. E. (2002). Validity of controlled clinical trials of psychotherapy: Findings from the NIMH Treatment of Depression Collaborative Research Program. *American Journal of Psychiatry*, *159*, 775–783.

American Psychiatric Association. (2013). *Diagnostic and statistical manual of mental disorders: DSM - 5* (5th ed.). Arlington, VA: American Psychiatric Association.

American Psychological Association (2002). *Ethical principles of psychologists and code of conduct. American Psychologist*, *57*, 1060–1073. Washington, DC: Author.

American Psychological Association. (2012). *Recognition of psychotherapy effectiveness*. Retrieved from http://www.apa.org/about/policy/resolution-psychotherapy.aspx

Andersen, T. (1987). The reflecting team: Dialogue and meta-dialogue in clinical work. *Family Process*, *26*, 415–28.

Asimov, I. (1969). *Asimov's guide to the Bible*. Vol. 2, *The New Testament*. New York: Random House.

Bateson, G. (1972a) *Steps to an ecology of the mind*. New York: Ballantine Books.

Bateson, G. (1972b). A theory of play and fantasy. In G. Bateson, *Steps to an ecology of the mind*, 67–73. Chicago: University of Chicago Press. (Original work published 1954.)

Baumrind, D. (1968). Authoritarian vs. authoritative parental control. *Adolescence*, *3*(11), 255–72.

Bordin, E. (1979). The generalizability of the psychoanalytic concept of the working alliance. *Psychotherapy: Theory, Research, and Practice*, *16*(3), 252–260.

Brook, P. (1993). *The open door: Thoughts on acting and theatre*. New York: Random House.

Bruhn, A. (1990). *Earliest childhood memories*. Vol. 1, *Theory and application to clinical practice*. New York: Praeger.

Buirski, P. (2005). *Practicing intersubjectively*. Lanham, MD: Aronson.

Buirski, P., & Haglund, P. (2001). *Making sense together: The intersubjective approach to psychotherapy*. New York: Aronson.

Butler, J. (1990). *Gender trouble: Feminism and the subversion of identity*. New York: Routledge.

Cattell, R. B. (1946). *The description and measurement of personality*. New York: Harcourt, Brace & World.

Christakis, N. A., & Fowler, J. H. (2009). *Connected: The surprising power of our social networks and how they shape our lives*. Boston: Little, Brown.

Clinton, W. J. (1993, November 13). Remarks to the convocation of the Church of God in Christ in Memphis. Retrieved from http://www.presidency.ucsb.edu/ws/index.php?pid=46115

Coates, T. (2015). *Between the world and me*. New York: Spiegel & Grau.

Dawkins, R. (1976). *The selfish gene*. Oxford: Oxford University Press.

Dewey, J. (1934) *Art as experience*. New York: Perigee Books.

Diamond, J. (2013). *The world until yesterday: What can we learn from traditional societies?* New York: Penguin.

Edmondson, A. (2014, May 4). Building a psychologically safe workplace. TEDxHGSE. Retrieved from https://www.youtube.com/watch?v=LhoLuui9gX8

Edwards, V. J., Holden, G. W., Felitti, V. J., & Anda, R. F. (2003). Relationship between multiple forms of childhood maltreatment and adult mental health in community respondents: Results from the adverse childhood experience study. *American Journal of Psychiatry*, *160*(8), 1453–1460.

Ellis, A., & Harper, R. (1975). *A guide to rational living* (3rd rev. ed.). Chatsworth, CA: Wilshire.

Ericsson, K. A. (2006). *Cambridge handbook of expertise and expert performance.* Cambridge, UK: Cambridge University Press.

Fisch, R., Weakland, J. H., Watzlawick, P., & Segal, L. (1982). *The tactics of change: Doing therapy briefly.* San Francisco, CA: Jossey-Bass.

Fisher, R., & Ury, W. (1981). *Getting to yes*. London: Penguin.

Fletcher, G. J., Simpson, J. A., Campbell, L., & Overall, N. C. (2015). Pair-bonding, romantic love, and evolution: The curious case of Homo sapiens. *Perspectives on Psychological Science*, *10*(1), 20–36. doi: 10.1177/1745691614561683.

Foss, S. K., & Griffin, C. L. (1995). Beyond persuasion: A proposal for an invitational rhetoric. *Communication Monographs*, *62*, 2–18.

Freud, S. (1923/1961). Two encyclopaedia articles: Psycho-analysis and the libido theory. In J. Strachey (Ed. and Trans.), *The standard edition of the complete psychological works of Sigmund Freud* (Vol. 18, 233–259). London: Hogarth.

Freud, S. (1930/1961). Civilization and its discontents. In J. Strachey (Ed. and Trans.), *The standard edition of the complete psychological works of Sigmund Freud* (Vol. 21, 57–145). London: Hogarth.

Fry, R. (1920). *Vision and design*. London: Penguin.

Garratt v. Dailey, 49 Wn.2d 499 (Wash. 1956).

Goffman, E. (1959). *The presentation of self in everyday life*. New York: Doubleday.

Goffman, E. (1963). *Stigma: Notes on the management of spoiled identity*. New York: Simon and Schuster.

Goffman, E. (1967). *Interaction ritual.* New York: Doubleday.

Goffman, E. (1974). *Frame analysis: An essay on the organization of experience*. Boston: Northeastern University Press.

Goodwin, J. (2001). *Challenging and transforming deadly spaces of authority: Steps towards a responsible and responsive educational body*. Paper presented at Borderlands: Remapping Zones of Cultural Practice and Representation. University of Massachusetts Amherst. March 31, 2001.

Goodwin, J. (2016, October). *You are reminded that your safety is your own responsibility.* United Solo Theater Festival, New York.

Haidt, J. (2012). *The righteous mind: Why good people are divided by politics and religion.* New York: Pantheon.

Haley, J. (1973). *Uncommon therapy: The psychiatric techniques of Milton H. Erickson*. New York: Norton.

Haley, J. (1976). *Problem-solving therapy*. San Francisco: Jossey-Bass.

Harari, Y. N. (2015). *Sapiens: A brief history of humankind.* New York: HarperCollins.

Hayes, S., Follette, V., & Linehan, M. (Eds.) (2004). *Mindfulness and acceptance: Expanding the cognitive-behavioral tradition.* New York: Guilford.

Heilbrun, K., Marczyk, G. R., & DeMatteo, D. (2002). *Forensic mental health assessment: A case book.* New York: Oxford University Press.

Heller, J. (1961). *Catch-22*. New York: Simon and Schuster.

Hicks, D. (2010, April). *Within and without: An exploration of stories*. Faculty lecture. Regis University, Denver, CO.

Holmes, O. (1881). *The common law*. Boston: Little, Brown.

Horney, K. (1950). *Neurosis and human growth*. New York: Norton.

Huxley, A. (1956). *Adonis and the alphabet and other essays*. London: Chatto and Windus.

Jacobson, E. (1971). *Depression: Comparative studies of normal, neurotic and psychotic conditions*. New York: International Universities Press.

Janoff-Bulman, R. (1982). Esteem and control bases of blame: Adaptive strategies for victims versus observers. *Journal of Personality, 50*, 180–191.

Johnstone, K. (1981). *Impro: Improvisation and the theatre*. New York: Routledge.

Jones, E. E., & Nisbett, R. E. (1971). *The actor and the observer: Divergent perceptions of the causes of behavior*. New York: General Learning Press.

Jung, C.G. (1969). Psychology and religion (R. F. C. Hull, Trans.). In H. Read et al. (Series Eds.), *The collected works of C.G. Jung* (Vol. 11). Princeton, NJ: Princeton University Press. (Original work published 1938.)

Kahneman, D. (2011). *Thinking fast and slow*. New York: Farrar, Straus and Giroux.

Karson, M. (1980). Is aesthetic judgment impaired by neuroticism? *Journal of Personality Assessment*, 44, 499–506.

Karson, M. (2001). *Patterns of child abuse: How dysfunctional transactions are replicated in individuals, families, and the child welfare system*. New York: Haworth.

Karson, M. (2006a). Nomothetic versus idiographic. In N. Salkind (Ed.), *Encyclopedia of measurement and statistics*. Thousand Oaks, CA: Sage.

Karson, M. (2006b). *Using early memories in psychotherapy: Roadmaps to presenting problems and treatment impasses*. Lanham, MD: Jason Aronson.

Karson, M. (2008). *Deadly therapy: Lessons in liveliness from theater and performance theory*. Lanham, MD: Jason Aronson.

Kernberg, O. (1984). *Severe personality disorders*. New Haven, CT: Yale University Press.

Kernberg, O. F., Selzer, M. A., Koenigsberg, H. W., Carr, A. C., & Appelbaum, A. H. (1989). *Psychodynamic psychotherapy of borderline patients*. New York: Basic Books

Kierkegaard, S. (1983). *The sickness unto death: A Christian psychological exposition for upbuilding and awakening*. (H. V. Hong, & E. H. Hong, Trans.) Princeton, NJ: Princeton University Press. (Original work published 1849.)

Kohut, H. (1971). *The analysis of the self.* New York: International Universities Press.

Kruger, J., & Dunning, D. (1999). Unskilled and unaware of it: How difficulties in recognizing one's own incompetence lead to inflated self-assessments. *Journal of Personality and Social Psychology*, *77*(6), 1121–1134.

Langs, R. (1978). *The listening process*. New York: Aronson.

Linehan, M. M. (1993). *Skills training manual for treating borderline personality disorder*. New York: Guilford.

Madanes, C. (1981). *Strategic family therapy*. San Francisco: Jossey-Bass.

Madanes, C. (1990). *Sex, love, and violence*. New York: Norton.

Madison, J. (1945). The particular structure of the new government and the distribution of power among its parts. In A. Hamilton, J. Madison, & J. Jay, *The Federalist* or *The new constitution*, No. 47, 321–329. New York: Heritage Press. (Original work published 1788.)

McWilliams, N. (1999). *Psychoanalytic case formulation*. New York: Guilford.

Miller, S. D., Hubble, M., & Duncan, B. (2008). Supershrinks: What is the secret of their success? *Psychotherapy in Australia, 14*(4), 14–22.

Minuchin, S. (1974). *Families and family therapy*. Cambridge, MA: Harvard University Press.

Morris, H. (2016, August). *The vengeful client: Warning signs and strategies for intervention*. Paper presented at APA annual meeting, Denver, CO.

Mukherjee, S. (2016). The improvisational oncologist. *New York Times Magazine*, May 12.

Ogden, T. (1981). *Projective identification and psychotherapeutic technique*. New York: Aronson.

Ottati, V., Price, E. D., Wilson, C., & Sumaktoyo, N. (2015). When self-perceptions of expertise increase closed-minded cognition: The earned dogmatism effect. *Journal of Experimental Social Psychology*, *61*, 131–138.

Parker, P. (2016). *The complete works of Pat Parker*. New Haven, CT: A Midsummer Night's Press.

Peebles, M.J. (2012). *Beginnings: The art and science of planning psychotherapy*. 2nd ed. New York: Routledge.

Reik, T. (1948). *Listening with the third ear: The inner experience of a psychoanalyst*. New York: Arena.

Rosenzweig, S. (1936). Some implicit common factors in diverse methods of psychotherapy. *American Journal of Orthopsychiatry*, *6*, 412–415.

Schafer, R. (1981). *Narrative actions in psychoanalysis*. Worcester, MA: Clark University Press.

Schwartz, R. C. (2001). *Introduction to the Internal Family Systems model*. Oak Park, IL: Trailheads Publications.

Shedler, J. (2010). The efficacy of psychodynamic psychotherapy. *American Psychologist*, *65*(2), 98–109.

Shedler, J. (2015). Where is the evidence for "evidence-based" therapy? *Journal of Psychological Therapies in Primary Care*, *4*, 47–59.

Shedler, J., Mayman, M., & Manis, M. (1993). The *illusion* of mental health. *American Psychologist*, *48*, 1117–1131.

Shriver, L. (2016, September). *I hope the concept of cultural appropriation is a passing fad*. Keynote speech, Brisbane Writer's Festival, Brisbane, Australia.

Skinner, B. F. (1953). *Science and human behavior*. New York: Free Press.

Skinner, B. F. (1957). *Verbal behavior*. New York: Appleton-Century-Crofts.

Sutton-Smith, B. (1997). *The ambiguity of play*. Cambridge, MA: Harvard University Press.

Tolstoy, L. (1873/1965). *Anna Karenina*. (Constance Garnett, Trans.) New York: Modern Library.

Vaillant, G. (2002). *Aging well: Surprising guideposts to a happier life from the landmark Harvard study of adult developmen*t. Boston: Little, Brown.

Van der Kolk, B. (2015). *The body keeps the score: Brain, mind, and body in the healing of trauma*. New York: Penguin.

Wachtel, P. L. (2010). Beyond "ESTs": Problematic assumptions in the pursuit of evidence-based practice. *Psychoanalytic Psychology*, *27*(3), 251–272. doi: 10.1037/a0020532.

Wampold, B. E., & Brown, J. (2005). Estimating variability in outcomes attributable to therapists: A naturalistic study of outcomes in managed care. *Journal of Consulting and Clinical Psychology*, *73*(5), 914–23.

Watzlawick, P., Weakland, J., & Fisch, R. (1974). *Change: Principles of problem formation and problem resolution*. New York: Norton.

Whitaker, R., & Cosgrove, L. (2015). *Psychiatry under the influence: Institutional corruption, social injury, and prescriptions for reform*. New York: Palgrave Macmillan.

Wilmot, W. W., & Hocker, J. L. (2007). *Interpersonal conflict*, 7th. ed. New York: McGraw-Hill.

Winnicott, D. W. (1972). *Holding and interpretation*. New York: Grove Press.

Index

About the Author

Michael Karson, PhD, JD, practiced psychotherapy with individuals, couples, and families for 29 years before entering academia in 2003. He is currently a professor in the Graduate School of Professional Psychology at the University of Denver. Karson is the author of *Deadly Therapy: Lessons in Liveliness from Theater and Performance Theory* and *Using Early Memories in Psychotherapy: Roadmaps to Presenting Problems and Treatment Impasses*, as well as three other books.